FINDING GOLD IN THE DARK

FINDING GOLD IN THE DARK

Reflections on Modern America, Virtue, and Faith

John Aroutiounian

The Abigail Adams Institute
CAMBRIDGE, MASSACHUSETTS

Cluny
PROVIDENCE, RHODE ISLAND

Essays from *Yale Daily News* and *The Logos* appear by the kind courtesy of *Yale Daily News*; essays from the *Devils' Advocate* appear by the kind courtesy of Henry Clay High School; "Abortion in Ireland" appears by the kind courtesy of *First Things*.

This volume is a publication of the Abigail Adams Institute, printed and distributed by Cluny Media LLC.

For information, please address:
The Abigail Adams Institute
14 Arrow St., Suite G10
Cambridge, MA 02138

For more information on The Abigail Adams Institute, please visit WWW.ABIGAILADAMSINSTITUTE.ORG.

For more information about Cluny, please visit WWW.CLUNYMEDIA.COM.

FINDING GOLD IN THE DARK

ISBN: 978-1685952372

Cover design by Clarke & Clarke
Cover image: Louis Michel Eilshemius, *New York Roof Tops*, 1908, oil on cardboard on wood panel
Courtesy of Wikimedia Commons

To God, my parents—Rouzan and Aris—and grandparents,
my friends, and my country:
all my past and future successes are yours,
and all my failings are mine alone.
I love you always.
Psalms 121 & Matthew 5.

(*The Yale Graduation Banner 2015*,
Vol. CLXXIV, p. 130)

CONTENTS

the words of john aroutiounian

An individual I look to as the best example of a servant leader is: Mother Teresa, who recognized that her mission was to lead by example and by serving others. She succeeded, and will remain a shining beacon of hope to those struggling and impoverished around the world, because she understood that she was serving something much higher than herself and never lost sight of that goal. In doing so, she empowered people around the world to do the same.
FROM: National Conference of YMCA Youth Governors Profiles (June 12-17, 2010)

Today, thanks in large to the media, our democracy has been reduced to nothing more than a game, a hysterical back-and-forth between incompetent talking heads that is the equivalent of verbal wrestling. Unlike wrestling, however, where nobody really gets hurt in the end...playing games with democracy means people get hurt.
FROM: "William Randolph Hearst, Ted Turner, and Tuscan: Information Overload Is Driving Americans to the Edge" (January 16, 2011)

Our success as people is defined by how well we provide for the continuity—the passing on—of wisdom and knowledge of truth to those who come after us. Part and parcel with this is respecting, honoring and building upon the collective human inheritance passed down to us. It is through this careful and caring passing down of inheritance...that we succeed in our fleeting roles on this Earth.
FROM: "Reflection, Over the Atlantic" (April 21, 2012)

Existential threats to American primacy in the world, or at least immediate ones, appear farther off than ever before. The Third Reich is gone, Communism isn't really a competitive candidate

for world domination anymore, and even the alarming specter of festering jihadist terrorism has receded as American intelligence has adapted to dealing with the threat. It almost makes you think that we should consider ourselves lucky that our political fights, however loud, are much smaller threats to America's stability than what we've dealt with in the distant-to-near past. But, with so much to do nationally to make sure the United States retains its position as top global leader and innovator, why are we having these protracted battles at all? And why are they so deafeningly loud?
FROM: "Beyond Governing by Crisis" (September 30, 2013)

Poverty takes many forms. Its material form is the most obvious and calls for our most immediate attention. But its more deeply rooted form, that of emotional poverty or the "poverty of satisfaction," is subtler and much harder to get rid of. It can affect the rich and the poor just as harshly, and I have personally seen it both inside and outside Yale's walls. And to understand poverty in America, we must come to grips with both forms.
FROM: "The Price of Emotional Poverty" (October 7, 2013)

We should not laud all changes as progress and change does not necessarily conserve what is best and true. We must embrace Mother Prudence! We must cultivate keen eyes able to filter the past and discern what ought to be kept and what is actually detrimental for a society. Otherwise we will succumb to the folly of the man full of warm, speculative benevolence who wishes his society constituted differently than how he finds it. Rather, a true citizen must always consider how he shall make the most of the existing materials of his country—each tradition is a potential treasure and the past is filled with gifts.
FROM: Remark at the Yale Federalist Party Debate (2013)

Everyone has heard the cliché that you should be yourself, because everyone else is taken. But what do you do when you're already taken? Everywhere you look, personal lives are individualized and planned: parenthood, relationships, even relaxation. This makes the urge to distinguish yourself on established, tangible terms very strong, and it suggests something deeply wrong with American university life. It leads to inadvertent close-mindedness, and it phases out a deeper connection to intangibles.
FROM: "Salmon, Not Pink" (April 17, 2014)

It is a paradox of history that our interconnected age features so much social decomposition and personal fragmentation. It is a prime moment for the Church to act as "salt, light, and leaven" in emphasizing the transcendent meaning of human dignity across the world, in shining a light on those forgotten in a society that worships power and ability above all, and in breaking through polarized discourse to reorient our politics toward the pursuit of true human flourishing. But this can only achieved by prayerful individuals, guided by the Holy Spirit, laboring each day in solidarity with one another.
FROM: Cover Letter, The Leonine Forum (August 5, 2018)

testimonials to john aroutiounian

John Aroutiounian, One of my best and funniest students ever, dies of cancer at 26. Once, over coffee, he leaned over and said, "we're so hungry!" Spiritual hunger he meant.

I wish I still had the papers John wrote for the courses of mine. They were outstanding. And characteristic of his first class and generous mind. He left such a lasting impression on me.

David Brooks, *The New York Times*

I often hear it said that we're well into an age of secularism, and that young people are leading the way. Maybe so, but that's not what I see in my students. Having grown up surrounded by instabilities—racial tensions, polarized politics, diminished economic expectations, climate change, and now a global pandemic—they crave the stabilizing anchors of faith. John Aroutiounian was a leader among them, and through these writings can still be.

John's writings reflect insights that would be impressive at any age, but are all the more so in someone as young as John was when he wrote them.

John Lewis Gaddis, Yale University

Once every few generations someone steps up from college experience to send a message about America's younger cohort to the population at large, like W.E.B. Dubois from Fisk and Harvard in The Souls of Black Folk; *F. Scott Fitzgerald from Princeton in* This Side of Paradise; *Jack Kerouac from Columbia in* On the Road; *William F. Buckley, Jr,.* in God and Man at Yale. *Here [in John] is Yale again, in a current form.*

The national character of America was challenged and changed by the upheavals of the 1960s with a pessimistic, adversarial, virtue-shifting and career potential dimension churned in uncertain ways. Then in the post-Cold War period globalization, quantification, and a finance-driven world spun the American psyche further from clarity. JA's [John Aroutiounian's] thought and example as he confronted these world and national-historical phenomena speaks powerfully to young America and the elder stewards of our society from a unique angle of vision.

CHARLES HILL, Yale University

John's an academic whirlwind, a talented public servant, a passionate public speaker and an experienced leader but how do I adequately illustrate for you that he is so much more? In an increasingly self-centered and competitive world, John has managed to hang onto those singularly old fashioned values of sincerity and integrity.

ASHLEY S. BARBOUR, Henry Clay High School,
Lexington, Kentucky
(Excerpt from the Letter of Recommendation for Yale University)

This is very moving—what a loss, we need his voice now! Ross Douthat was a colleague about ten years ago at the Atlantic *(time is passing) and John reminds me a bit of Ross, though more intense.*

REVIEWER, Harvard University Press

A special moment through and through.

REVIEWER, St. Martin's Press

acknowledgments

"Finding Gold in the Dark" is the title of one of John's essays written back in 2013. Yet, it wouldn't have become the title of this book without the encouragement and approval of the three of John's professors at Yale—John Gaddis, Charles Hill, whom we sadly lost, and David Brooks—to go forward with the idea of a book four years ago, in 2019. Our deepest gratitude to these amazing mentors of John who believed in him while he was their student, and carried their trust in him throughout these years. We are forever grateful.

Early on in this journey, we had the fortune of being introduced to Charlie Goodyear—a young Yale author who had studied under the same professors as John. As John's father Aris and I started to put this book together, Charlie served throughout as our guide, editorial and strategic advisor, and committed friend. It is impossible to count the hours that Charlie invested in creating and formatting the book proposal and trying to get it through tirelessly. We are immensely grateful for his dedication, unwavering commitment, and generous contribution in commemorating our son's legacy.

We are thankful to John's close friends, Eric Sirakian and Sharon Chekijian from Yale, who shared their important suggestions and insights at the early stages of this book project; Stephen Adubato, who shared with John a deep devotion to the Church, for his continuous support and interest in this project; Quinton Cannon, John's friend from the U.S. Senate Page Program, for volunteering to transcribe some of John's speeches. We also thank John's dear friends Isabel Marin and Kelly Schumann-Andino from Yale, and Anna Ghnouly from the U.S. Senate Page Program, for their contribution in reviewing the book proposal and their valuable and impactful feedback. And our special thanks to Isabel Marin, who stood by firmly every step of the way, and whose wise and practical advice was invaluable.

We are grateful to Margarita Mooney Clayton, John's professor and mentor at Yale, and later a loyal friend, for introducing a new generation of scholars at Scala Foundation to John's thoughts and aspirations through his writings.

Our heartfelt thanks to the following friends of John who graciously contributed the letters they had received from John for the purpose of this book publication: Isabel Marin, Eric Sirakian, Kelly Schumann Andino and Eduardo Andino, Grace Hirshorn, Kirsten Schnakenberg, Anna Ghnouly, Quinton Cannon, Abby Cave, Brittany Gunn, and Stephanie Nevel-Alejo.

Our deep gratitude goes out to Danilo Petranovich, John's professor at Yale, and later his supporter and friend, for the critical role he played in getting the manuscript to the point of publication. Our years' worth of hard work would not have come to its fruition and John's legacy would not have come to light in its entirety without Danilo's personal and decisive involvement in this process. Thanks to the personal generosity and vision of Alice (La) Wang and Scobie Ward, Danilo also established the John Aroutiounian Fellowship for student scholars affiliated with the Abigail Adams Institute.

This resulted in a collaboration with John Emmet Clarke and the wonderful team at Cluny Media. We are tremendously grateful to Cluny for its interest in getting John's message out, its extraordinary professionalism and receptive attitude throughout all the stages of manuscript advancement, and its exquisite esthetic taste.

Lastly, exceptional thanks to my ninety-five-year-old mother, John's grandmother, long-retired pediatrician Karmen Mejlumian, whose strong and unwavering support for John's legacy has accompanied us throughout this journey. We also express sincere thanks to all our extended family and friends who wholeheartedly supported us in our efforts to make John's book a reality.

John shall be rejoicing with us!

ARIS AROUTIOUNIAN (1949–2020)
and ROUZAN KARABAKHTSIAN

INTRODUCTION

by David Brooks

I GOT TO know John Aroutiounian not at first through his writing, but through his presence. He took a couple of my classes at Yale, and we got to know each other inside and out of class. Some students try to project a serious demeanor and others show anxiety, but John radiated warmth, enjoyment and delight. In my memory, the guy was just always smiling, in the smart, knowing way that the art historian Sir Kenneth Clarke once called "the smile of reason." It is a smile that flows from a good faith that whatever the world throws at us, we will be curious about it and we'll be able to figure it out.

This smile was unusual in a place where self-seriousness is a common commodity. Even more striking than that was his immense sincerity. In any school, there is a natural incentive to want to please the teacher but through our friendship John struck me as utterly guileless, without some kind of an agenda. He enjoyed being around people and I was swept in by the lasso of his enthusiasm.

He wrote several excellent papers for me, and then, while taking a biography class with John Gaddis, pulled me aside one day asked if he could write a biography of me, to fulfill that course's final assignment. Not only did he want to write about me, he said, but he wanted to write the essay in my prose style. Audacious. The resulting paper was tremendous and his take on my prose was witty and knowing. I felt well and truly seen!

But what I really remember were the times we got together, nominally to talk about me, but really to have a series of ranging conversations about life in all its aspects. Years have gone by and I generally have a terrible memory, but I remember one bright Spring day sitting outside on a park bench near the library, him wearing a pair of roughly plum-colored slacks, while we talked on and on. He was a lively, cheerful guy to spend an afternoon with, and his topics were the big ones—the good, the true and the beautiful.

The mind you will encounter in these pages is wide-ranging, self-directed and compassionate. He is exploring an astonishing array of topics—from the State of the Union address to the subject of abortion, to the many merits of his friends. You can see him using his writing, from an astonishingly early age, to explore—expression as a way to understand his own mind.

You will also see an astonishing level of energy and curiosity. Many people have high IQs, and obviously John did, but he was noteworthy for the energy he brought to life, his eagerness to engage with the world. He seemed to be involved in everything—Yale Political Union, student government and debate in high school, serving as a Senate page, the Armenian club he founded, the Yale Daily News. Thriving in high school and at college is hard and time consuming, and John found time to add an extra few educations on top of the one that we in the faculty were assigning to him. Where did all this energy and enthusiasm for life come from? I think the key is found in the conviction that John mentions in one of the essays deep in this book: Love conquers all. That phrase often means that love between two people conquers all obstacles, but in John's case I think it meant that love for life conquers all. He was driven not so much by career ambition as much as zest for the wonders of the world—the need to explore, to experience, to reflect. Some of my favorite pieces in this book are the little notes he wrote to himself, on what he valued and how he should be.

There is also incentive, especially while young, to be a conformist, to fit in. John was a contrarian. As you'll discover, he was more nakedly patriotic than many of his peers, more religious, more conservative and his views on things like abortion were not the standard Yale fare. He held these minority positions with courage and without rancor. I read these pages with a little nostalgia, especially when John is talking about the Yale Political Union. It was a time in American campus culture when debate was more open and freewheeling, when you could state unconventional views without the certainty that you would be hounded, hated and denounced.

John had a wonderful attitude toward Yale—properly appreciative of all its glories and properly suspicious of its elite trappings. In several of these pieces, he captured what it was like to be one of the golden children of the meritocracy, lifted up on the superhighway toward career success, aware of the competitiveness and anxieties that route necessarily inflames, sympathetic to those around him, alert to the snares.

He struck me as shockingly oblivious to status games. He could move from New York City to Kentucky without any big city condescension. But mostly he struck me as a man with an earnest, idealistic and questing soul. That is what you will find in these pages most often—just the earnest desire to understand the good and how to be kind, generous and empathetic. What a warm and grateful faith he had. As your memory of the specific incidents that John writes about fades, I suspect you will be left with his persona. You will be amazed at how much he could cram into a tragically short life, and you will be even more amazed by how much he radiated outward, words of wisdom and curiosity, earnest intentions and well-earned truth, but also that smiling attitude toward the world, which emanates from every page and remains when the covers of the book have been closed.

FINDING GOLD IN THE DARK

John Aroutiounian's voice was distinctive within his generation. This volume will ensure its being heard by others to come.

– John Lewis Gaddis, Yale University

CHAPTER I

National Discourse

1. *High School Years*

I BELIEVE IN THE TORCH OF LIBERTY

(*Lexington Herald-Leader, November 10, 2007*)

I BELIEVE IN the bright, flaming bronze torch of Lady Liberty. Now, you might be saying, "Couldn't have been more original," in a sarcastic overtone. Liberty. Wayyyyy overrated. But the torch of the Statue of Liberty, located in my hometown of New York, New York, means much more to me than just "liberty" or "freedom." Sure, that's part of it. But to me, it represents much more than this simple, much-used, over-applied concept. It means survival. It represents change and the passage of time.

First, let's get the obvious out of the way. The whole "liberty" thing. We've got to remember that we're the one and only true functioning democracy on the face of the Earth, and have been since the day of our conception. Only in the United States can you say what you want to say with no fear of retribution by governing forces. Only in the United States can representatives of the people stand in the highest legislative chamber of the land—the

Senate—and speak until their throats get dry. Only in the United States can representatives of the people stand in the highest chamber of the land—the Senate—and speak until their throats get dry. Only in the United States can we be so critical of billionaires, or establishment political machines, or major institutions with the guarantee that what we have to say will be respected, if not agreed with. We need not look far for examples where citizens are much less fortunate; Myanmar, Sudan and even now-advanced nations such as Russia and Turkey are suppressing citizens for speaking their mind against government policies.

That torch of Lady Liberty reminds me to say my extra prayers each night to be living in a place where I don't have to worry about being gunned down, stoned or censored for exercising my God-given rights. So liberty is definitely a part of what makes the torch on Lady Liberty such an important symbol for me. It represents liberty and freedom—concepts which are cherished more in no other nation on Earth.

But this is just the tip of the iceberg. For me, the Statue of Liberty's flaming bronze torch represents survival. I am a born and raised New Yorker, having moved to Kentucky only a year and a half ago (I know what you're thinking—"what a change"). I was 8 years old (and only several miles away) when the two iconic buildings of the metropolis that is New York City came crashing to the ground. Lady Liberty looked on and undoubtedly shed tears, along with the rest of America. Tears for the nearly 3,000 mothers, fathers, sisters, brothers, wives, husbands, relatives and friends who died that day. But her torch was not quelled. The terrorists avoided striking the Statue of Liberty. It survived. The terrorists also did not strike the morale of Americans. Not in their wildest dreams. And so the torch burns on, as fiery as it ever has been. And it is burning so vibrantly for one reason alone—because it has survived.

Lastly, the torch on top of Lady Liberty, to me, indicates change through passage of time. I have evolved as a person many and many a time over since growing up in New York, along with the physical aspects of my environment that have changed. So the torch on the Statue of Liberty serves as the proverbial "eternal flame" symbolizing where I came from, and where I'm going. It's the flame that burns inside me, to keep me going, to keep me hoping, to keep me believing.

Once upon a time, visitors could climb up the arm to the torch of the statue; now, the farthest tourists can go is the top of the pedestal. But so what? It's there. You bet it's still there.

LESSONS NOT LEARNED

(*Devils' Advocate, September 2010*)

SEPTEMBER 11, 2010 marked the ninth anniversary of the World Trade Center attacks. It was nine years ago. Nine. I keep saying that to myself and still can't believe. I remember waking up on that beautiful morning in Manhattan, and crossing the street to P.S./I.S. 187—my elementary school which, like so many others in New York City, was nameless because there were simply too many schools to name them all. I lived in Washington Heights, Manhattan's northernmost neighborhood. We were only a couple miles up from lower Manhattan. Not enough, though, to avoid smelling the debris rising in plumes of smoke from the wreckage that evening.

The lucid memory of that day's events has stayed wedged in my mind as bright and clear as the day it happened. It was nine years ago that my third grade teacher got a call saying a student was going home. Five minutes later, she got another one. Then another. And then she called my name out. "Why would I be going home?" I thought.

In the days, weeks, and months that followed, the world would come to realize what had happened and how. We would hear stories of the brave men and women who risked and lost their lives for others, the people who went to work as if it was another day—never to come home. Then there were the passengers onboard the doomed fights, whose heroism stopped United 93 from reaching a far more disastrous target. The people who overslept their alarm clocks and were late to work at the World Trade Center that day. And of course, the pathetic terrorists—led by Muhammad Atta—who carried out the attacks orchestrated by Osama bin Laden. But we are still asking ourselves why. Why?

No one will ever fully know. Everyone has an answer, but each and every one is always clouded by bias and opinion. Yet in the aftermath of the attacks, our nation and its leaders resolved to embrace the terrible lessons of that day and move forward stronger and better. Have we? This September 11 was marred by a controversy we had never seen before on a 9/11 anniversary. The plan for the so-called "Ground Zero Mosque" and the debate that ensued revealed deep tensions in our nation still. It also revealed that much of what we promised to do after 9/11—become more understanding of each other and more sensitive to different values, so we could avoid hostility—has not materialized.

The mosque issue has been used as a relentless campaign tactic, by the likes of Rick Lazio, a candidate for Governor of New York (who lost his primary bid on September 14), and other reactionary critics to stoke feelings of fear for political gain. Pundits called the mosque a "giant middle finger in lower Manhattan," an insult to America and those who died. Anti-Islamic sentiment abounded.

But the other side was equally insensitive, if not more so. What was Imam Rauf, the "Ground Zero Imam," thinking? Many Americans associate Islam—or at least a radical element of it—with stoking the violent ideology that led to 9/11. Either Imam Rauf is severely unaware of American public opinion, in which case he shouldn't be a public figure for Islam, or he simply doesn't care. His defense is that Islam is a religion of peace, and Americans' fear and opinions are untrue. But that doesn't change American opinion. It doesn't change the fact that people are going to be offended, and will see Islam as more of a threat to their way of life than ever before, due to Rauf's perceived arrogance. So really, his claim that the mosque is meant to bring people together is totally bogus. It's done the exact opposite. It is clearly true that mainstream Islam rejects the violence of extremists. But from a public relations standpoint, building a mosque so close to Ground Zero was not the way to make people understand that.

The inflammatory, anti-Muslim rhetoric being used for political gain must stop. But the mosque must also be relocated. We all need a crash-course in the very lessons we promised ourselves we'd learned after September 11, 2011. It is said that both sides of the debate used the situations to their advantage, trying to promote the interests of their political or ethnic group before that of the nation as a whole. Yet it's important to remember that America has, in the years following September 11, made inroads in becoming more sensitive to different ethnic groups. It is now politically incorrect to denounce people of any religious group, which is a good thing. But this move was designed to push people's buttons—to test the limits of American's sensitivity.

Some say this story might never have emerged if not for the slow August news cycle, which made a quiet plan erupt into a national controversy. But I'm glad that it did. This debate has made us all question our true loyalties and has shed sunlight on wounds that never really healed. But most importantly, it has forced us to consider whether we are many groups of people living under the convenient but false pretence of being one—or whether we truly are a nation united.

REFORM STINKS OF SOCIALISM

(*Devils' Advocate, October 2009*)

AMERICANS ARE SCARED. Between hearing about "death panels," the supposed long lines to see a doctor, and angry town hall protestors waving "Obama lies while Granny dies" signs, we're terrified about the future of healthcare. Should we be? After all, who would truly believe that those so-called "panels" would ever really exist? Granted, a version of H.R. 3200, the House of Representatives' most current version of the healthcare bill, includes coverage for "end-of-life counseling." Could these counselors make "Do not Resuscitate" orders signed by ill patients a more attractive option for healthcare recipients? Possibly.

Would they bring up "assisted suicide" options for patients, even when these patients had never considered it as an option? Certainly—no conversation on the "comprehensive options" available to an end-of-life patient would be complete without mention of assisted suicide. But what am I saying? Surely, Congress would never propose anything to cut costs on the backs of seniors and the terminally ill. How dare I insinuate the government would do such a thing? After all, government is supposed to look out for us! How dare I, indeed...

I confess: I'm being cynical. Although H.R. 3200 called for the government to cover such counseling once every five years, it didn't require individuals to receive it. And there's very little guarantee, especially after all the uproar, that this provision will make the final version of the bill, anyway. A discussion about healthcare reform warrants careful and intellectual debate. Government is not out to destroy us, nor is it out to save us. So let's have a conversation, and let's not forget—as the great Mark Twain once said, "Irreverence is the champion of liberty and its one sure defense."

First and foremost, let's crunch some numbers. We've got to address the supposed 46 million people without healthcare. Who are they? How much of their costs will be covered? And what about average citizens, who enjoy their healthcare? Will their care be affected? 46 million is an awfully large number. The notion that one-sixth of Americans don't have healthcare in such a bountiful nation is distressing indeed. But let's read between the lines. In 2003, the Congressional Budget Office tried to answer the question of how many Americans were uninsured. Two studies were conducted. According to *The Spectator*, "One study pegged the number of people who were uninsured for the entire year at 31 million, while another put it even lower, at 21 million. In either case, the number was significantly lower than it was in 1998's Current Population Survey, which found 43.9 million uninsured." But the numbers get even better. Among the uninsured, 14 million qualified for Medicaid or State Children's Health Insurance. Many of the uninsured can afford coverage, but *choose* not to purchase any. So where do the numbers truly stand? "[A] 2003 BlueCross BlueShield study determined that 8.2 million Americans are actually without coverage for the long haul, because they are too poor to purchase health care but earn too much to qualify for government assistance," according to *The Spectator*. Still large. But certainly a long haul from the 46 million originally claimed. What is even more revealing is the sense of ease many Americans now have with regards to medical expenses. More Americans are confident that they will be able to pay their health care costs, according to a new poll by Reuters out last week. According to the most recent Gallup poll, conducted last November, a large majority of Armenians want to keep the current health care system in place, with only 39% agreeing that replacing the current system is the way to go. And that's what the President and the majority in Congress want to do.

So what's going to happen? What do current plans have in mind to cover the uninsured, whatever their numbers may be? Speaker of the House Nancy Pelosi has repeatedly called for a bill containing a "public option." Such an option would offer citizens without health care the opportunity to receive coverage from the government, and the option would be at least partially, if not fully, taxpayer-funded. Those who have coverage and are satisfied with it, Congress and the President claim, would be allowed to keep it. But would they? Critics have brought up the fact that if this government plan is indeed instituted, it would rival private health care in price—but not necessarily quality. If private insurance—because of the wider range of services it covers—becomes unable to complete, either it will reduce its coverage or go completely out of business. Either way, quality goes down.

In the President's speech to Congress on this topic he claimed that when the costs are added, "...the plan I'm proposing will cost around $900 billion over ten years." But the numbers simply don't add up. The Congressional Budget Office, a nonpartisan agency, released a report in July—based on the most current versions of the bill—that put the true cost of the plan at $1.6 trillion. That's $1.6 trillion coming from your pocket and mine.

Americans don't want a plan like this. And the poll numbers prove it. We can cover the uninsured by expanding state health programs, cutting taxes for families who purchased health insurance, and working with insurance companies to make health care more affordable. Let's make care more efficient, without making it less comprehensive. Let's enhance Medicare and Medicaid for low-income Americans. Let's cap insurance premiums and create health savings accounts, so people who want to buy care but can't afford it can get help saving for it. The alternatives are out there. But do Congress and the President want to consider these choices, or are they fixed on creating a government monolith that crushes quality and choice in this country?

We shall see. The voters are waiting.

KENTUCKY SENATORS TAKE CAMPAIGN TO A WHOLE NEW LEVEL OF NASTY

(*Devils' Advocate, November 2010*)

WELL, NO ONE died. But someone did come pretty close. After the last televised debate between U.S. Senate candidates Attorney General Jack Conway and Dr. Rand Paul took place on Oct. 24, a liberal activist was wrestled to the ground and stomped by Paul supporters. She's lucky to have escaped with only a concussion, for in this volatile climate, anything could have happened.

The national media dubbed Kentucky's senatorial race "the nastiest in the country," after Conway's now-infamous ad linking Paul to drugs, harassment, and the worship of "Aqua Buddha." The ad caused a virtual firestorm, that culminated in Paul's refusal to shake Conway's hand at a debate in Louisville.

But the Lexington debate appeared to begin the denouncement of this embarrassing campaign year. This night's exchanges were civil and, I daresay, more substantive—not much more.

The debate, hosted by mild-mannered KET anchor Bill Goodman, began with a few softball questions about the importance of family and neighbors, which both candidates seized upon as an opportunity to boast about their Kentucky roots. When asked about the most important issue facing America today, Paul responded that jobs trumped all the rest and that "regulatory burdens" were stifling growth. (The argument could also be made that a lack of "regulatory burdens" caused the economic downturn.) He reiterated his opposition to health care and banking reform, both of which cleared Congress this year. Conway also answered "jobs," (clearly the response of the evening) claiming he could create 750,000 jobs by closing overseas job loopholes. (A great idea with a 0% chance of actually happening.)

A back and forth ensued during which Paul accurately pointed out that banking regulations are placing an inordinate burden on small banks, while Conway tried to make the claim that "leaving banks alone got us into this mass." But Paul persisted with his argument about overbearing government regulation and spending, rather poignantly pointing out that it was political machination at its worst to call the stimulus a success because it "created or saved" millions of jobs. (He was right—there is no way to measure how many jobs were actually "saved," something the Obama administration has repeatedly tried to do as a way of justifying the stimulus.) Invoking a bit of morbid humor, Paul also pointed out that 77,000 stimulus checks were issued to dead people, and seemed to win the point, by leaving the audience with stark examples of waste and noting the inadequacy of Conway's justifications.

The debate also featured questions on foreign policy and education, which got polished answers from both candidates. Paul favors decentralizing the Department of Education, an idea which Conway attempted to paint as extreme but in reality is an idea espoused by many mainstream conservatives. Such a move, Paul argued, would eliminate unfunded mandates and give local school systems—who are more informed about the educational situation in their respective districts—power to make decisions. Conway responded with a question about student financial aid programs. Paul's rather vague response was that the money would be "moved somewhere else" but still be available.

Then came the topic of the healthcare bill. Paul cited the $500 billion in Medicare cuts and the need for a "market-oriented" approach as his justification for favoring repeal. Convey claimed he wanted to "fix" the bill, not repeal it—though he failed to elaborate very much on how this was to be done.

The most contentious point of the evening came when Conway

repeated one of his favorite lines, claiming Paul wanted to institute a 23% sales tax and force seniors to pay a $2,000 Medicare deductible. He repeated this line ad nauseam, despite Paul's stated opposition to the deductible and clarification that the 23% sales tax would be accompanied by an elimination of the federal income tax.

This topic prompted one of the most heated exchanges of the evening, with Paul accusing Conway of having a "simplistic worldview." Conway responded by asking if his opponent was "talking down to me" and asserted that Paul did not "really want to present the facts" prompting the Tea Party candidate to assert "You really don't want an intelligent discussion." The moment was a stinging reminder of the nastiness of this campaign.

Paul seemed to emerge from the debate looking like the more direct and honest of the candidates, whereas Jack Conway came off as the more conventional politician. On Tuesday, Kentucky voters obviously agreed.

And even though the candidates ended the last debate of the campaign with a cordial handshake, fists were shaking just a couple feet away outside.

WILLIAM RANDOLPH HEARST, TED TURNER, AND TUCSON: INFORMATION OVERLOAD IS DRIVING AMERICANS TO THE EDGE

(*Devils' Advocate, January 16, 2011*)

IN THE LATE nineteenth and early twentieth centuries, news giant William Randolph Hearst became widely known for his incendiary "yellow journalism," which presented ordinary stories in gut-wrenching, sensationalized detail in order to make the news more entertaining and consequently, easier to sell. Hearst and his rival, Joseph Pulitzer, soon developed a tug-of-war to see whose newspapers could come up with the wildest extensions of the truth and still sell the most copies at the newsstands.

It worked. Americans loved yellow journalism. The public sopped up the countless stories about farfetched crimes, sex scandals, and supposed international developments. The news became just another form of entertainment. As that love continued to balloon, so did the power and influence of the media magnates.

Soon, however, a seemingly harmless *quid pro quo* between the media moguls, who enjoyed ever-increasing sales, and the public, who delighted in this newfound form of entertainment, became a dangerous cycle. Hearst used his bully pulpit to smear his foes and advance his own Democratic political agenda. And, when tensions with Spanish-held Cuba began to escalate, Hearst sensed an opportunity to profit.

The Hearst newspapers began publishing farfetched accounts of Spanish atrocities in Cuba, most of them false and unsubstantiated. When a wire came in from artist and Hearst newspaper illustrator Frederic Remington, reporting that nothing remotely close to war was on the verge of breaking out in Cuba and that he was ready to come home, Hearst replied, "Please remain. You furnish the pictures and I'll furnish the war." The Spanish-American War eventually broke out on April 25, 1898.

The connection between yellow journalism and the declaration of war is far from direct, and it is completely possible that the War would have occurred notwithstanding the sensational news stories. But there is no question that the media played a discernible role in inflaming public angst and support for military action against Spain.

Today, thanks in large part to the media, our democracy has been reduced to nothing more than a game: a hysterical back-and-forth between incompetent talking heads that is the equivalent of verbal wrestling. Unlike wrestling, however, where nobody really gets hurt in the end (including the wrestlers, who act out the whole abominable episode), playing games with democracy means people get hurt. The unemployed don't get their checks. Crucial services remain unfunded as politicians bicker over vital appropriations legislation in order to score political points, and the media provides hype for all the legislative battles. And, perhaps worst of all, the public comes to accept the nasty words they see on television as reality—as the normal method for exchanging thoughts in a public discourse. As Joseph Goebbels, Adolf Hitler's propaganda chief once said, "If you repeat a lie long enough, it becomes the truth."

It wasn't always this way. Granted, America always had its share of social ills. Those who yearn for the "courtesy" of the 1950s often tend to forget that America had just emerged from a World War then, and that a temporarily toned-down discourse was likely a result of the public's heightened sensitivities and aversion to any more hostility after a bloody conflict. People also tend to forget the brutality of the 1950s and 1960s with regards to America's treatment of African Americans, who experienced countless assaults while Congress sat, for the most part, idly by. So America has never had a calm, friendly national political dialogue. The idea of such a serene tone runs counter to the idea of democracy, where often antithetical opinions are debated in the public sphere. Democracy demands sharp, heated dialogue. But something is markedly different about the tone of discussion now. It is manufactured, repeated, and talking points are drilled into citizens' heads. And I would argue that to truly understand it, we need to turn to the nation's media outlets, which are at their core in the *business*—not the reporting—of news.

On June 1, 1980, modern media mogul Ted Turner announced the creation of the Cable News Network, the world's first 24-hour news station. Shortly before the launch, he promised that "We won't be signing off until the world ends."

Turner's farfetched remarks were a telling sign of the kind of network he wanted to create: one which saturates the viewer with all-day, 24/7 news. CNN marked a shift away from the message and towards the messenger. CNN did not aspire simply to be a news agency. It aspired to be a *brand*, no different from McDonald's or Starbucks in the making and delivery of its streamlined product. This was the first time that news was made into an assembly-line product. The modern information industry was born.

In the decades since, a litany of similar corporations have been created: right-wing FOX News, owned by media mogul Rupert Murdoch, and left-wing MSNBC, owned previously by General Electric, one of the largest multinational corporations in the world with an openly horrendous environmental record. Make no mistake: these organizations don't necessarily support the views they sell (yes, sell). But that's just it: what they say *sells*. And all that matters to a corporation and its shareholders is the bottom line.

So, finally, the most important question: How does all this affect the American psyche and what relation, if any, does it have to the deadly shootings in Tucson, Arizona? For those who watched the news coverage of the tragedy, it was nauseating to see pundits begin to blame and scream at one another only hours after the shots were fired. To answer the first question, the effect on people's minds is profound. The public becomes conditioned to expect outrage, cynicism, and argument on a daily basis. Politicians, for their part, become more wary of talking to reporters and being transparent, worried that every little comment they make may someday come back to haunt them. Gone are the days of characters like Daniel Patrick Moynihan, Ted Kennedy, and conservative commentator William F. Buckley. The quality of intelligent argument has taken a nosedive since the era of these men, replaced with cheap talking points and a refusal even to accept some of the most valid points of the other side as having any merit.

The second question is a bit more difficult to answer. Like Hearst and the Spanish-American War, there is certainly no direct relationship between the mass media, killer Jared Loughner, and the massacre that occurred in Tucson. The man was purely insane, and the ensuing debate in the media over who was to blame (Sarah Palin? Glenn Beck? Communists?) showed us just how despicable the "news" has become in the interest of sparking outrage, allowing itself to point fingers without any substantiation of charges. But there is no doubt, much like there is no question that Hearst helped create a setting conducive to war, that the talking heads on television have created an age in which it is much easier for already-boiling people to lose their top. Did it happen here? Probably not. But then again, we don't know for sure.

The solution to this problem is certainly over my pay grade. It is, I would argue, over the head of any one person, expert, or institution. Some have suggested government ownership of the news, which would trigger an entirely different set of problems. Others have called for more public television stations, which are non-profit and do not operate on a *business* model. Both of these proposals run into serious first amendment issues.

Another approach might be to limit news broadcasting to only a few hours every day, in order to push news agencies to focus on delivering the stories rather than creating controversy. But we are still ignoring the internet, and the often-incendiary rhetoric that emanates daily from countless sites and blogs. Government measures to more strictly regulate any of these outlets would be met with censorship accusations, and could conceivably lead to serious free speech violations.

There might not be a practical way to "tone down the rhetoric" pervading today's public discourse. But the issue should be discussed, with a firm understanding of the history of the role of media in America and how the negative aspects can be mitigated in a way that keeps both our tradition of free speech and the promise of transparent democracy alive and robust. At the end of the day, it will likely fall on the people to demand more from the suppliers of news. After all, if consumers don't purchase a low-quality product, the manufacturer must improve it lest it goes bankrupt. The business model, as luck would have it, works both ways.

THE STATE OF THE UNION: A STATELY WASTE OF TIME

(*Devils' Advocate, January 28, 2011*)

STATE OF THE Union addresses are, by nature, boring. The speech is a relic from a time when communication between the President and Congress was infrequent (we're talking late eighteenth century) and legislators wanted to be kept abreast of the chief legislator's agenda.

As the speech gravitated farther and farther away from its original purpose, it became a platform for the President to momentarily re-enter campaign mode, raising support for key agenda items by appealing to core American values, all while behind the powerful emotional backdrop of a huge American flag and facing the rest of the most powerful people in the country.

Few State of the Union speeches are remembered for their originality or passion. We tend to remember one-liners that encapsulated the then-current national mood, like Bill Clinton's declaration that "the era of big government is over" following the Republican Revolution and Gerald Ford's "the state of the union is not good" following the tumultuous Nixon scandal. More recently, America fell in love with George W. Bush's "axis of evil" in the post-9/11 days of increased threats to domestic security.

Presidents and their staff, for their part, go into the speech mainly as an opportunity to press upon Congress to enact their agenda. The speech is carried live across the country, having the effect of placing pressure on legislators to respond with appropriate body language: Should the opposition remain mum when the President mentions a popular policy item and risk looking bad, or clap quietly and pretend they didn't hear? Should the President's supporters clap uproariously at the risk of looking claphappy (cue Nancy Pelosi last year), or remain modest and risk looking unenthusiastic? What if a rogue member decides to pull off a stunt ("You lie," anyone?). All in all, it's an arduous affair.

No wonder very few people watch it, and the ones that do mostly realize that they've wasted an unentertaining hour of their time sitting on the sofa. Add the opposition party response and some analysis by "professionals" (who, by the way, don't know what their talking about any better than the average educated voter...Roland Martin, Piers Morgan, and Sean Hannity all fall into this category), and you've easily wasted two hours. That's two hours that could have gone into watching the infinitely more entertaining *MTV* (I hear "Skins" is a hit), *Lifetime*, or, if you're feeling really eccentric, an archaic intellectual pursuit called "reading."

I was one of the unwise souls who chose to watch this year's State of the Union. I've watched it every year for as long as I can remember, though I still can't seem to figure out exactly why. Perhaps it's the hope each year that this speech, finally, will bring about something truly substantive. Or perhaps it's the cynical delight in seeing the President propose a laundry list of legislation and seeing close to none get passed by the time he leaves office. No, it's more likely the entertainment value of seeing half the room rise in uproarious applause while the other half wishes they weren't there, complete with occasional close-ups on disgruntled lawmakers' (or Supreme Court justices') faces. Sometimes the cameras even catch the occasional Congressman texting on his Blackberry while the

President is recounting the heart-wrenching story of a citizen he met in some working-class town (probably in the Rust Belt), pulling three jobs just to make ends meet. But alas, even most of the traditional tug-of-war between applauding Democrats and still Republicans (or vice-versa) was eliminated this year, as Congress chose to sit together in a "show of unity." The thing was a complete stunt. Most members of Congress are friends anyway. They just don't vote on each other's legislation. Sitting together is not going to change that, but it had the overwhelmingly negative effect of doing away with the only entertaining part of the whole charade.

If nothing else, at least the speech gives Americans a sense of what the President is thinking and what his policy goals are going forward. The State of the Union is a policy speech, in which the President outlines legislative priorities. This year's speech, in this one remaining worthwhile regard, was a colossal flop.

Obama begun by rightly congratulating Speaker Boehner and asking for prayers for the recovery of wounded Rep. Gabrielle Giffords. The emotional remarks should have ended there. Instead, Obama embarked on what was almost purely a speech stuffed with, for lack of a better word (or perhaps it's the perfect word), fluff. He talked about "differences" and "robust democracy." He tugged at America's heartstrings with talk of the "American family." He mentioned the need for jobs, but stopped grossly short of proposals to actually remedy the unemployment rate (which, by the way, he initially promised would never get past 8%).

"The future," Obama declared with oratorical expertise, "is ours to win." And then, in what I desperately hoped would be followed with detail, he announced his desire to "take responsibility for our deficit" and make people "prosper" for the future. "And tonight," he announced, "I'd like to talk about how we get there." He didn't. Sure, he glorified American innovation and identified this very moment as "our generation's Sputnik moment." Obama does this a lot—the moment he is presently in is always the most important moment, the most important speech. (He shares this style with Glenn Beck and his momentous sermons, but the similarities between the two end there.)

In any case, Obama continued with the soaring rhetoric. Occasionally, he did mention a policy proposal—some of which were great ideas, had they been expanded upon just a little. He proposed eliminating tax breaks for oil companies and lowering the corporate tax rate. He argued for a permanent tuition tax credit, announced a domestic spending freeze, and nudged Congress to pass the DREAM Act (which would allow illegal immigrants to receive in-state tuition at American universities). These are all ideas which the writer of this column supports. But for an hour-long speech, a few sentences of content is grossly deficient. Obama utterly failed to provide a direction forward for bringing the nation's staggering deficit under control. The President also proposed a few agenda items which, as I am sure he is well aware, are very unlikely to gain any traction in the near future. He proposed sourcing 80% of American energy from "clean" sources by 2035, a lofty goal that stands little chance of being realized. At a time of unprecedented debt and economic crisis, he seemed to contradict himself as he proposed a tremendously costly nationwide high-speed rail system. Some other odd proposals included a vague initiative to conduct a "reorganization" of government to streamline agencies and to increase Americans' faith in the system. Perhaps he'll start another agency to get that done. We don't know. He didn't delve into details.

Overall, President Obama looked disconnected, idealistic, and aloof throughout the hour. A common critique from the campaign was that President Obama's ideology and rhetoric are better suited for the dreamy world of the college campus rather than the practical, down-and-dirty world of government. This critique carried the hour.

The powerful orator the nation saw in Tucson several weeks ago could have followed up his moving address to the nation with a practical policy roadmap for the future. Instead, he told us that he continues to think in broad, idealistic brushstrokes and remains unable to get into the detail which the nation now so badly needs.

So if you watched President Obama's fluff fest this year (not to mention Representative Ryan and Bachmann's lackluster rival Republican and Tea Party responses), my condolences for the killed time. Better luck watching "Skins" next time—if it's not cancelled for blatantly pornographic content by then, that is.

MUBARAK OUSTED: THE BLINDING EFFECT OF POWER

(*Devils' Advocate, February 15, 2011*)

History has a very nasty and well-documented record of repeating itself. You'd think someone, out of all of now-deposed Egyptian president Hosni Mubarak's illustrious advisers, would be kind enough to remind him of that. But alas, no one did. And so, amid high unemployment, poverty, public disgust over the state of corruption in government, and widely-acknowledged vote rigging, an untold number of Egyptian protestors took to the streets, and remained for three weeks—withstanding intimidation, reports of beatings, and countless threats—until the Mubarak government couldn't stand the heat anymore. Mubarak finally left Cairo discretely and quietly, having his vice president, Omar Suleiman, make the announcement of his departure as he was already likely on his way to the resort enclave of Sharm el-Sheikh.

The rapid pace of the deterioration of the situation in Egypt—and the subsequent fall of the government—raises one fundamental question: How? It was less than a month ago when most Americans hadn't a clue who Hosni Mubarak was, and had only perhaps heard of slight rumblings in nearby Tunisia. Protests there preceded those that rocked Egypt (albeit by only a few days). How could an able and skilled politician, who had ruled his nation with a strong grip on power since the early 80s, fall in such a brief period of time?

The Mubarak downfall illustrates what I like to call the "Byrd effect," after the late Senator Robert Byrd (who served in the United States' upper body for over fifty years before passing away last year). When politicians are in power too long—no matter how wise, smart, or cunning they might be initially—they lose touch in the end. This is particularly true of nondemocratic, authoritarian systems where leaders aren't even required to actively campaign and don't ever have to leave the halls of power. As time goes by, a bubble begins to form between the inside world of politics and the public tension brewing outside the ivory tower. Leaders lose touch. People revolt. And eventually, the bubble bursts.

The phenomenon of politicians losing touch is well-known in the United States, where the news is separated by what is happening "inside the Beltway" and what is happening on your average "Main Street." Even politicians who have to campaign every two, four, or six years forget—after a few terms—that they are there for a broader reason. But tunnel vision sets in as the political culture envelops legislators who might have originally arrived in Washington truly to "do the right thing."

Egypt is a case-in-point. The signals leading up to the peaceful revolution were blatantly obvious. Widespread corruption and a stagnant economy led to bitterness among the citizenry. But before a single protestor had the thought to walk into Tahrir Square, where the protests were headquartered, the government could have begun some sort of power-sharing deal to at least create the illusion that control was no longer solely in the hands of the Mubarak regime. Cases could have been brought against the most corrupt officials (which did happen, but only after the protests began). And Hosni Mubarak could have slowly walked into the Egyptian sunset, loved by his people for shepherding the nation for thirty years and then moving on when it was his time to go. Instead, he chose to leave Cairo a hated "tyrant."

The former Egyptian leader was a friend of the United States. The military is currently in command, but there is no telling who will fill the power vacuum once elections are held later in the year. Maybe it will be the Muslim Brotherhood. Maybe it will be the secular, democratic government the West hopes for. It is very difficult to accurately predict the outcome at this point. But the elections will decide if America and Egypt are able to maintain the alliance that existed under the Mubarak government.

Similar revolts are brewing in other nations with pro-American regimes, including Jordan and Yemen. This could spell trouble for American interests and the stability of the region as a whole. The silver lining is that similar revolutions might be coming down the pike for Iran and Algeria—nations which haven't been American allies and who have violently suppressed democratic opposition. French writer Victor Hugo once remarked, "No army can stop an idea whose time has come." If the time has come in these nations, it is difficult to believe that the tide can be controlled ad infinitum.

One principle remains constant: when power is not shared, power corrupts. It corrupts so much that those who have it cannot even see their own self-interest, let alone that of the people. Rulers always forget this—and this holds true across time and across continents. Here too, history repeats itself.

REP. KING TO ISLAM: WE NEED TO TALK

(*Devils' Advocate, March 22, 2011*)

NO FORM OF bigotry is more insidious than one disguised as compassion and empathy. Such was often the case with eugenicists in the nineteenth and twentieth centuries who argued that sterilization was in the best interest of minority groups who were "...human weeds" and "reckless breeders...who never should have been born," as Margaret Sanger (who incidentally founded Planned Parenthood, the modern family planning and abortion agency) so eloquently stated. Secretly, any desire to "help" people who, in their view, cannot help themselves is nothing but racism. "We do not want word to go out that we want to exterminate the Negro population," Sanger once said, fearing that the African American community would discover the true intent of her "family planning" work.

Other examples of bigotry masked by compassion abound in human history.

European imperialists spread Christianity to the "savages" of the New World to "civilize" them. And, in the Holocaust and Armenian genocides of the twentieth century, mass extermination campaigns were initially disguised as deportations for the purpose of "relocating" people to "safer" places.

Contemporary examples of bigotry packaged as compassion abound in politics today. On March 10, Congressman Peter King (R-NY) held hearings in the House Homeland Security Committee (which he chairs) regarding Islamic radicalization in America. The committee heard testimony from those who have examined the extent of radicalization—inside the Muslim community and in other communities—at length. Panelists included Muslim scholars, law enforcement officials, and community organizers who have worked with youth and have observed patterns of radicalization.

At one point, the committee heard testimony from Melvin Bledsoe, whose son was radicalized in America and went on to fatally shoot an American soldier outside an Arkansas military recruiting station in 2009. Bledsoe, a private citizen, gave a heartrending testimony about how his son's behavior and outlook changed as he grew more radicalized.

Bledsoe's painful recount about the loss of his child to an insidious ideology would have been fascinating to the public, a large sector of which still struggles to grapple with a movement very foreign to the American psyche. Sadly, his testimony did not make network news. Interestingly enough, I did not happen to see any of the panelists' provocative testimonies—all of which could have sparked a national conversation regarding what America is doing wrong when it comes to the trend of Islamic radicalization—covered on the news. Not even soundbites.

But I did hear about this: At one point in the hearing, the committee heard testimony from a Muslim member of Congress, Rep. Keith Ellison (D-MN), who recounted the life story of Mohammed Salman Hamdani, a Muslim NYPD cadet who rushed into the World Trade Center to save lives on 9/11. Ellison, in tears, painfully recalled how "some people spread false rumors and speculated that [Hamdani] was in league with the attackers only because he was Muslim." He used the story as a resounding condemnation of the hearings, implying they demonized Muslims. (Somehow, all the other Muslims who testified didn't seem to). The treatment Hamdani received, Ellison seemed to say, demonstrated America's profound intolerance towards Muslims. Clips of the congressman's tearful testimony were broadcast that evening throughout American media.

There's only one problem. Ellison was crying about the details of a story he made up. That very same day, the *National Review*'s

Matthew Shaffer decided to do a little digging into Ellison's claims: "There's little evidence of the 'rumors' of which Ellison speaks... none for sites or news reports accusing Hamdani of being a terrorist, and many thousands of pages honoring him as a hero while claiming he was 'widely accused' of being a terrorist."

Only one report—a *New York Post* article dated Oct. 12, 2001—ever even mentioned the possibility of Hamdani being linked to the attacks. Now, juxtapose that with the hundreds of articles praising Hamdani's heroism on 9/11. Very few of the countless other heroes of 9/11—firefighters, policemen, EMS workers—were honored as much as Hamdani was. Shaffer reported that Hamdani "was eulogized by the *New York Times*, had scholarship funds named after him, was honored by Mayor Michael Bloomberg and Police Commissioner Ray Kelly (both of whom went barefoot to honor Muslim practice) at his funeral, and has been celebrated over and over again by the media."

Representative Ellison is a philistine buffoon who shed fool's tears over a story which he didn't even bother to fully understand. Unfortunately, this is typical of left-wing bigotry, which masks a divisive agenda with claims of victimization and helplessness. Here he was, a lonely Muslim Congressman, speaking in front of a committee composed mainly of congressmen adhering to the "white man's religion," as Louis Farrakhan once put—*clearly* trying to suppress and portray innocent Muslims as radicals.

Ellison does a disservice to America and shames the institution which is Congress. Instead of tackling a serious issue head-on, he is playing the "victim" card—although, as facts show, he's no ace at the game. When 180 of the past 220 of those arrested in connection with terror are Muslims, as committee panelist Dr. Zuhdi Jasser noted in an interview after the hearing, we've got a problem. Not a *Muslim* problem. A *Muslim radicalization* problem.

Bigotry and racism are awful, evil things. This country has had a history with both—in the form of white supremacy, xenophobia,

Islamophobia, and others. But bigotry and racism are not exclusive to white perpetrators. The main source of today's violence (as evidenced by arrest statistics and unfolding terrorist acts) comes from the radical Islamic community. A fringe group is being allowed to hijack Americans' perception of an otherwise peaceful religion.

It is time we overcame the bigotry, masked as compassion, of those on the political fringe who would rather continue to demonize America rather than address a serious national security issue. Americans of all stripes should give these hearings a chance to uncover what could be vital information about how to reverse what is a very dangerous trend if left unchecked. The safety of all Americans—left, right, Muslim, Christian, Jewish, atheist, and everyone in between—depends on it.

LADY GAGA: THE ESSENCE OF AMERICA

(*Devils' Advocate, April 2011*)

Lady Gaga's Louisville "Monster Ball" was nothing short of epic. She was loud, she was ludicrous, and she made it very clear that she was extremely proud of being "born this way." That evening will stand out as the night I saw more cross-dressers in an hour than I have in my life (having been to Key West, that's saying something). I, on the other hand, was more modestly adorned in my vegetable superhero outfit and matching makeup. But I digress. My point is that even I, a fire-breathing conservative, enjoyed the concert. And I think more conservatives—particularly foreign policy hawks, of which I am not one—should also like Gaga. After all, her message runs parallel to American foreign policy: love me or go to Hell. In fact, shouldn't Americans of all stripes like Lady Gaga, if not for her music then for the fact that she is the embodiment of everything American? Let me explain...

Stefani Germanotta's life story is a classic modern American pop star success tale. Raised in a middle-class New York household, she was ostracized as an eccentric oddity in high school but went on to study at New York University's prestigious Tisch School of the Arts. She dropped out within two years' time, started experimenting with drugs, stopped talking to her parents, and launched her music career: the basic American pop star trajectory.

Within a few years, she was Lady Gaga—not widely known yet but already making the rounds in clubs and small venues nationwide. As she reminded her audience in Louisville last week, she went from an audience of eighty the last time she was in Kentucky to over twenty thousand.

Why? Her songs are good, but are they *that* good? Or has Gaga struck a chord somewhere in the American psyche?

Individualism. Pride. Self-promotion. These are concepts which define the American mindset and way of life. Most of us are still programmed with the brash (but successful) frontiersman mentality that guided early settlers in what was then hostile territory. In the nineteenth century, transcendentalist Walt Whitman's *Leaves of Grass* embodied this early way of thinking that celebrated self-promotion and an unyielding love of self. Lady Gaga captures this continuing thread of Americans' belief in our own capabilities, our innovation, and our "self-made" futures. Our belief in ourselves—which has been frequently construed as overconfident and arrogant—is as strong today as it was when portraits of "Manifest Destiny" floating west were popular.

In the last century, American democracy has become one of our chief exports. We package and sell it (sometimes by force, much like Britain did in China with opium in the 1800s) to societies around the world. Some societies love it and use it. Others find our brand of rabid capitalist democracy to be a low-quality product that diminishes community and creates a culture of egotistical snobs. Gaga is a cultural ambassador and chief marketer of this individualist message. Some turn away in disgust. Others use it as license to feel good about being different—whether that means dressing differently, acting differently, or loving differently. It is, then, no surprise that gay rights is one of Gaga's pet causes. Her message—crafted around her own personal experience—fits like a glove with the gay rights cause.

It is not for me to say whether Lady Gaga is good for society, much like it is unclear whether America's net contribution to the world is good or bad. Do America and Gaga promote self-centered, egoist lifestyles that toss tradition and community—tenets of societal structure—out the window? Or do they offer freedom from repression and help for those who have long reached for self-actualization, the very top of Maslow's hierarchy of human psychological needs?

From our vantage point, it is hard to say. Those who opine about this issue are simply editorializing; it is a debate that will continue for centuries to come. Meanwhile, Gaga's "Little Monsters" fill stadiums and American missiles fall over Libya.

MODERATION REVISITED

(*Devils' Advocate, May 27, 2011*)

Stereotypes and rigid political dogmas define American political life. You are either a Democrat or a Republican, a liberal or a conservative. When you think of the typical Democrat, you are likely to come up with the image of an urbane, well-dressed subway rider, toting a bag made from recycled bottles and caring for the poor in whatever spare time is available amidst the many social commitments and active lifestyle. A graduate of Harvard or Columbia, he or she eats arugula three times a day and chugs several cups of fair trade certified coffee an hour. That is, if you're a Democrat. Otherwise, your mind will likely conjure up an image of a morally depraved, foolishly idealistic, self-absorbed fashionista, eager to tax you more so that your money might feed the undeserving masses—and to give your daughter free birth control. He or she lives in a one-bedroom apartment, infested with rats and adorned with poor-quality photos of Che Guevara and Jimi Hendrix smoking something otherworldly.

How are Republicans viewed? As keepers of the guard, of course. The Republican is the true American, perhaps a farmer or a businessman, who has employed thousands of people and run a successful business. He still wears his old ripped Levi's jeans, even though he can probably afford much more—because he is humble and remembers his roots. He prays daily and attends church weekly, and he always blasts country music in his pickup—donning a Confederate flag bumper sticker.

Or, your typical Republican might be an old, grumpy white male, whose idea of fun on the weekends is shooting defenseless deer while wearing tacky camouflage. *He*—definitely a male—thinks everyone who is an illegal immigrant is Mexican, wants taxes so low that people on welfare starve to death, and has never been to New York. Worse, he has no desire of ever going.

Not one of these four descriptions exactly define anyone, nor do they come close to describing the political parties—the Democratic party was prevalent in the rural South before it gained a foothold in the pro-labor union North, and the Republican Party was almost exclusively a northern party with roots in nineteenth century abolitionism. There are African American Republicans in New York and white Democrats in Alabama. But nuance and moderation is no longer a part of the political culture in America—Republicans have to appeal more and more to their Southern, gun-toting base and Democrats to their labor unions and feminist groups of the North and West for political victory. And they are still securing victories, no doubt. But it does not seem the same can be said for the country as a whole.

Over the past two decades, America's dominant political parties have swung more and more to their sides of the room—daring to come close to the middle less and less. The Democrats have lost many of their subgroups over the years: pro-lifers, of which the most famous Democratic dynasty in American history—the Kennedys—was part of, are almost all gone. They've lost most of the "Blue Dog" members of their coalition in Congress, consisting of members who were particularly economically more conservative than their typically northeastern counterparts. What is left is primarily a group of quasi-socialist, radically pro-choice members who are unwilling to talk tax cuts or reasonable restrictions on abortion. On the flipside, the Republicans have lost quite a bit of their constituency, as well—particularly in the Northeast, where only two of New England's twenty-two Congressmen are Republicans. If a Republican were to come out in favor of environmental restrictions, union rights, gun control, or gay rights, they can effectively kiss their next primary election—now dominated by fringe "Tea Party" groups—goodbye. Just ask former Senator Bob Bennett of Utah, or failed presidential candidate Rudy Giuliani.

But what's wrong with mixing things up a bit? Parties function today as sources of negative groupthink and conventions where everyone confirms each other's beliefs instead of challenging them. What if I'm a pro-union, pro-environment, pro-gun control Republican who wants my taxes reasonably low and my borders secure? Or what if I'm a Democrat who believes in a government that takes care of all Americans, but also find myself in the pro-life camp? Do I have no room in my party?

The short answer is "no." Such candidates cannot win primaries, because—even if they won't admit it—both parties have litmus tests for their candidates. Entrenched major party donors and bosses won't allow it, because any shift from the conventional platform would alienate a key voting bloc. And so, the American people, time after time, are forced to choose between two rigid dogmas that very few voters actually fully agree with.

In business, the only antidote to monopoly is competition. The same goes for politics. But how on earth can the moderate, questioning middle compete against interests so entrenched, so rooted in money and power? The generation that answers this question will have a modern American political realignment—a revolution, of sorts—to call their own.

LATE BREAKING: OBAMA TO RUN IN 2012 AS A REPUBLICAN; SECRETARY CLINTON ANNOUNCES CAMPAIGN

(Parody | Spring of 2011)

IN A MOVE that has sent shockwaves throughout the political world, President Barack Obama announced today that he is kicking off his campaign for re-election by breaking ranks with the Democratic party and will instead run as a Republican in 2012.

In his press conference announcing the party switch, the President said, "After two years of record deficits, a healthcare bill that will cost billions and accomplish close to nothing, a war in Afghanistan that seems to have no end, and a failing economy, I have seen the light."

Obama's punny religious reference was well-received in comedians' circles, since the President is widely regarded as "The Messiah" and the "second coming" of Jesus Christ among the educated elite. A recent Gallup poll of those who live in ivy-covered buildings (and/or in and around the Berkeley, California area) found that an overwhelming 96% of residents answered "Barack Obama" when asked the poll question, "Whom do you regard as your eternal savior?" Only 4% answered "Jesus Christ or an equivalent figure lesser in stature and glory than Barack Obama." Elected officials throughout Washington had mixed reactions to the stunning announcement.

In a swift response that sent similar (but not quite as impressive) jolts throughout the Capitol Beltway, Secretary of State Hillary Clinton submitted her resignation to the White House today, and announced her bid to be the Democratic candidate to challenge President Obama.

"Today we start anew," Clinton said in a speech that was occasionally interrupted by her loud bouts of maniacal, seemingly uncontrollable laughter. "We are beginning the process of taking back this country. With your help, the White House will be mine, all mine!"

When asked about the remark, spokesman Richard Morris issued the following statement: "President-to-be Clinton simply misspoke; Ms. Clinton meant to say that the White House will be 'ours,' as in belonging to the people. She meant 'mine' in the sense that although the presidency will be hers, she will share it with the rest of America." Morris directed attention to former President Bill Clinton's use of the word "is" as another example of definitions being taken out of context.

Former President Clinton could not be reached for comment regarding his wife's decision to seek the office he once held. His spokesman reported that Mr. Clinton was in Lyon County, Nevada, for an economic development forum. The county has the unique distinction of being the home of The Moonlite "Bunny" Ranch.

In Wasilla, Alaska, gunshots were reportedly heard emanating from the home of former Alaska governor Sarah Palin within minutes of the morning announcement. While neighbors expressed the fear that Palin's "final screw had come loose" upon hearing she would not be able to seek the presidency in 2012, a Palin spokeswoman later clarified that the former governor was simply "catching breakfast."

The President's prospects for 2012 suddenly look very different, as the electoral map is suddenly reversed and Obama will have to spend more time campaigning in conservative states to maintain his edge.

Elsewhere in Washington, other top figures reacted with surprise to the announcement. Vice President Joe Biden, seen leaving Duffy's Irish Pub, could only offer a phrase he has used often to describe significant moments in the nation's history: "This is a big f***ing deal," he said.

A KINDER, GENTLER NATION

(*Devils' Advocate, June 2, 2011*)

IT REMAINS TODAY one of the most adroitly phrased and prescient wishes for the future of Amerca—President George H. W. Bush's desire, as stated in his 1988 speech to the Republican National Convention, to see a "kinder, gentler nation." With the culture of radicalism, arrogance, and corporatism that feeds the political discussion in America today, it is fitting that the last article this columnist ever writes for the *Devils' Advocate* be about the future of our societal discourse.

Bush's quote should strike close to home for all of us—but let us begin with his own political party and its adherents. What has become of H.W.'s Republican party? Simple observations can prove that it's not the party it once was—the party that, in Bush's 1988 election, won states as varied as Louisiana, Pennsylvania, and Texas—but also painted Illinois, Michigan, California, Connecticut and Vermont red. Sure, the demographics of those states have changed somewhat in the past twenty years, but even moreso has the party which used to fare so well in the West and the Northeast. It has lost touch with its kinder, gentler side: its loudest talkers have abandoned center-right economic policy in favor of drastic cost-cutting solutions which the Democrats effectively paint as death knells for entitlement programs that millions of American depend on to get by. It has allowed itself to be labeled anti-immigrant because it permits fringe groups to carry the dialouge on immigration. And, in a final affront to Northeastern and Western voters, it has embraced a solidly and unapologetically anti-gay anything (marriage, civil union, etc.) platform without really engaging the gay community to join the dialogue and reach a compromise. On its abortion position, the Republican party has refused to hold a substantive debate about the issue, which—if it does—it can likely win: most Americans, according to Gallup, identify as pro-life and would rather see taxpayer dollars withheld from abortion funding. An overwhelming majority of Americans also believe abortion should only be legal in certain circumstances, and do not embrace the Democratic party's abortion-on-demand position. But, here as well, the Republican party has boxed itself in by refusing to get beyond party talking points, and it has been labeled anti-woman by groups on the Democratic side as a consequence. The Republican party, largely by its own fault, is no longer viewed in many parts of America as an even-minded party—and is consequently fading into irrelevance in states where it was once extremely competitive.

But the same may be said of the Democratic party—which has

transformed itself from a big-tent orgnanization encompassing union strongholds in urban centers to the "Dixiecrat" South into a party which can't really get past urban areas, women voters, and minority populations. Since the 1970s, the Democratic party has adopted a quasi-socialist (in its openly stated economic redistributionary policy and affinity for government investment), dangerously open-borders, and almost exclusively feminist and pro-union plank. The Democratic party uplatform under President Obama is farther to the left than it has ever been before and, on paper and in practice, arrogantly falls out of line with the political opinions of a country which considers itself center-right. Intraparty debates over spending, border security, and abortion law have been silenced in the name of party unity, and moderate Democrats find it increasingly difficult to survive both their comeptitive primary and general elections (as a case in point, most of the moderate-to-conservative "Blue Dog" Democrats in Congress were wiped out last year, replaced by Tea Party Republicans—leaving a mostly hard left Democratic minority in Congress).

So the question in all this remains: where do the allegiances of the middle class lie? It is difficult to say. Do they lie with a party whose intention it is, as demonstrated in states like Wisconsin and Ohio this past year, to crush long-held union benefits and power and replace them with corporate power structures? Or do they lie with a party who has embraced rampant deficit spending with the promise of paying its way out of recession, only to find that economic growth continues to stagnate just as before? A party who is split on immigration policy between xenophobes who want everyone out and corporatists who want illegals to stay so they can continue to live in the shadows and be exploited for economic gain, or one which favors legalization and reduced enforcement in order to pander to ethnic groups which they know will soon become potent political voting blocs? Which party is kinder and gentler to the interests of that silent majority which consitutes the middle class?

Contrary to popular belief, each and every problem posed in today's political discussion has a reasonable solution. Deficits can be cut and budgets balanced. A strong border enforcement policy can be instituted that is coupled with a "back of the line" program for those immigrants here already. The solutions are out there, but the climate and the political will is not.

George H. W. Bush's call for a "kinder, gentler nation" should not go unheard in today's political atmosphere. A kinder, gentler conservatism could go a long way in solving many of the nation's problems: one which is tolerant and accepting of different faiths, ethnicities, genders and orientations but stands firmly in favor of American Judeo-Christian tradition—and one which acknowledges the need for government to exist in a limited, effective, and direct capacity. It has been done in other countries and it can be done here: in the Netherlands, the center-right Christian Democratic Party (CDA) encompasses members who are ethnically Dutch, but also those who are Muslim, gay, or otherwise who believe in the West's liberal democratic and Judeo-Christian tradition. Other examples of such moderate and all-encompassing parties abound throughout the world's varied political landscape.

America remains, and likely will remain for some time, a center-right nation. The "frontier mentality," which places trust in the individual over the constraints of collectivism, is what has made America great. But unless the modern conservative movement acknowledges a responsibility to the collective, along with its reverence for the individual, it will be spurned as narrow-minded and will find itself electorally stranded. America is an individualistic, but also a kind and gentle nation—if conservatism can grasp both the former and the latter aspects of the American psyche, it will certainly catapult itself into huge electoral success.

2. *College Years*

YALE FEDERALIST PARTY SPEECH

(*September 1, 2011*)

History's tendency to repeat itself is particularly poignant today with regards to America's military—which, like the standing armies of antiquity, has increasingly proven that it cannot stand still for too long. America's continually escalating radical interventionist foreign policy has spread our armed forces thin from a tactical standpoint, but as we well know, it threatens a more significant disunity, as well: divorcing the armed forces from society, and removing the rank-and-file from the public's view. The result, as former House Armed Services Committee Chairman, Democrat Ike Skelton said, is a state in which "those who protect us are psychologically divorced from those who are being protected." According to former Defense Secretary Robert Gates, as the army becomes more exclusive—with less family members or friends known to the general public who serve—bonds are broken, or never made. More people just don't care, emotionally detached from unknown people fighting in unknown places for an ambiguous cause, at best. The proof is in the military pudding—movies about Iraq and Afghanistan perpetually perform poorly at the box office, a December Defense Department report discovered that 25% of military applicants can't pass the exam, and 75% of recruit-age Americans are obese, or—have drug problems.

What is to be done? And more importantly, what is the root cause of this demise in a once military-loving, reverent culture? Some would attribute it to a degeneration in America's moral fabric. That is happening, to be sure. But I'm not sure it's to blame for this particular phenomenon. The true reason lies in our army being spread vastly too thin, putting an exorbitant strain on servicemen who must endure perpetually extended tours of duty. It has also lead to the armed forces relaxing its standards as to who can join. The army is appealing to people it wouldn't have before as a direct result of frivolous wars begun without any sense of public consensus and conducted poorly afterwards.

America need not fear military versus civilian government conflict paralleling that of Turkey, where the army is the guardian of secularism against an increasingly Islamist government. Our problem going forward will be to bridge the growing stratification between the armed forces and their families and a society which doesn't understand them—nor has any particular desire to. The result is alienation and misunderstanding on both sides, meaning less morale amongst the force and less competency and understanding amongst the civilian leaders who send the force into battle.

So the solution lies not only in returning ROTC to campuses, and promoting our military in film—which, as Saving Private Ryan proved—can be done well, but also by scaling back America's unrestrained military interventionism—and our ugly leading export which is nihilistic multiculturalism. Then, I think we will find that ROTC programs are not shunned by students and faculty in academia to the degree that they are. To those ends, I agree with Miss Marin and Mr. Landry, respectively. To make the military more respected at home and abroad, as failed candidate John Kerry once said in a temporary moment of likely botox-induced lucid insight, we must prove to the American people that our military decision-making is rooted in the constitutional duty to defend American citizens—and nothing more. Leave the evangelizing—the spreading of the freedom agenda gospel—to the churches. Our men and women in uniform don't deserve—at their livelihoods' expense—to be the pawns of our leaders' pretentious ideological imperialism.

"YOU DIDN'T (SAY) THAT!"

(*Light & Truth, Volume 19, Issue 1, September 2012*)

SOUND BITES ARE rarely fodder for even five minutes of substantive discussion about high-priority national issues, let alone the weeks and weeks of mindless coverage the Great Triumvirate of public civic education—CNN, FOX News and MSNBC—can be regularly found affording them. But every once in a while, a candidate's one-liner or inanity will be a revelatory moment. And, in this age of closely guarded candid-moment paucity, these statements have a tendency of becoming some of the most revealing moments of the campaign. A tired Ronald Reagan's "Shut up!" to a heckler on the last day of campaigning brought out a down-to-earth humanity in the candidate that the audience instantly loved. Hillary Clinton's crying in New Hampshire was met with both genuine empathy and allegations of crocodile tears. And now, there's "You didn't build that!"

Much can and has been made of President Obama's comment, but the words surrounding the sound bite reveal quite a bit about his thinking:

> "If you've been successful, you didn't get there on your own... I'm always struck by people who think, well, it must be because I was just so smart. There are a lot of smart people out there. It must be because I worked

> harder than everybody else. Let me tell you something—there are a whole bunch of hardworking people out there. If you were successful, somebody along the line gave you some help. There was a great teacher somewhere in your life. Somebody helped to create this unbelievable American system that we have that allowed you to thrive. Somebody invested in roads and bridges. If you've got a business—you didn't build that. Somebody else made that happen."

First, the context illustrates that the remarks certainly were not a slip. Obama slowly builds up to the punch line with examples of how successful people receive help along the way, seeming to assert the entire time that an entrepreneur is not wholly responsible for his or her company's success. Part of the utterance is, essentially, a truism. Of course businessmen don't single-handedly build their businesses—they have supportive families and friends to thank for helping them out when times got difficult; they have their communities to thank for working with them; they have America to thank for the system of education, infrastructure and a spirit of entrepreneurship that made their businesses possible. Duh. One might even call the gratitude for all of this taken together "patriotism," which an overwhelming majority of American businessmen no doubt feel. It affects everything from their politics to their charitable giving. No one is questioning these notions.

Unfortunately, these ideas do not seem to be what President Obama meant. In fact, he evolves (as he is wont to do) from saying "you didn't get there on your own," a charge few people who have been successful in business would deny, to saying "you didn't build that." And, more importantly, "Somebody else made that happen." He essentially moves from expressing, you had help to you're not responsible for success within seconds of each other—a leap, if there ever was one.

And yet, fact checkers like the website *PolitiFact* have rated reactions to Obama made by Romney and other Republicans on this episode as "False." The website argues that these Republicans have "misled viewers and given a false impression" by taking the words out of context since the rest of the speech (apparently omitted) makes "clear that Obama was talking about the importance of government-provided infrastructure and education to the success of private businesses." Maybe Obama didn't really mean to insinuate this after all, but Romney's interpretation is by no means an outlandish one. In the part of his speech where he is mocking entrepreneurs for believing in their own success, Obama makes fun of the notion that, "it must be because I worked harder than everybody else. Let me tell you something," the knowing president continues, "There are a whole bunch of hardworking people out there." The intelligent reader must discern for himself whether President Obama here did in fact suggest that one's success does not spring from one's own hard work, but rather on aid from others. It seems difficult to brand Romney's indictment of the way Obama downplays the role of hard work in determining success as "a lie."

Of course, this speech hardly comes as a surprise—only, rather, furthering the public's insight into Obama's mentality. It builds upon the message Obama relayed in Osawatomie, Kansas, back in December. There he said, "As a nation, we've always come together, through our government, to help create the conditions where both workers and businesses can succeed."

Roads are great. Public schools are great—even essential. And public services to help the needy in a compassionate society are also great. That is why Americans consent to paying the high taxes that we do; it is why we engage in substantially more charitable giving than most societies on earth, according to the World Giving Index. This is nothing more than a semantic debate, and a bad one at that. But what isn't up for debate is that presidents are in charge of setting the national agenda and the national mood—in both of these respects, phrasing and morale matter a great deal. Attempting to belittle the community tasked with generating wealth—wealth that Obama as President has had no aptitude for or experience in creating—is plainly senseless.

Then again, dear Mr. Bonaparte, you were painfully correct that stupidity in politics has never been a handicap.

GOP SENATE HOPES FADE

(*Yale Daily News, November 2, 2012*)

WITH THIS YEAR'S election cycle coming to a close, Republicans hope to reclaim a Senate majority for the first time since 2006 are facing a spate of final polls showing GOP candidates leading in only four of the country's 11 competitive Senate races. With 33 races taking place this year, the latest polling puts Democrats in position to hold at least 52 seats in the Senate after Election Day, maintaining their majority despite having many more seats up for re-election.

Republicans came into this election cycle defending 10 Senate seats, while Democrats were forced to defend 23, a situation that Yale political science professor John Bullock '01 said could result in a perceived loss for Senate Republicans this November.

"If the Democrats keep control, it should be regarded as a big blow to the Republicans. The Democrats had a slim majority. They had to defend many more open seats. And they had a few highly vulnerable candidates," Bullock said in a Wednesday email to the News. "A year ago, I don't think that any informed, objective observer would have given them a 50-50 chance of keeping their majority. I certainly didn't."

But political science professor David Mayhew disagrees. Excluding the presidential race, Mayhew said 2012 was "a real bad year for challengers, regardless of party."

"Ninety-five percent of incumbent senators who are running again, 95 percent of House members who are running again and 100 percent of governors running again are running ahead," Mayhew said. "Despite the low [polling] standing of Congress, there is virtually no evidence of any voter kickback against House Republicans, Tea Partiers or otherwise."

Pundits expect the Republican party to maintain its control in the House of Representatives.

In Connecticut's open seat to replace retiring Sen. Joe Lieberman '64 LAW '67, Democrat Rep. Chris Murphy has pulled ahead of Republican businesswoman Linda McMahon, maintaining a five-point average lead in polls after having run neck-and-neck with McMahon earlier in the campaign. In neighboring Massachusetts, incumbent Republican Sen. Scott Brown is trailing Harvard professor Elizabeth Warren by over four percentage points, though pundits still consider the race a toss-up.

Geoffrey Skelley, chief political analyst for the University of Virginia's Center for Politics, said the race is Warren's to lose.

"Unless Elizabeth Warren had turned out to be a complete zero of a candidate, it was always going to be tough for Brown to win re-election in a presidential year," Skelley said. "The Democratic tide in Massachusetts is just too much."

Democrats also lead narrowly in Virginia, where former Democratic Governor Tim Kaine currently bests former Republican Senator George Allen by a narrow one-point margin, and Wisconsin, in which former Republican Governor Tommy Thompson is running 0.3 points behind Democratic Rep. Tammy Baldwin. While these races are close, Democratic incumbents have seen significant polling leads ahead of Republican challengers in Florida and Ohio, even while both remain swing states in the presidential election, with Democratic Sen. Bill Nelson '65 and Democratic Sen. Sherrod Brown '74 leading by five- to six-point margins in Florida and Ohio polling averages, respectively.

While Republicans began the 2012 Senate election cycle hopeful about retaking the Senate by running moderate candidates with bipartisan appeal in New Mexico, Hawaii and New Jersey, all three are behind Democrats in polls. In Missouri and Indiana, two races in which Republicans were long presumed to be favorites, the Democratic candidates are now once again competitive in light of comments made about abortion in the case of rape. Competitive Senate elections in which Republicans currently lead in polls are in Montana, North Dakota, Nebraska and Nevada.

Skelley said he recommends looking to the 2014 elections, when it will be "difficult" for Democrats to stay in control given the number of vulnerable seats they will be defending. RealClearPolitics political analyst Caitlin Huey-Burns, meanwhile, suggested watching Pennsylvania in the final days of the election, where Democrats are favored to win in both the Senate and presidential election but Republicans are showing signs of closing the gap in the final days of campaigning.

Election Day is Tuesday, Nov. 6.

FORUM: ELECTION EVENING

(*Yale Daily News, November 6, 2012*)

REPUBLICANS MAY OR may win the presidential election this year, but this time—at least compared to last time around, which was a sleeper of a race as far as Republican offices around the country were concerned—they've campaigned like a party shocked back to life.

I remember walking into regional Republican campaign offices throughout the swing-y regions of northern Kentucky and Ohio in 2008. There were usually one or two lonely senior citizens making calls. Campaign paraphernalia was in short supply. The entire operation felt like a dead man walking, because, well, it was. The night before the election, as I walked out of GOP headquarters after making a last round of dispirited phone calls, the regional coordinator called out to me to take the last of the yard signs—"Honey, why don't you just take these and put them up around?"

But this weekend, I traveled to New Hampshire—the swingiest of swing states—to volunteer. I got to see what the mood was like there. The office was packed, the phones were ringing and random citizens were coming in for all sorts of Romney gear. Volunteers brought their babies and their dogs. Others supplied donuts, and a continuous stream of coffee flowed. Whether or not we were projected to win, the 2008-era resignation was gone. Entire streets were lined with Romney yard signs; we knocked on door after door to receive smiling assurances that Romney had the support of someone living inside.

This is all anecdotal evidence, of course. Romney may or may not win tonight, but Republicans are back to compete on a presidential level. Whether it will be enough to counter the Democratic turnout advantage remains to be seen, but what's certain is that if the election were decided by independents, as Politico reported, Romney would win in a landslide.

CONGRESS POISED FOR MORE OF THE SAME

(*Yale Daily News, November 7, 2012*)

As THE DUST clears after one of the most expensive election cycles in recent memory, many political analysts are predicting that the newly elected Congress will continue to face legislative gridlock.

With Republicans maintaining control of the House of Representatives and Democrats hanging on to their Senate majority, President Barack Obama will enter a new term with his work cut out for him. Not only has the president faced an uncompromising atmosphere in Congress since Republicans won the House in 2010, but political moderates in Congress also faced losses last night that may speak to the polarization of both parties. "No one is going to break through the gridlock this year. In fact, Congress will be more polarized than before. The last of the moderates are losing," said Michael Tanner, senior domestic policy fellow at the libertarian CATO Institute.

Brian Darling, senior fellow for government studies at the Heritage Foundation, a conservative think tank, said he thinks it is unlikely that congressional Republicans will agree to raise revenues in the coming session.

"I would expect more of the same we've had over the past two years," Darling said of a Democratic win for both the Senate and the presidency. "It will be virtually impossible to extend all of the Bush tax cuts, but otherwise I don't think Republicans are going to accede to the idea that we need more tax revenues. The federal government spends too much, and Republicans will have the incentive to continue focusing on cutting spending."

Darling said that had Romney won and the Senate tightened, Republicans would have been likely to pursue further spending and regulation cuts.

Elizabeth Henry '14, the president of the Yale College Republicans, said she thinks Obama's re-election will determine congressional action.

"The president determines the dynamic, and what happens in Congress will depend on whether we have a president who is committed to bipartisanship," Henry said. "Every major Obama administration initiative was passed with almost no Republican votes."

But Yale College Democrats President Zak Newman '13 said that even with both Obama's re-election and a divided Congress, Republicans will have to compromise more frequently.

"They can no longer be the party of 'no,'" Newman said.

Darling identified Obama's often-touted jobs proposal as a potential legislative priority that might attract bipartisan support in the coming session.

But Tanner said he is not optimistic about the prospect for compromise given a recent spike in party polarization. He identified Republicans like New Hampshire Rep. Charlie Bass and Massachusetts Sen. Scott Brown as members of an endangered breed of party moderates who lost in highly contested races last night. He also noted how "Blue Dogs," the name given to moderate and conservative Democrats in the House and Senate, suffered heavy losses in 2010 as a "more polarized electorate" voted for conservative, Tea Party-backed Republicans instead.

"The Senate is likely getting more polarizing figures on the left and right, like Massachusetts candidate Elizabeth Warren and Texas Solicitor General Ted Cruz," Tanner said.

Other moderates, like Republican Sen. Richard Lugar of Indiana, were defeated by Tea Party conservatives in primary elections. Such polarization is expected to continue because most of those elected to Congress in 2010 will remain in office.

Due to Congress' inability to compromise on significant legislation, three analysts interviewed said they fear the new legislative session will be marked by more "stopgap" measures that offer temporary fixes to immediate budgetary issues but will be more cautious when it comes to seriously tackling budgetary reform and other major priorities, including entitlement reform and Medicare. But Tanner said he predicts the newly elected Congress will still tackle immigration reform, given bipartisan interest in resolving the issue.

Prior to yesterday's election, the Senate was split between 53 Democrats and 47 Republicans. The House of Representatives had 241 Republican members and 191 Democratic members.

FISCAL CLIFF THREATENS CONN. ECONOMY

(*Yale Daily News, November 14, 2012*)

As Congress attempts to negotiate an agreement on taxes, spending and the debt ceiling, businesses in Connecticut and across the country are growing uneasy about what the impending "fiscal cliff" could mean for their operations.

If a compromise is not reached before the end of the year, the Budget Control Act of 2011—which was passed last year as a temporary solution to increasingly raising the debt ceiling—stipulates that a combination of tax increases and heavy cuts to government programs will take effect at the start of 2013. "Sequestration," as the automatic budget trigger is called, would mean the end of measures such as payroll tax cuts and components of the Bush-era tax cuts. As many as 1,000 government programs will also feel the impact, with Medicare weathering a 2 percent cut in spending and other mandatory non-defense social programs bearing a 7.5 percent reduction. Facing a 10 percent budget cut, mandatory defense spending will be the most severely influenced; and with an active defense industry, Connecticut could feel an outsize portion of the impact.

"A lot of companies have lost confidence in Congress' ability to do something," said Benjamin Zimmer LAW '12, director of the non-partisan Connecticut Policy Institute. "Last time, the presumption was that at end of the day, they'd figure it out. They didn't."

Zimmer said a number of studies have predicted varying job losses, including one from the National Association of Manufacturers that estimates 9,000 to 10,000 lost jobs. Other studies have placed as many as 50,000 jobs at risk, but Zimmer thinks such estimates are generally above realistic projections.

Zimmer said the state will inevitably lose jobs if sequestration goes forward. Sikorsky Aircraft Corporation, located in Stratford, Conn., is a large supplier of military aircraft for the U.S. Air Force. Military contractor General Dynamics also maintains a facility in Groton, Conn., which has long served as a primary supplier of submarines for the U.S. Navy.

Another issue, Zimmer said, is that many of these spending reductions are affecting budgets for departments that do not need to be cut. Defense as a share of spending has not been increasing, he said, adding that long-term debt reduction is going to involve a "serious" look at entitlements, which have grown as a percentage of total federal outlays.

"Cutting funding for PBS—or raising taxes on the wealthy, whether or not it's the right thing to do—isn't going to solve the debt problem," Zimmer said.

Connecticut Independent Senator Joseph Lieberman '64 LAW '67, who will take part in negotiating a budget deal before his retirement in January, is opposed to considering any cuts to defense spending as part of the agreement, said his communications director Whitney Phillips.

"Our armed forces are already under unprecedented strain given previous cuts and aging assets," Phillips said.

John Piecuch, a spokesperson at international rating agency Standard & Poor's, said sequestration would not automatically mean a devastating economic impact. Increased tax revenues and cuts in spending visible by the end of 2013 can be "credit-positive," Piecuch said, "provided that the recession didn't result in large numbers of people removed from the workforce to the extent that their skill sets permanently deteriorate."

With regards to the U.S. credit rating, which was downgraded following the 2011 debt ceiling crisis, Piecuch said that another drop given sequestration is a possibility but not a certainty. The last downgrade was fueled by a negative appraisal of the debt trajectory and the current political situation, two of the five "pillars" used by S&P when evaluating credit ratings, he explained. Neither is likely to improve this year, but it is unlikely that these scores will come down even further, he said.

But the Defense Technology Initiative, a research group based in Massachusetts, released a study in November warning that the defense industry in Connecticut "has driven economic growth for the region over the last decade," and that cuts would mean a more sluggish recovery. Companies like General Dynamics are not yet laying workers off, but Congress might force their hand in the coming months.

The fiscal cliff's year-over-year changes for 2012–'13 include a 19.63 percent increase in tax revenue and 0.25 percent reduction in spending.

U.N. SECRETARY-GENERAL PUSHES FOR "GLOBAL CITIZENSHIP"

(*Yale Daily News, November 14, 2012*)

In a speech entitled "Shaping Solutions for a World in Transition," United Nations Secretary-General Ban Ki-moon discussed the major problems facing the world and the need for people to consider themselves global citizens.

Speaking before an audience of roughly 200 in Luce Hall Tuesday afternoon, Ban discussed his push for immediate global attention to continuing conflicts in the Middle East, climate change and the lack of basic resources in some of the world's poorest regions. Provost Peter Salovey, who will become University president on June 30, 2013, served as master of ceremonies for the event and introduced Ban, praising the Secretary-General's ongoing commitments to sustainable development, women's empowerment and arms control. During his lecture, Ban urged professors to cultivate "global citizenship" in their students, adding that students must approach their futures with an eye to international problems.

Ban said the modern era is one of dramatic transformation.

"We are living in an era of inequality, instability, injustice and intolerance, but people are demanding freedom, accountability and equal opportunity," he said.

Citing the continuing violence in Syria, Ban said the Arab world has undergone a period during which regimes content with a "repressive" status quo have been falling apart. The Secretary-General said he remains "gravely concerned" about the situation in Syria, particularly with regard to the brutal force the Assad regime has employed against peaceful protestors and its refusal to honor a truce during the important religious holiday of Eid. Ban said he has appealed to both the Assad government and the opposition to stop the use of violence and to begin the process of political dialogue immediately.

Ban also voiced support for the Obama administration's promises to curb climate change, and discussed U.N. efforts to bring critical resources to communities in need. He said the creation of Every Woman Every Child, the Zero Hunger Challenge and Education First during his tenure helped create stable living conditions and gave historically underserved populations worldwide the tools necessary to have an active role in the 21st century. He stressed that these goals are inextricably linked to global security challenges.

"Terrorists don't fear governments' guns, but they do fear education," Ban said. "They fear girls with a textbook. When people are educated, there remains no place for terrorists to stand."

During his lecture, Ban emphasized the importance of the United States' partnership with the U.N., remembering his own childhood and recalling that U.S.-backed international forces from the U.N. fought against North Korea during the Korean War.

He also reminded the audience he was in tune with contemporary culture.

"I guess you came to hear a Korean on the international scene," Ban said, "But I'm not going to dance Gangnam Style."

Four students interviewed said they were disappointed that Ban did not bring a new perspective to the issues he addressed in his lecture.

"His speech was entirely rhetoric," Luis Schachner '15 said. "I was expecting thought-provoking new ideas about international problems but they weren't there."

Ban became Secretary-General in 2007.

MENTAL HEALTH BUDGET OVERHAULED

(*Yale Daily News, February 14, 2013*)

IN THE WAKE of a renewed national focus on mental health services after a gunman left 27 people dead in Newtown, Conn., last December, Gov. Dannel Malloy has released a budget for the Connecticut Department of Mental Health and Addiction Services that increases funding for young adult services, but may leave some of the state's most vulnerable patients without public assistance.

The proposed budget calls for an increase in support for home and community-based services, in addition to brain injury placements and help for adolescent and early adult patients. But the plan also reduces funding for legal services and testing, including eliminating $1.3 million for research at the Yale-affiliated Connecticut Mental Health Center.

Jan VanTassel, attorney and executive director of the Connecticut Legal Rights Project, said the cuts will have a "serious" effect on her organization's ability to provide mentally disabled individuals and their families with the legal representation they need to stay in their homes and get much-needed care. The agency works with clients who face eviction, whose housing subsidies are threatened, and individuals who need disability assistance to be able to enter and exit their homes. CLRP did not anticipate the elimination of a significant portion of its state funding.

"I was stunned," VanTassel said. "We have always had a very strong working relationship with [the Department of Mental Health and Addiction Services], and we often get direct referrals from DMHAS staff."

CLRP employees have been operating under a salary freeze for the past two years, and VanTassel acknowledged that the cuts, if enacted, will result in "immediate layoffs" of legal personnel.

"We will need an additional $493,000 to be operational in the next fiscal year. What this means in terms of impact on clients is that we're not going to be able to conduct housing and disability advocacy," VanTassel added. "Some will likely lose their housing."

Malloy's press secretary Juliet Manalan declined to comment on the cuts and referred the News to the budget speech the governor delivered last week in Hartford, in which he proposed reducing services spending by $1.8 billion.

"The governor has made it very clear that budget cuts were necessary," she said.

Connecticut is projected to end the current fiscal year on June 30 alone with a budget deficit of $140 million.

The cuts will also have an immediate impact on services in New Haven, where the Connecticut Mental Health Center is located. State Rep. Juan Candelaria, D-New Haven, told the New Haven Independent in a Feb. 8 article that the elimination of funding will directly affect the care that patients in the city receive through the research funding used by the center for treatment. He said he opposes the proposed cuts in Malloy's budget for DMHAS.

But DMHAS spokeswoman Mary Kate Mason emphasized that the budget for the department will increase as a result of "caseload growth" among young adults requiring mental health services. Mason also said that the budget figures—including the cut in CMHC funding—reflects an anticipated increase in assistance from the federal government, with continued implementation of the Affordable Care Act of 2010.

"The governor's proposed budget for DMHAS increases funding for available community services and accounts for the reduction in need for state subsidies for under- and uninsured individuals as a result of the Affordable Care Act," Mason said. "Mental health services are one of the core services provided for under the Affordable Health Care Act, so it is anticipated that mental health services will be more widely available."

It remains unclear, however, whether those who are not covered by the Affordable Care Act and who do not receive public health benefits will be able to receive mental health treatment following the implementation of the budget for fiscal year 2014.

The overhaul also has other groups, including the Connecticut chapter of the National Alliance on Mental Illness, concerned. Sara Frankel, part of the public policy team at the organization, expressed mixed feelings with the projected budget.

"We're pleased to see an increase in the line item for young adult services, and we're thankful that Gov. Malloy recognizes the need to expand the state's work with more young adults," Frankel said.

But she also called the proposed cuts "concerning," noting that legal advocacy often represents the key factor in guaranteeing a patient's unhindered access to needed care. While state laws differ, many have regulations that do not accept new patients in the public system until they prove themselves "dangerous" by hurting themselves or someone in the community.

In explaining her surprise at the decision, VanTassel said that the governor has previously been receptive to the need for effective legal services for patients with mental illness.

"At a reception last year for people in the profession, Gov. Malloy called legal services the 'safety net of safety nets,'" VanTassel said.

Another problem with cutting legal advocacy funding is the "ridiculously low" salaries that are generally offered to attorneys who are recruited to work on behalf of mentally disordered patients, VanTassel said.

Malloy's proposed budget increases spending overall by 5.1 percent in fiscal year 2014.

NEGROPONTE HIGHLIGHTS FOREIGN POLICY CHALLENGES

(*Yale Daily News, February 26, 2013*)

Speaking to an audience of about 20 students in Linsly-Chittenden Hall Monday night, Yale lecturer and former ambassador John Negroponte '60 commented on a wide range of foreign policy issues facing the Obama administration today.

The former ambassador identified what he described as the three key elements of American foreign policy: to protect the country's security, to enhance economic interests and to promote and defend American values. Negroponte also argued that the core of U.S. foreign policy involves the ongoing need to build positive diplomatic relations with other countries. He called for the new secretary of state, John Kerry '66, to continue the emphasis on keeping diplomatic channels open and to articulate the need for more economic and military agreements between nations as a strategy for deterring new challenges.

Negroponte also spoke of the consistency that has characterized American foreign policy since the end of World War II.

"When you take a look at what is actually done, foreign policy doesn't broadly change from administration to administration or party to party," Negroponte said.

The former ambassador said the international situation and the national mood mean that President Barack Obama is unlikely to start any new foreign engagements in the near future, adding that Obama will likely opt instead to concentrate international relations in the context of a national focus on the economy and internal rebuilding. He cited the president's State of the Union address in January, which alluded sparsely to foreign policy but mentioned a potential free-trade agreement with Europe, as an example of a shift in focus.

Negroponte also touched on issues he predicted that America and its allies will soon have to face, including the changing role of NATO and a still-resurgent Russia. While there have been positive relations between the United States and Russia on issues like arms control, nuclear nonproliferation and counterterrorism, Negroponte acknowledged "some daylight" in terms of human rights and democracy issues that must be managed strategically.

In speaking about the Obama administration's policy on the decadelong war in Afghanistan, Negroponte said the president seems committed to ending the war quickly, though he recommended leaving a small military presence to indicate long-term American interest in the region.

The former Bush administration diplomat also took questions from the student audience, fielding inquiries about current and past political issues.

When asked about the American military's controversial drone program currently under international scrutiny, Negroponte said the president has been enthusiastic about the program and the administration is looking to expand the program by installing a new launch base in central Africa.

Toward the end of his speech, Negroponte spoke of climate change as an issue he would like to see addressed.

"This is an area where it will take the president's personal leadership to get things done," he said, recommending a focus on China and India as two of the world's largest polluters.

Linh Nguyen '15, who organized the event, praised Negroponte for sharing his views, adding that his personal experience enriched his opinions.

Miranda Melcher '16 said Negroponte's perspective allowed audience members to consider foreign policy over time.

"People our age tend to forget that the people making the

decision are a lot older than us," she said, adding that this time frame shapes the way high-level government officials make decisions.

The ambassador's talk was sponsored by the Yale International Relations Association.

CLOSING THE TRUST GAP

(*Yale Daily News, April 19, 2013*)

STERLING PROFESSOR OF political science David Mayhew once noticed that "Probably half the adverse criticism of Congress by elites is an indirect criticism of the public itself." Few truer observations about contemporary political discourse have been made in recent memory. The public gripes about an inactive Senate, but within that institution, there are Senators, and behind Senators, there are primary and general elections. The blame, then, is meant really for the voters themselves.

Money talks, but few issues or candidates without the potential for widespread appeal catch fire among the electorate, no matter the financial advantage: see Romney, Mitt. Similarly, some sociopolitical shifts are so great that it makes no sense to try to wage political campaigns on them, as will be the case for gay marriage for the foreseeable future.

Over the last 40 years, this same kind of a shift happened with gun politics. The popular notion that the National Rifle Association was once a gun control-loving fraternal organization is not exactly true. In fact, the NRA began vocally opposing various federal measures in the early '70s, after originally having supported certain elements of the Gun Control Act of 1968.

But the narrative that the American voting public was in favor of stricter gun control in the past certainly is correct. Indeed, in the late '60s, public support for tightening gun laws hovered between 60 and 70 percent.

As gun control measures were passed, and new ones were increasingly being suggested, mobilization against them grew more sophisticated. But even in 1994, 61 senators and 235 representatives (including 46 Republicans) passed a 10-year ban on specific assault weapons. But in 2004, things changed. Despite continuing violence, the political wind behind gun control was gone, revoked by the people.

Is it because ignorance in America grew? Did the people in what coastal cosmopolitans consider "flyover country" become more reactionary? A disturbing number of people I talk to at Yale think so. Certainly, opposition to gun restrictions became better organized—but, nationwide, citizens' trust in their government also declined rapidly.

The bottom has fallen out of trust in national government. Congress's approval rating hovers in the single digits, and a litany of surveys also find that people want private organizations and state governments to replace the federal government in a wide swath of executive functions.

This narrative of alienation has been getting louder since the Kennedy assassination and the Vietnam War (before then, Americans liked their government a whole lot more). It grew also as a result of the repeated squandering of political goodwill, from Johnson to Nixon to Clinton to Bush. People want to see their choices for political leaders vindicated. They tolerate one big mess, or two—but eventually, after years of disappointment, they just throw up their hands. And so, alienation invades. This is especially true for gun control legislation, where stories of government malfeasance have dominated the pro-gun discourse.

The response from steadfast supporters of the state, instead of turning a critical eye towards government waste and incompetence, has been to condescend those who've felt alienated. "Of course government can be trusted! Take your conspiracies elsewhere!"

PayPal founder Peter Thiel has often observed that New Deal-style engineering simply cannot be envisioned today. To wit, a very postmodern skepticism has set in about the limits of government.

The answer to this trust gap is more normativity, not less. We need more "values" rhetoric that asserts American exceptionalism and capability, and more politicians who, instead of shying away from proposing Fourteen Points or manifestos for fear of being lampooned, sketch out a vision for a new American century.

And the private vs. public distinction as it's currently understood needs to vanish, too. Presidents kiss babies, they lead the nation in grief and they represent American vitality. If they were Politburo-style technocrats, perhaps they could live immoral personal lives. But they aren't, and they can't.

People's views towards gun control were different in the second "era of good feelings" leading up to the '70s. Yes, the NRA was a different organization then—but so was the government. No matter how reasonable the gun control regulation, a critical mass won't be in favor if people think they are living in a banana republic.

We're not, of course. But there's enough government garbage to make many think so. A new era of virtuous example in leadership—and a rebirth of moral language, responsibly used—is sorely needed in today's public discourse to reverse the "leave me alone" narrative of alienation. Only then do significant gun control laws, and an American renewal, stand a chance.

SAVING SINCERITY

(*Yale Daily News, September 23, 2013*)

An oversimplification of Kant's discourse on why we should not break promises goes something like this: to break a promise, or to make one with no intention of keeping it, renders meaningless the very act of promising itself. It's a simple point made in the broader argument for his categorical imperative, which has been the subject of must philosophical debate. But it seems pretty clear that anyone with a reputation of not following through on their word loses authority and respect.

The promise—along with the very concepts of responsibility and sincerity themselves—are always under attack in public political discourse, since politics reflects man's sinful and self-interested nature. No surprise there. And while there is definitely nothing new under the sun, every once in a while an instance of dirty politics reminds us how hypocritical we are.

Calls for more civility in politics abound from the left and right, as we are constantly besieged with cable news headlines that carry on pointless (and often hurtful) semantic battles between one talk host and another. The organized response to such brinksmanship has taken on forms like the non-profit group "No Labels," which has proposed some good, but unimplemented, structural changes to the executive and legislative branches. Most of these proposals have gotten little media coverage, taking a backseat to flamethrowers whose relentless political maneuvering (most recently over an impending government shutdown) is much better material for keeping the few people watching still tuned in.

Enter, briefly, the world of former House Speaker Nancy Pelosi, who has repeatedly called for an "increase in civility" in politics. A few days ago, she branded her party's fiercest opponents in the latest government budget battle "legislative arsonists." Within the past week, she has also called President Obama "a nonpartisan president," and accused Republicans of wanting to "take down" his presidency because his nonpartisanship is "very hard for them to cope with."

Speaker Pelosi is not a media host—she is not Bill Maher or Glenn Beck, whose careers were built largely on draining the reserve of public decency by taking cheap partisan shots at their opponents. Pelosi's comments are thus inexplicable. No constituent, interest group or lobbyist could have demanded that she voice this opinion of her political opposition. And if anger is to blame, politicians have a responsibility to save most of their personal frustration for private conversation. Taking every thought to the public discredits political authority, since we have a lot of thoughts, even the leaders among us, that aren't worth sharing out loud. Politics is personal, but get too personal and you begin to lose virtue and professionalism. You appear insincere and inconsiderate, engaged in the same old game that everyone hates.

It's pretty intuitive that as the fourth estate of American politics has made content readily accessible and constant for the information consumer, the quality of their product has gone down. But while the news itself is an information product, its quality affects the quality of what it's delivering to the consumer: a politician's speech, for instance, or a televised debate. The media cycle encourages newsmakers to share the basest thoughts that come to mind. But for what? For whom? The only plausible answer is for itself. Calling your opponents "arsonists" neither helps your side nor the political processes. It merely helps a struggling cable channel retain a small portion of the viewers who are leaving in the mass exodus from content drained of real political significance.

We have a responsibility to restore sincerity, virtue and—perhaps most importantly—meaning into most of what passes as political discourse on television and in print. As citizens, we have a duty to boycott media that refuses to respect the process it works under. As Yalies, we have a responsibility to make sure that our discourse about issues we care about doesn't become self-defeating by becoming too emotional, flippant or self-righteous. In short, we have a responsibility to teach ourselves to become good citizens, and to check ourselves when we realize we fail. A more humble, sincere approach to politics is better for its own sake, but it also produces better results—an effect we should all be able to get behind.

THE ETHICS OF COMPROMISE AND CONFRONTATION

(*Keynote Speech, The Nantucket Project, September 27, 2013*)

I AM SO honored, thrilled, and I think, appropriately, just a little intimidated, to be among so many of the sort of, brightest minds out there in the United States, here on Nantucket right now. I am John Aroutiounian, and as Tom mentioned, I am the Speaker of the Yale Political Union at Yale University. It's one of the oldest debating societies in the United States, and is the largest campus organization at Yale. Over the years our organization has hosted people like President Franklin Delano Roosevelt to William F. Buckley, Carl Rove to John Kerry, and Larry Summers to Hermain Cain.

As Speaker, my job is to do as little speaking as possible. Our style is a parliamentary-run debate, beginning with an argument from the guest, followed by affirmative and negative speeches on either side of a given resolution or question. The guest stays until the very end of the debate, hears everything happened, asks questions, and then we vote on the topic.

Much in keeping with this year's motto at the Nantucket Project, the YPU comes together every year, or every week really. Every year we're in business since 1934, but we come together every week to seek truth and to endure the consequences, no matter what happens to the resolution on any particular evening.

As a student of political ethics at Yale, I study trends in the way people think of their polity and their particular role in their government as citizens. And I think one of the amazing things about living in a democracy as vibrant, as active, and as diverse as ours, is that you're allowed to live and let live. People with very colliding ideologies, very different life plans, can live on the same street, can be neighbors, and sometimes can even be spouses, even though that latter category is pushing it sometimes.

This tolerance—a staple, absolute fundamental building block of our society, can also lead, though, to some social compartmentalization: "My neighbor lives the way he wants to live, I live the way I want to live, and we're just not going to question that, not even going to think about it. Why bother? What is it of any import to me?" And I sort of detect the same thing happening just across the board at Yale sometimes. You know, "You're a student, you hold your view, I hold my view, and we're just going to keep subsisting that way, "Don't tell me about it. Nobody wants to hear, sort of long-winded impassioned manifestos."

Which brings me to the United States Senate... This morning, the Senate Chaplain, Dr. Barry Black, who I met and spoke a lot to when I was a Page in the US Senate—which is basically just sort of a Senate minion; you run papers around, you get to be a sort of fly on the wall in all of the rooms—this very morning, he started his prayer by saying "Lord, deliver us from governing by crisis." So, divine help was requested on the floor of the United States Senate this morning. He continued by saying, "Use judicious compromise, Senators, for the mutual progress of all."

How do we do that? What does "judicious compromise" look like? Well, yesterday, also, Senator McCain said, you know, the sort of political wrangling over the budget battle going on this week is the worst he's ever seen. And respected US Senator Tom Harkin of Iowa said "We're in one of the most dangerous," that's his word, "points in history." All in the past 24 hours.

So....there are senators in the audience, so I want to be really careful about what I say. But I was a Page once, which is basically a Senate minion...and it still ranks as some of the best couple months of my life. Most Senators care very deeply about the issues that they are invested in. And each one—and I spoke to quite a few in sort of the Senate basement and the hallways, just you know, catching them for a minute—and almost everyone has a reason for getting into politics, and for becoming so involved.

At the Yale Political Union, my job is to make sure intellectual confrontation—sometimes ugly, sometimes easily resolvable—happens every week. If that doesn't happen at the debate that week, I failed. If people leave during the debate because they're disengaged, I failed, I'm in trouble. Maybe that explains why even though you can't really see it when you watch on C-SPAN, most of the time there are no Senators in the chamber. No one's saying anything new, and if they are saying anything new, you can watch it on TV. It's sort of a tradeoff of having C-SPAN in the room, which was introduced a couple of decades ago. Everything's on TV, so direct engagement, physical engagement is not as frequent.

And also yesterday Senator Harry Reid said, "There's no need for a new conversation on the budget. We know what we have to do. We know what the Executive Branch wants us to do." So, it reflects a very palpable and understandable frustration with the gridlock. We feel it as American citizens, I feel it as a student and as a prospective participator in that dialogue, and Senators and Congressmen—people who are currently in the system—feel it, too. But when he says, "there's no need for a new conversation right now," my question is: have we been having one at all in recent years? Was there a conversation to begin with?

Both sides have very large reasons to fuss, right? One side thinks that this, sort of, healthcare bill that's being wrangled to, trying to worked through in the budget process was rammed through early on in 2009, or 2010. And the other side is sort of going to block it at all costs. So, there are reasonable arguments on both sides, that the other side isn't listening. But the ethics of compromise and confrontation, which is sort of the title of my speech today, as practiced in the United States—it's time for a new political dialogue.

Some of you might be familiar with Professor David Mayhew, a political science professor who said, "Probably half the adverse criticism of Congress by American citizens is an indirect criticism of its people, of the American system itself." Which is more than half right.

A lot of the time, we don't want to listen to what the other 50% or what the other 47% wants to say. But it doesn't have to be totally right. There can be a way forward, and there are politicians from left and right, like Bill Christie, Tom Booker, doing it. We say that the media has to change, but that's also a lofty goal. First, it takes politicians who understand what the media is for. Nonpartisan groups like No Labels don't work because there is no political endgame, and no one embraced it.

Politicians, I would submit to you—this is sort of my big point—need to be ranked on how well they do, not on the positions they take, not on their profiles, but their "talk-to-walk" ratio, case work, the effect of the speeches they give. For example, Ted Cruz's recent remarks on the Senate floor, lasting 20 hours, would probably get a low grade. Rand Paul's, even if you don't agree with him, raised the stakes on an issue that wasn't being talked about.

When politicians talk now it seems like they're doing it less for themselves or their constituents, and more for the media. Most of the time, no one really is watching—I mean, have you checked the ratings of the cable networks?

Politics requires real confrontation. The confrontation not just of dialogue, but of actual interests coming together with a deadline present. The real solution is not more confrontation like we've been seeing on TV (the TV-style confrontation), but more actual confrontation. This means we need more diverse congressional districts. It means we need campaign finance reform. But it also means, less structurally, we need more actual debate happening outside of the media circuit.

So, in conclusion I would just like to say that the Yale Political Union can't really exist in real life. You can't have ideals and notions detached from their consequences and from public opinion. It's much too confrontational, and you need some sort of dressing, some artifice—but the current situation can't really exist, either.

"We don't care what you think," the YPU is fond of saying, "but that you think." Our structure is fine, it's one of the best in the world. It's hard to imagine a better one. But it's not hard to imagine a media more focused and less repetitive. Because media, after all, isn't just a channel for conveying information. It actually affects what it's conveying. It affects the people that it's bringing to.

I have found that at Yale, and just about everywhere else in America, you can't make everyone care. You just can't. But you have to convince people that they can do Big Things. And Big Things require communities—every single voice in that community.

It's an interesting thought that our ideological battles are really smaller than they've ever been before, compared to 50 years ago—existential threats are gone, communism is gone, segregation is gone. But it seems like our battles are louder than they've ever been before. How does that make sense? We have less to battle over, but then they're louder than they've ever been before. It doesn't make sense, and I think we can change it together.

If you're ever in New Haven, please come and visit the Yale

Political Union and see what we do. I think that through more confrontation, we can actually come to the point with more compromise and more things actually getting done. Thank you very much!

BEYOND GOVERNING BY CRISIS

(*Yale Daily News, September 30, 2013*)

ANOTHER DAY, ANOTHER government "crisis," and another few hundred people think they're being original by posting excerpts from W. B. Yeats' apocalyptic poem "The Second Coming" to their Facebook walls:

> *Things fall apart; the centre cannot hold;*
> *Mere anarchy is loosed upon the world.*

Too bad Yeats wasn't talking about a petty and thoroughly unnecessary political fight over whether or not to fund the fledgling Irish government—but rather invoking Biblical imagery to describe a Europe laid to waste by the horrors of the First World War. Invoking "The Second Coming" is probably a step too far.

Existential threats to American primacy in the world, or at least immediate ones, appear farther off than ever before. The Third Reich is gone, Communism isn't really a competitive candidate for world domination anymore, and even the alarming specter of festering jihadist terrorism has receded as American intelligence has adapted to dealing with the threat. It almost makes you think that we should consider ourselves lucky that our political fights, however loud, are much smaller threats to America's stability than what we've dealt with in the distant-to-near past. But, with so much to do nationally to make sure the United States retains its position as top global leader and innovator, why are we having these protracted battles at all? And why are they so deafeningly loud?

The immediate, superficial answer is simple—two rather intransigent actors chomping at the bit for chances to undercut the other politically, with a media all too happy to amplify the noise in the fading hope of reviving dying circulations and (by and large) sagging television ratings. The Affordable Care Act, the cause of the government shutdown that began at midnight, was a highly partisan bill—passed by a president without Lyndon Johnson-like force of personality or the will to form the strong personal friendships in Congress to squelch major dissent. The force wasn't strong enough in the beginning to avoid a costly political insurgency from the inside that has, arguably, handicapped the remainder of his presidency (even though healthcare wasn't on Obama's radar long before his administration took office). And that's to say nothing of the insurgency that rolled in after 2010, full of Congressmen who wouldn't talk to the President if he begged—representing "mad as hell" constituents who had watched the process unfold and who were determined to stop a repeat with other liberal priorities being passed on party-line votes. Had Obama taken a piecemeal approach to health insurance reform, his presidency might have looked quite differently now—then again, who knows what would and wouldn't have gotten through.

But that postmortem aside, the scary question is this: Are we in for a long stretch of governing by crisis? Not even during the deeply divisive Bush years did we have the now-very real possibility of close to a decade of protracted budget battles, assuming (not unreasonably, but also not with certainty) six more years of a Democratic president and a Republican Congress. House districts have *become less diverse*, meaning the incentive to compromise is low on both sides. *Innovative proposals* are out there to reform state-by-state redistricting, from the independent commission (which has been implemented in several states) to proportional "superdistrict" representation. Unfortunately, these ideas have little to no political traction in most states for the foreseeable future. The possibility of campaign finance reform—somewhere in between the ill-fated McCain-Feingold and nothing—also isn't going anywhere, and won't while President Obama is in office. Meanwhile, don't expect the blaring "BREAKING NEWS" screens or repetitive pundits to be headed out anytime soon, either.

But the good news is that Congress still has to weather elections every two years, and eventually the president (and his leadership style) departs. New tools, such as *Nikita Bier's* innovative database *www.outline.com*, may soon allow citizens to vote based on knowledge of how policy proposals in campaigns will likely affect them in dollar amounts—knowledge based on data that few people have the time or the resources to access. Of course, many other issues decide campaigns—but Bier found that 6% of trial users in his system switched their voting preference. More knowledge means more power in the hands of constituents to pressure politicians, and it also means that radio and television hosts will likely hold less monolithic sway over their listeners' and viewers' voting preferences. Citizens in the future will be better empowered to access data and make more independent value judgments without having to sift through a tiresome story or artificial political narrative, whether it's coming from the left or the right. For such tools to be used effectively, *technology education*—and education in general—will have to be crucial.

There's further good news in that the next president will come in keenly aware of the gridlock we're currently experiencing. It's going to take rhetoric, but of a very different kind compared to President Obama's. The next president will need to echo calls for a new era of American leadership and big thinking, but he or she will also have to work to avoid seeming only annoyed each time he's attacked politically. The president will have to confront opponents head-on, depoliticizing issues in the name of national interest.

So even though you can't visit a national park starting today, don't be too upset. The government shutdown is rattling everyone's nerves, but if past shutdowns are any indication, we're pretty close to rock bottom, and the future of civic involvement appears—at least from this low point—significantly brighter.

MALLOY'S DESPERATE MOVES

(*Yale Daily News, September 23, 2014*)

THE MASS HAD just ended. I had already moved on to contemplating Sunday brunch options. But don't leave just yet, the priest suddenly exclaimed. We've got a special guest!

Before I could make a beeline for the holy water, Connecticut Gov. Dan Malloy comes darting toward the pulpit. What followed next was a brief bio, with references to political positions omitted. A word about growing up in a Catholic home and delivering a eulogy. Something about how good it was to see everyone today. A passing mention to the other Masses he's off to after this one.

Goodness, I'm thinking. Several Masses in one day? Why would you go to more than one? Maybe he missed a few Sundays and he's trying to make up for them on this early September morning—but it doesn't really work that way. Maybe the man just really loves communing at Christ's table—practically a saint! Oh, wait. He's up for reelection this year.

A few more words and he stepped away, en route to church number two. The congregation clapped politely. Never mind that he had just turned a religious gathering—whether the parishioners liked it or not—into a political one. Never mind that his political record points to deliberate disregard for Catholic teaching. Never mind, because the damage had been done.

What damage? Clapping is like smiling. Even if you do it out of politeness, the very action reinforces positive feelings. You clap, and you might approve of the speaker just a little bit more—maybe enough to check his name at the ballot box, especially if you've got absolutely nothing on the other names.

Dan Malloy is running for reelection against Republican Tom Foley, a moderate who's also served as U.S. Ambassador to Ireland. Four years ago, Malloy edged out Foley in one of the closest races in state history after some late ballots came in from Bridgeport. It's understandable why Malloy's getting desperate: the polls show him losing. The church blitz may not be illegal or unconstitutional. But it is mighty unsavory. Candidate forums and speeches at churches have been pretty common in American politics, but usually parishioners get a chance to react in real time. Not here. No question time. No meet-and-greet afterwards.

Just the speech, then obligatory applause.

And in case you too were a victim of the Malloy stump speech while trying to say your prayers, here's a snippet from his relevant political record: He's called for Pope Francis to change "just about everything" in the Church. His stances and statements on abortion are to the left of even pro-choice Democrats like Joe Biden. And, perhaps most importantly, he appointed a state senator to the Connecticut Supreme Court who in 2009 proposed a bill to take away the Catholic Church's power over the budgetary decisions its own parishes made. It was universally regarded as a direct attack on the Church's constitutional rights.

All this from the man who's been called "America's progressive governor" in these very pages. I'd like to believe I'm for progress, too, without supporting a far-left agenda out of step with most voters across the country. And that's not to discount the positive achievements in Connecticut during Malloy's tenure. But they've been few and far between, as his poll numbers—and the public's views on the condition of the state—attest. In 2011, Malloy passed the largest tax increase in Connecticut's history, amounting to $1.5 billion in hikes on income and various sales and service taxes in the midst of an economic recovery. Gallup found that 49 percent of Connecticut residents want to leave the state, second only to Illinois. Public sector liabilities remain tremendously high, with little improvement in public schools to show for it and low job growth again in 2014 to pay for it.

And who's forgotten his 2011 executive orders to unionize day and home care workers subsidized by the state? It was widely opposed by recipients of care, and the U.S. Supreme Court ruled this summer in favor of two employees in Illinois who didn't want to pay union dues by stating that these workers were exempt from such fees.

It all makes sense, though, since Malloy has been governing in machine politician, you-scratch-my-back-I'll-scratch-yours style, every chance he's gotten.

None of this is to tell you who to vote for. It's just to tell you what Governor Malloy, standing at the pulpit week after week, won't.

CONDESCENSION ISN'T COMPASSION

(*Yale Daily News, November 11, 2014*)

IT'S AS PREDICTABLE as it is insulting: Cocooned Democratic pundits predict victory in an election, Republicans win, blogs light up and students take to Facebook to bemoan how sad it is that so many dim-witted Americans just voted against their economic interests. It happened in 2000 and 2004, even resulting in the publication of a book on the topic, "What's the Matter with Kansas?" This year, it's déjà vu all over again.

And it's pretty ubiquitous, too. Pretentious columnists at *The New York Times* pull the argument off the shelf every so often ("Most voters don't know much about policy details, nor do they understand the legislative process," Paul Krugman opined last week), as do pretentious columnists at the *Yale Daily News*. The Internet is filled with various iterations of this same message, coming from people who apparently don't mind that they might still have some friends who disagree with them.

So, besides the obvious condescension, what's wrong with the argument that voting Republican is almost always against your interests? On the simplest level, it betrays the cognitive dissonance engulfing the left's "we're all in this together" rhetoric. The left wants us to be together, as long as "together" means some kind of a push towards redistribution. It's troubling that some of the bluest cities in the country are actually those with the most social imbalance and economic inequality. Despite liberal policies, the rich and poor shop for groceries in different places, they pray in different places and they travel in different ways. A genuine platform of "togetherness" would seek to bridge these day-to-day lifestyle gaps that contribute heavily to many facets of inequality.

"Togetherness," then, doesn't really mean unity at all. It's appropriated as a weapon of class warfare. They're Robert F. Kennedy's words coming out of Saul Alinsky's mouth. "Togetherness" used in this way shouldn't be conflated with fostering fairness and community cohesion, great things that most Democratic policies haven't come close to accomplishing.

The "What's the Matter with Kansas" argument is also fundamentally flawed because it reduces voters to purely self-interested agents.

For the sake of the argument, let's say that maybe a Kansas voter doesn't agree with the Republican candidate's position not to raise the minimum wage. But perhaps she's appalled by the fact that America has some of the most draconian abortion laws in the world, far to the left of countries such as France, Germany and Italy—where federal laws often mandate waiting periods and where abortion is usually legal only through 12 to 16 weeks. In the United States, it's often legal past 24 weeks, despite poll after poll showing that majorities find this horrific and favor a 20-week limit, which Congressional GOP leaders have proposed. Are these voters foolish for prioritizing protecting the defenseless over their economic gain, however just their economic demands may be?

There's also the economic side of the coin that, no matter how hard some try, can't really be separated from people's hopes and values. First, it shouldn't even require mentioning that there are many circumstances that can determine the course of a person's economic future and overall success. Many of these factors are outside one's control: racial discrimination, lack of education, lack of family support, poverty. But Americans like to believe—and if it's a myth, it's been a pretty empowering one through the generations—that underneath it all, just about everyone can pull off a decent measure of success in life, and maybe much more. It's what my parents came to the U.S. believing. And even though there were institutions in the U.S. that made things harder for them, they kept believing this promise.

Obviously, some people have had to deal with much worse, and progressives in America have worked in certain areas to make opportunity more accessible to more people. On the issue of economic inequality and the minimum wage, progressive arguments have a lot of salience. But it seems that their rhetoric and policy has gone from "giving everyone a fair shot" to "making sure the government is there every step of the way."

Here's a disconcerting thought: What if even the voters who

have a lot to gain through broader economic safety nets vote against those policies to preserve the importance of true freedom? Maybe the voters in Kansas don't want to be treated differently. Maybe they want to preserve the existential value of free will—something many Yale students, with privileged backgrounds that are lifelong insurance policies of their own, just don't understand. Or is it that giving voters far more credit than they could possibly deserve?

CHAPTER II
Disparities & Empathy

---

1. *High School Years*

MORNING IN AMERICA: WILL OBAMA REALLY DO AWAY WITH AMERICA'S CONSCIENCE?

(2010)

THE ABORTION DEBATE has been, by some accounts, the most divisive issue in modern American politics. This is certainly believable, seeing that the debate centers on whether the United States has, since the 1973 Supreme Court decision entitled *Roe v Wade*, allowed for the largest murder of innocent life in history to be carried out on American soil. This is no walk in the park as far as political issues go, to be sure. And the public knows this, too. Polling has put American public opinion on abortion on shaky ground—71 percent of Americans think abortion should be illegal or legal only under certain conditions (with 57 percent saying it should be illegal in most or all circumstances), according to 2008 Gallop poll numbers. At the same time, when Americans are asked whether they consider themselves to be pro-life or pro-choice, it's a dead heat.

As a result, the pro-life and pro-choice communities have always been able to make compromises, in a nation almost evenly split on whether abortion-on-demand should be legal. Partial-birth abortion, the procedure where a developed fetus is destroyed and removed from the mother's body, is banned in the United States. Many individual states have parental notification laws and require women to see an ultrasound of their babies before choosing whether to terminate the pregnancy. And the "conscience clause," put in place by the Bush administration, allows doctors and hospitals who believe that abortion constitutes murder to graciously ask women seeking the procedure to go somewhere else. It allows pro-life medical professionals to know that they haven't pulled what they feel is a trigger on any human life. For now, anyway.

The heavily pro-abortion Obama administration is reportedly considering forcing doctors to pull that trigger, whether they want to or not. The administration established a mandatory "review period" in its early days to begin the process of determining how to repeal the conscience clause, and is expected to make a public announcement soon. The administration's reasoning? Laws already exist protecting medical providers from providing abortions. Not so, says Tony Perkins, president of the D.C.-based Family Research Council. "The lack of regulations resulted in confusion and a lack of awareness within the health care community, leaving health care personnel vulnerable to discrimination and forcing them to drop their specialties at a crucial time of health care scarcity." The Provider Refusal Rule, as the clause is formally known, closed loopholes that allowed for discrimination and reprimands directed towards pro-life doctors. So what will happen if it goes?

The answer to that question lies in explaining what won't happen if the clause is repealed, rather than what will. For example, Catholic hospitals around the country, which adhere to the

Catholic teaching equating abortion to murder, will simply close in areas where their services are crucial—as they have made clear to the Obama administration already. People won't have access to the kind of medical care they need, especially in rural or disadvantaged areas—precisely where many Catholic and other religiously-affiliated hospitals operate. Skilled doctors won't see patients, because their hospitals will simply close their doors to all patients seeking help rather than partake in what they believe is murder. And more people will turn to clinics and organizations where they can't get nearly the same level of care that they can receive at large medical institutions. And whose fault will this be?

President Barack Obama said in his campaign numerous times that his intent on the abortion issue was to "move away" from the decisiveness the issue had brought the concerned American public in the past. But his actions to this day on the issue indicate that such statements were so insincere that they could fuel a hot air balloon's trip twice around the world. In only four months in office, Obama has already allowed taxpayer funds to be allocated for the United Nations Population Fund, an organization that funds abortion overseas and that has been implicated is assisting China's policy of forced abortions and sterilizations—a massive human rights violation. He has lifted the ban on embryonic stem cell research, which many Americans believe amounts to experimenting on human life. But what is unraveling in this string of decisions is the true stance of the Obama administration on the issue of life, which is marked not by a resolve to cooperate on the issue, but rather consists of a decidedly one-sided agenda.

Obama's recent decision shed light on a history of positions regarding abortion which he vociferously tried to hide during the campaign. On April 2, 2008, *Washington Post* columnist Michael Gerson wrote about the true nature of Obama's abortion record. "...Obama's record on abortion is extreme. He opposed the ban on partial-birth abortion—a practice a fellow Democrat, the late

Daniel Patrick Moynihan, once called 'too close to infanticide.' Obama strongly criticized the Supreme Court decision upholding the partial-birth ban. In the Illinois State Senate, he opposed a bill similar to the Born-Alive Infants Protection Act, which prevents the killing of infants mistakenly left alive by abortion. And now Obama has oddly claimed that he would not want his daughters to be 'punished with a baby' because of a crisis pregnancy—hardly a welcoming attitude toward new life." So maybe this was the real Obama all along.

What the president fails to realize is that doctors who uphold their values and refuse to terminate women's pregnancies are simply upholding the Hippocratic Oath, the millennia-old document which every doctor once swore to. The document made doctors vow "to do no harm" to their patients, a clause that has been subject to many interpretations. What many people are not aware of, however, is that the clause following the "do not harm" statement in the Oath reads, "I will not give a lethal drug to anyone if I am asked, nor will I advise such a plan; and similarly I will not give a woman a pessary to cause an abortion." If President Obama overturns the conscience clause, he will be overturning the right of doctors to adhere to the Oath so many of them forever swore to. He would be opening the door to a society where doctors' sole purpose, in certain settings, would be to do harm to fellow human beings. Is this Western medicine at its best? Hippocrates, the father of Western medicine, would be ashamed.

WINNING THE BATTLE AGAINST INFANTICIDE: A MILLENNIA-OLD STRUGGLE

(john_ar@insightbb.com, March 17, 2011)

THE PRACTICE OF infanticide has spanned the entire length of human existence. In ancient Rome, babies were often left on hilltops to die when they were unwanted by their families. Certain tribes practiced infanticide well into the twentieth century. And, in China, sex-selective infanticide is brutally practiced to this day. In fact, anthropologist Laila Williamson notes that "Infanticide has been practiced on every continent and by people on every level of cultural complexity, from hunter gatherers to high civilizations, including our own ancestors." Williamson is correct, but fails to note that the practice did not stop with our ancestors. Rather, it continues today under the brazenly institutionalized and convenient euphemism of "abortion."

A grossly political, philistine, debate today exists about this issue and the supposed "choice" of a mother to kill her child. The debate has been dumbed down by pro-abortion radicals to appeal to the American psyche, in which freedom of choice and individualism are strong themes. But we know, as any basic student of biology knows, that exercising your "right to choice" on an unborn child is terminating a viable life.

Now, you do not need me to tell you that the battle we are fighting is not yet being won. Despite the fact that I am growing up in the most pro-life generation since *Roe v. Wade*, the abortion rate remains high and is now growing. So how are we to win the battle over public opinion? Taking the recent effort to block federal spending for Planned Parenthood as an example, the pro-choice lobby is clearly better funded and better stocked with public relations operatives. They were able to effectively turn the public discussion into one about women's health. No one ever paused to say, "Wait a minute. If Planned Parenthood gave up the abortion part of its operation, no one would try to cut its funding." Planned Parenthood is a nasty international organization whose true goal is population control. I have been on PPFA's website, and have looked through it thoroughly. Looking at its content from the point of a view of a teenager, I got the impression that the site was an "app store" for sex. Want to have casual sex? There's an app for that—use a condom or birth control. Condom breaks? There's an app for that—the morning after pill. Found out about your pregnancy late? No worries. There's an app for that. Have an abortion. Didn't bother to check until you realized you were several months pregnant? Don't you fret. There's an app for that. Get a late-term abortion. Yup, there's an app for just about anything in the Planned Parenthood App store. Sex has become a responsibility-free, no-stress activity. Behind this innocent, insidious cover, thousands are dying every day in the genocidal organization's abortion mills.

So how does the pro-life movement battle this well-funded opponent whose playbook is designed to appeal to individuals' weaknesses? Fight back just as hard. The abortion debate has to experience a paradigm shift; it needs to become an ethical, scientific, and social discussion. Not a dumbed-down political one, full of the old used talking points and one-liners. We cannot win the debate the way. So we need to reach out to more human rights groups and minority groups. Pro-life speakers must diligently make our intellectual case to universities, high schools, and religious and non-religious people alike. We need to show people that abortion—not only the procedure, but also the mindset—ruins families and creates unhealthy personal relationships.

We must also change our tactics. Everyone might not agree with this point, but I believe that one of the best ways to win the public policy war on abortion is to argue for universal, free access to contraceptives. Don't get me wrong—I know that increasing contraceptive use does not decrease the abortion rate. But from a public relations perspective, we must acknowledge that we are often pigeonholed by Planned Parenthood who accuses pro-life organizations of not being realistic in insisting on abstinence. Abstinence is no doubt the best option, but the overwhelmingly hypersexual culture we live in simply cannot be countered by rational explanations on the danger of premature sex. Too many innocent lives will be aborted while we try to win that battle. However, if we also insist on universal, free access to contraception, we effectively disarm Planned Parenthood and NARAL of the most effective tool in their arsenal. It gives us license to ask, "So contraception is available to everyone, yet some are still grossly irresponsible enough to choose abortion?" In a society which places high emphasis on personal responsibility, we will have the unique opportunity to turn their argument against them. One million abortions per year is simply unacceptable. We also need to encourage social programs that help women see alternatives to abortion, and the government ought to support life in and out of the womb.

I'd like to end where I began. As noted earlier, infanticide has been around since humanity's earliest days. How can we be so foolish as to think we can abolish such a longstanding human problem? Keep in mind that slavery, too, existed for thousands of years before humanity recognized the inhumanity and sheer stupidity of not recognizing humans as such because of their skin color. With God and this audience as a witness, I stand here before you to say that the unborn child will also one day be conferred the rights of all humans. Humanity will look upon the abortion era with shame and disgust at how so many could turn a blind eye to the senseless genocide of the weakest among us, just as those pro-abortion advocates shake their heads today at slavery but yet so blindly fail to see the modern parallel.

We are all the William Wilberforces, the William Lloyd Garrisons, and the Susan B. Anthonys of our time. So let us stand up for humanity in all its forms. Let us stand up for life, the gift given to us by our Creator that only He can take away. Let us stand up today and every day, until we can truthfully proclaim about every human on this Earth, as Dr. Martin Luther King Jr. did, that we are "free at last, free at last, thank God almighty, we are *all* free at last."

FREE EXPESSION: THE EVOLUTION OF A RIGHT CENTURIES IN THE MAKING

(*Constitutional Speech Contest, March 20, 2011*)

It is but the most often-quoted, vigorously defended, universally revered phrase found anywhere in the United States Constitution: "Congress shall make no law respecting an establishment of religion, or prohibiting the free exercise thereof; or abridging the freedom of speech, or of the press; or the right of the people peaceably to assemble, and to petition the Government for a redress of grievances." The first amendment to our Constitution. It has united Americans of every stripe behind it, from the ideological right and left. This constitutional freedom has been yearned for in all parts of the world, but rarely has it been achieved in the form that it has in America. In fact, even noted socialist intellectual Noam Chomsky once admitted that he lived in "the greatest country in the world," adding later that America's advances "particularly in the area of free speech, that have been achieved by centuries of popular struggle, are to be admired."

Chomsky, of course, was alluding to the centuries-old struggle that culminated in the free speech laws we are privileged to enjoy today. Efforts to create a free society have existed as long as man has on this Earth. When Socrates was brought to trial in Athens for speaking against the state in 399 BC, he proudly declared that "If you offered to let me off this time on condition I am not any longer to speak my mind...I should say to you, 'Men of Athens, I shall obey the Gods rather than you.'" Needless to say, he was promptly sentenced to death. In the year 1215, the Magna Carta was signed in England, finally wresting away King John's unlimited power and setting the basis of liberty in Britain. But alas, in 1633, censorship famously reared its ugly head again when Galileo Galilei was brought before the Inquisition, after his blasphemous claim that the sun did not revolve around the Earth, but vice versa. He was subsequently imprisoned.

But time brought progress in the advancement of free speech. The 1689 English Bill of Rights granted "freedom of speech in Parliament" after the overthrow of King James II. Less than a century later, French philosopher Voltaire quipped to an opponent, "Monsieur, I detest what you write, but I would give my life to make it possible for you to continue to write." And in 1789, the French Revolution's *Declaration of the Rights of Man* finally codified universal freedom of speech in France.

Enter America. Fresh off of a costly war for independence, and struggling to create a stable governing model after the evident failure of the Articles of Confederation, a group of political thinkers called the Federalists, who advocated for a strong central government, were on the verge of winning the battle of public opinion. They proposed a stable constitution, which would lay out their vision for a strong federal government. As the ratification debate ensued, critics raised the concern that the document did not codify the rights which Americans had so tirelessly fought to earn: free expression, religious liberty, and protection from an oppressive regime, among a laundry list of others. Anti-federalist George Clinton, writing under the pseudonym "Cato," warned that the people were about to "risque much, by indispensably placing trusts of the greatest magnitude, into the hands of individuals, whose ambition for power, and aggrandizement, will oppress and grind you." Without any written legal protection, the people were effectively placing their trust in elected officials to uphold their rights. Their concerns were heard, and before ratification took place, a "Bill of Rights" was added to the Constitution to ensure that basic rights—first among them being free speech, religion, press, assembly, and petition—could never be taken away. We have James Madison, a prominent early American federalist who is today known as the "Father of the Bill of Rights," largely to thank for drawing up the language we know and hold so close in the American psyche today. He, in turn, was influenced by French Revolutionary thought and the centuries of progress made in the evolution of the rights spelled out in the first amendment. Since this time, first amendment rights in America have not gone unchallenged.

Indeed, only a few years following the ratification of the Constitution as amended, the majority Federalists secured passage of the Alien and Sedition Acts of 1798, which made it a criminal act to publish "any false, scandalous, and malicious writing...against the government of the United States." This included statements about government officials. Thomas Jefferson and James Madison, who were growing disillusioned with the Federalist party, were irate, and secretly wrote the Kentucky and Virginia Resolutions denouncing the acceptance of unjust laws. The Acts were subsequently killed when Jefferson became President.

This incident marked the first, but certainly not the last time that first amendment rights have been challenged in America. The dawn of the twentieth century brought with it fresh questions of which forms of speech were constitutionally protected. In the 1919 case *Schenck v. United States*, the Supreme Court ruled that speech which presented a "clear and present danger," quoting the majority opinion written by Justice Oliver Wendell Holmes, Jr., could be constitutionally censored. But the Court turned on itself and overruled precedent in *Brandenburg v. Ohio* in 1969, instead saying that government had no right to restrict incendiary speech. The exception, the Court reasoned, would be in cases where the purpose of speech would be to incite "imminent lawless action." This ruling on the limits of free speech continues to stand today. But the debate has raged on, culminating in cases dealing with free expression in schools, in the workplace, and in various media outlets. Most recently, the Supreme Court ruled in *Citizens United v. Federal Election Commission* in 2010 that the first amendment prohibits limitations on corporate spending during elections.

So the final question we need to ask ourselves is a simple one: Where are we today in the evolution of the right to free expression? Despite, as Chomsky noted, the advances made over time, what challenges does the world still face? In 1929, Justice Oliver Wendell Holmes said "The principle of free thought is not free thought for those who agree with us but freedom for the thought we hate." Echoing Voltaire, Holmes was highlighting tolerance as a fixture of the continued vitality of free speech. The state of tolerance in the world leaves much to be desired.

Despite the right to free speech being enshrined in the 1948 United Nations Declaration of Human Rights, it continues to be under assault everywhere. In Iran and Pakistan, free speech might to this day cost you your life. In 2004, filmmaker Theo van Gogh was assassinated by Islamic extremists in the Netherlands following the premiere of his film regarding violence against women. In Russia, freedom of expression is a right promised but not always delivered.

So how about here in America? Here, we face a bit of a different conundrum. Free expression is alive and well, but many in the public sphere seem to have forgotten that in order for free speech to work, there have to be those who are willing to listen. The 24-hour news cycle has created an atmosphere not conducive to an intelligent dialogue about the important issues facing our country today. So it is our civic responsibility to demand more from our media and from our leaders. It is our duty to refuse to buy into news as entertainment and demand that those entrusted with protecting our constitutional rights—the first amendment chief among them—execute and take their responsibility seriously. It is up to us to vote, to write to our leaders and the press, and to make clear that our democracy, which is the model for the world to emulate, deserves better. That is the essence of today's call for civic responsibility. It is up to us to answer that call.

So in our free society—which has come farther than any other to perfecting the freedom of speech, the great new challenge of the day is a simple question: Speak we certainly may, but will anyone listen?

THE FUTURE IS ANYTHING BUT "BRIGHT"

(*April 20, 2011*)

YOU KNOW THE world is falling apart when twenty-five percent of 11-year-olds, according to a survey of West Philadelphia students conducted by the city's Health Department, are having sex. But what's an even surer sign that the world is going to hell in a handbasket is a city-sponsored website going up where children between eleven and nineteen can request that free condoms be mailed to their homes. **Eleven.**

But this tragic statistic and the city's response are not the main points. As Philadelphia health commissioner Donald Schwarz said, "Clearly, we don't think it's OK for 11-year-olds to be having sex. But we don't have the infrastructure in place to fix the problem fast. We can, however, make condoms available fairly quickly to whoever needs them." This translates roughly into, *Kids are having sex. We can't do anything to stop them. So, this is the next best thing we can do.* The whole situation, as *Philadelphia Inquirer* writer Ronnie Polaneczky put it, "makes me want to cry." To think that so many are being robbed of their childhoods and being thrown into a sexualized world that they don't even understand brings tears to one's eyes.

A city facing statistics like the ones aforementioned, and even more sobering incidents like HIV-positive 13-year-olds walking into city health clinics, has very few options. And so, it is doing the only thing it believes it can—to minimize the damage. In the short term, it might be effective in stemming the virulent growth of STDs. In the long term, however, distributing free condoms to all above eleven is the equivalent of trying to extinguish an oil fire with water—seeming to work at first but ultimately spreading the fire further. Transmission rates might briefly drop, but the drop will easily be made up for as the perception of supposedly foolproof "safe sex" augments the proportion of children engaging in it. True "safe sex" lies in a longstanding relationship where both partners have been tested for STDs and are not engaging in intercourse outside of their relationship. Leaving the possibility of contraction of a life-threatening disease to chance (in case of condom breakage, slippage, etc.) may very likely lead to transmission in the end. This is not a statement of opinion, but simply pure mathematics. The average condom breakage rate is 2.3%, or a 97.7% success rate (probably a high estimate), according to the American Sexually Transmitted Diseases Association. Raise the number to the tenth power, for ten instances of sexual activity, and the success rate falls to 79%. Raise it to twenty, 63%. To thirty, and the success rate is 49.8%.

This does not bode well for those who have their start at age eleven, and who are bound to engage in intercourse with innumerable partners going into adolescence and beyond. So Philly's efforts are a quick, short-term fix that will only make the problem worse in the long run if the epidemic of underage sex is not aggressively addressed. The solution, however, has nothing to do with sex. No—extinguishing this fire means cleaning up the oil first.

Before I go any further, a word about "comprehensive sex education" as a solution to this particular problem. It isn't. Comprehensive sex ed, which is designed to give adolescents information regarding all the options available to them (abstinence, birth control, etc.), remains controversial because some say it can be construed as condoning sexual activity and making what many believe are unethical options (such as abortion) sound universally permissible. On the other hand, proponents argue that those who will have sex will have sex and comprehensive sex ed simply informs adolescents about the options available. Key word—*adolescents*. Comprehensive sex ed, despite the countless oversimplifications made in the media, is a complex and controversial topic for another day. But an overwhelming majority of people are in agreement that 11-year-olds are not adolescents—and that this age crosses the socially accepted threshold of when sexual activity should be allowed. For goodness' sake, puberty in 11-year-olds has barely even begun.

So if not sex ed, if not condom distribution, then what? Hmm. I am willing to bet that a majority of the twenty-five percent who were found to be having sex at eleven come from poor households. I am also willing to bet that many, if not most, come from tattered households with one or no parent, where there is little family support to right the ship that so often veers in the wrong direction during the crucial preadolescent and adolescent years. But it wasn't always like this, was it?

Dr. Walter E. Williams is an American economist and distinguished professor at George Mason University. He grew up in the housing projects of Philadelphia, the city now at the forefront of this heartbreaking epidemic. As a Private in the Army in the 1960s,

Williams fought institutionalized segregation in the armed forces by writing to then-President Kennedy and standing up to military brass against racist policies. He writes, "My father deserted us when I was three and my sister was two. But we were the only kids who didn't have a mother and father in the house. These were poor black people and a few whites living in a housing project, and it was unusual not to have a mother and father in the house. Today, in the same projects, it would be rare to have a mother and father in the house. The welfare state has done to black Americans what slavery couldn't do, what Jim Crow couldn't do, what the harshest racism couldn't do, and that is to destroy the black family."

Needless to say, this is not a race issue. It is largely a socioeconomic issue, magnified in the African American community because of the extreme poverty present due to centuries of abuse and systematic oppression in America. But the example that Dr. Williams provides is a shocking view into the effects of welfare on the poor—it has destroyed the family, encouraged rampant promiscuity, and today those effects are being felt by the youngest members of the lower classes (who oftentimes mimic the behavior of the older people around them).

How does one connect the dots between welfare, the weakening of the family, and 11-year-old sex? Well, why do people get married in the first place? Normally, marriage takes place because two people love each other—but it does not end there. Marriage is also an economic institution, whereby two people agree to support each other by sharing expenses and earnings. Married couples usually have children who they expect will come to support them in old age. So, it is unsurprising that many people stay married long after they don't really "love" each other anymore (or at least, not in the same way they used to). They stay married because, economically, they have to.

Now consider welfare—which essentially came around in the 1960s and said, *No matter where you go in life, the federal government is standing ready with a paycheck.* Granted, it wasn't very much, but it was certainly enough to get by in West Philadelphia.

What became of the economic incentive to stay married? There no longer was one. Why marry and "tie yourself down" to a spouse and children—not to mention a boring *job*—when you can flee responsibility and still survive financially? And thus, the "deadbeat dad" phenomenon increased exponentially. Families broke apart. Single parents, particularly mothers, struggled to raise their children. And, when time for "the talk" came, there was likely no one at home to give it—leaving countless children essentially alone in trying to determine what was right and wrong in a world where the media tells you that what is wrong is right. Hence, the phenomenon of 11-year-old sex, in a very, very small nutshell.

Of course, welfare wasn't the only factor. Poor communities also continue to suffer from a lack of education, legal support, and financial help—all of which are critical if people are going to climb out of the cesspool which is poverty. But instead of working to put the best schools in urban areas, hiring social workers, and creating stable community financial aid programs, President Lyndon Johnson initiated a "war on poverty" through welfare programs that can more adequately be described as a "war on the poor." The poor are losing that battle.

Just ask Jill Foster, who leads pediatric and adolescent HIV care at a Philadelphia hospital. Her youngest HIV patient is 12.

2. *College Years*

YALE POLITICAL UNION SPEECH #1

(September 27, 2011)

I SAW THE best minds of my generation destroyed by madness, starving hysterical naked, dragging themselves through the negro streets at dawn looking for an angry fix, angelheaded hipsters burning for the ancient heavenly connection to the starry dynamo in the machinery of night, who burned cigarette holes in their arms protesting the narcotic tobacco haze of Capitalism.

This is "Howl," Allen Ginsberg's 1950s-era poem chronicling the emptiness, madness, and desperation haunting the generation growing up in what their families believed would be a dream. Many instead found themselves in a nightmare: full of bourgeoisie materialism, racism, and a suppressive uniformity. Their reaction to this way of life produced the cultural revolution of the 1960s, with its myriad sexual excesses and fierce resistance to the "system" of their forebears.

James Truslow Adams, who coined the term "American Dream" in 1931, defined it as "that dream of a land in which life should be better and richer and fuller for everyone, with opportunity for each according to ability or achievement." This definition—directly from the words of he who coined the term—applies to all who have searched for the American Dream.

If we take only the beginning half of this definition, the "better, richer, fuller" part, we must acknowledge that Adams believed the

Dream could bring us more happiness—happiness through the second part, achievement by work. So this is the fundamental premise we are critiquing this evening. Has our toil—our hard work, by alleviating material poverty, also made us happy?

It hasn't. Because the very idea of an "American Dream" doesn't allow it. In 1835, Alexis de Tocqueville identified the fundamental flaw of this thinking. He wrote, "In America I have seen the freest and best educated of men in circumstances the happiest to be found in the world; yet it seemed to me that a cloud habitually hung on their brow, and they seemed serious and almost sad even in their pleasure. The chief reason for this is that…[they] never stop thinking of the good things they have not got." That is why most international studies of "life satisfaction," including a 2006 University of Leicester study, which take into account people's rankings of their own well-being, rank the United States behind much of Europe, the UAE, and Bhutan—have you been to Bhutan? The point is that wealth is only one factor in a field of many determining quality of life—and it's not even the most important one—but it's the one around which is centered the American Dream.

Let me turn, in summation, to Robert F. Kennedy, Jr. In 1968, at a point where it was becoming clear that this dream wasn't exactly what many expected, he said "Even if we act to erase material poverty, there is another greater task, it is to confront the poverty of satisfaction—purpose and dignity—that afflicts us all. Too much and for too long, we seemed to have surrendered personal excellence and community values in the mere accumulation of material things. Our Gross National Product, now, is over $800 billion dollars a year. Yet the gross national product measures neither our wit nor our courage, neither our wisdom nor our learning, neither our compassion nor our devotion to our country, it measures everything in short, except that which makes life worthwhile. And it can tell us everything about America except why we are proud that we are Americans.

STANDING UP FOR PERSONHOOD

(*Yale Daily News, November 10, 2011*)

USING TIRED SCARE tactics to avoid fundamental ethical questions may be fitting of the caliber of debate in Washington or on cable television news, but not for Yale students. We should expect more than Planned Parenthood talking points that have not been revisited to check for accuracy or persuasive ability since—quite likely—1973.

Micha'le Simmons's guest column addressing Mississippi's Personhood Amendment ("Criminalizing a woman's right," Nov. 8), constituted a blatant attempt to focus on technical detail and glittering generalities to cloud what is at the heart of the abortion debate: the moral and legal status of the fetus.

It is true that the natural implantation of an embryo does not always take place—indeed, instances of death in nature abound. Humans become sick with cancer and die. Miscarriages take place. The fact that what some call "spontaneous abortion" occurs in nature does not give us license to advance it; to make this appeal to nature is a fallacy of relevance. Just because something is sometimes "natural" does not automatically make it just.

The perpetual claim that Initiative 26 would "ban birth control" is at best inaccurate and at worst a lie. By acknowledging the status of a fetus as a person from the moment of conception, the initiative bars it from being willfully destroyed. Contraception that blocks fertilization from taking place would not have been affected in any way. Indeed, the word "contraception" is a contraction of "contra," which Latin for "against," and "conception."

Simmons is right in deducing that the law would ban abortifacients—drugs and mechanisms that cause abortion—that we colloquially (and incorrectly) define as birth control. But the medical and scientific fact remains: Any form of "birth control" which causes the destruction of a fertilized embryo does not "control" anything. Indeed, it does nothing but destroy the embryo. Those are the facts.

In no broadly recognized and legitimate legal, ethical or religious text is abortion deemed a "necessary, basic human right." (Unless, of course, Simmons considers Planned Parenthood's charter to be this sacred—in which case I would caution her against putting so much faith in an organization which has its historical roots in the eugenics movement.) Contraception, for its part, would have been completely unaffected by the Personhood Amendment.

And now, to the crux of the issue: All the talking points consistently used regarding "more unwanted pregnancies," "stigma," and "basic choices about...fertility" are empty, extraneous words that only serve to mask the philosophical discussion to be had about fetal rights and the ethics of abortion. So are questions like "What kind of a life is the child going to lead?" when we consider the alternative is murdering the child. "Ah, but it's not murder!" We have arrived at the core issue.

When does a fetus become a person worthy of legal rights? For, as Justice Harry Blackmun admitted in 1973 in explaining his vote in favor of Roe v. Wade, the decision he reached would "collapse" if the "suggestion of personhood [of the fetus] is established." This question has but one logically consistent answer: conception. All other boundaries, including the "age of viability" that Roe suggests, are arbitrary and moveable.

But scientifically, there is a right answer. Before we were able to conclusively judge the world to be round, many people posited it to be round or flat. Both were entitled to express their opinions, but there indeed was an objectively correct answer. Other boundaries also fail to pass the consistency test: Many say that abortion becomes impermissible when the fetus can experience pain or is conscious. So, then, do we have no qualms about killing patients in comas or those suffering from familial dysautonomia—the inability to feel pain? No ethical or logical framework, except that which establishes conception as the beginning of life, passes this test.

The right to life—expressed in the Declaration of Independence and revered in this country and around the world—is the most fundamental, basic human right of all. It is well past the time for the law to reflect this reality.

YALE POLITICAL UNION SPEECH #2

(November 13, 2011)

LADIES AND GENTLEMEN, what cause do conservatives have to rise in favor of this resolution? On its surface, this seems like just another loony hippy idea, coming from Vermont no less: break down a hegemonic superpower, start sustainable farms and pass resolutions in our city halls declaring George Bush a war criminal. Granted, this may be the reasoning behind some of those on the affirmative tonight—but there is a very different reason for rejecting the Leviathan of a state in its modern form: its inability to allow us to reach, as Baruch Spinoza called it, "self-realization."

I hope I don't have to sell many of you on the idea that achieving material, appetitive, Epicurean pleasures is not what fundamentally makes us happy. It is no accident that some of the highest suicide rates in the world are found in the most industrialized of countries: Japan, South Korea, and France among them. People are the happiest if they can achieve the self-actualization pinnacle of Maslow's hierarchy of needs. So how can a society best be structured to help people do that?

The rapid industrialization and consolidation of political power in society is certainly not the way. For starters, technological advancement being pursued for its own sake—as opposed to its benefit in helping us live richer lives—is extremely wasteful: Jonathan Swift speaks of Gulliver going to the Grand Academy of Lagado—a parody of the Royal Society of London—and seeing sunbeams being extracted from cucumbers and discovering political conspiracies by checking the poop of suspects. Reminiscent, perhaps, of the National Science Foundation spending $500,000 of grant money THIS YEAR to research the running habits of shrimp. But I digress. Technological games have a more insidious downside, aside from the millions wasted—that is, the dehumanization of personal interaction.

When consolidation of government, corporations, or what have you is pursued for its own sake (some say it's efficiency)—it becomes very easy for those at the top to forget (perhaps willfully) that each sweatshop built—yes, I'm talking about you, Nike—destroys a community of. Wait for it, wait for it: people. When governments become too large, wasting money becomes so easy—because it's money coming out of the IRS for Senator (so and so), not the hard-earned tax dollars of a family struggling to make ends meet. And even with all the waste, people aren't happy.

Humans are, and have always been, tribal animals. We become self-actualized when we feel comfortable in our social environments and when we've established meaningful communities kept together by human bonds that serve as safety nets and social circles. But our social capital in this country is rapidly declining, because these bonds are being broken or are never being formed due to rampant depersonalization of culture. Forget reverting to states' rights—how about municipal rights? Neighborhood rights? What if each neighborhood were tasked with taking care of itself—where all had a vested interest in keeping the community afloat. Communitarian anarchy, if you will, held up, perhaps, by very a limited state which provided for the common defense of all. The family, the church, the neighborhood would be restored as the primary institutions individuals relied on—not corporatist entities that could care less about individual well-being.

Proximity breeds empathy, ladies and gentlemen. And empathy breeds understanding. A return to our immediate surroundings and our core family and local values will do far greater in solving social malaise than any "government solution" has or ever will.

GRAHAM DISCUSSES INTERPERSONAL ART

(*Yale Daily News, December 4, 2011*)

SINCE THE 1970s, Dan Graham's art and critical writings have provided new ways of looking at the cultural hallmarks of recent generations. On Monday night at the School of Art, Graham spoke to an audience of more than 80 graduate and undergraduate students about his work, recalling experiences of both creating and critiquing art. The lecture focused on his sculptures that employ glass and two-way mirrors to create "impressionistic effects" on spectators, causing them to reflect on their emotions and interpersonal interactions.

Graham said his works have been influenced by his upbringing in suburban New Jersey. The strict boundaries between types of properties in the American suburban landscape, for instance, continue to influence Graham to emphasize borders in his art. "Two-Way Mirror Punched Steel Hedge Labyrinth," a Graham piece located in Minneapolis, Minn., features borders that alternate in material construction between natural hedges and glass to create a maze.

"Hedges are important to me," Graham said, adding that they signify the boundary between "private space and the outside." Graham noted that the glass in "Two-Way Mirror Punched Steel Hedge Labyrinth" seems opaque from a distance but is transparent once the viewer approaches it.

Graham explained that he strives to create "intersubjective" work that emphasizes the idea of social connections playing a key role in shaping thought, rather than "minimal art." Many of his "pavilions," which allow the audience to step into an enclosed glass space, are placed in varied settings. "Two-Way Mirror Cylinder Inside Cube," for instance, is located on a New York City rooftop. Through their incorporation of reflected surfaces, such structures encourage spectators to "see each other seeing themselves."

The artist also acknowledged the significant impact of urban architecture on his work, while differentiating his style from the corporate, "reptilian" forms of city architecture in the 1970s.

"My work usually involves the materials of the city," he said. "The city is very cinematic. Storefronts take the reflection of a person passing by and project it against the product in the window."

Graham said he grew up with no formal art education after high school and largely taught himself how to create through reading and listening to music. He credited Jean-Paul Sartre with inspiring his early work and discussed his abiding love for rock music. This passion resulted in "Rock My Religion," the one-hour video art production that explores commonalities between themes in rock music and religion for which Graham gained national fame in the 1980s.

While Graham's numerous sculptures are a cornerstone of his artistic portfolio, he said he has increasingly turned to writing as he has gotten older.

In exploring the impact of his personal history on the development of his art, Graham discussed his struggles with mental illness. "My work represents the borderline between psychadelic usage and borderline schizophrenia," he explained.

Claudia Cortinez ART '14 said she had expected to hear mostly about Graham's sculpture work. Jonathan Peck ART '14 said that Graham's lecture lived up to his expectations.

"He seems to have an answer for everything," Peck said. "The lecture was much richer and more philosophic than I expected, which was great to see given his non-academic background. Graham seems really entrenched in placing himself among other artists."

Graham was born in Urbana, Ill. and lives and works in New York City.

JFA REFLECTION

(December 22, 2011)

CHOOSE LIFE AT *Yale*'s recent trip to Colorado to participate in *Justice for All*'s program on the campus of the University of Colorado at Boulder can only be described as an eye opening, inspiring, profoundly moving experience. Going into the 3-day event, I could have never expected the intellectual depth and unyielding compassion I would witness as JFA spoke to the people on the ground—nor could I have anticipated the wide breadth of intellectual and emotional responses our presentation received on campus.

On a personal level, the trip sparked within me a resurgence of will to become an active participant in the pro-life cause. I have been pro-life ever since I can remember, but—up until the JFA trip—never felt so called to be on the front lines of the movement. I'm very happy to report that my first semester at Yale has brought with it many new opportunities to take part in pro-life activism and meet fantastic people. Our organization has tremendous leaders—chief among them Isabel Marin, whose unfailing devotion to the cause is beyond inspirational—and I feel blessed to know and to have been able to go to Colorado with all of them.

Since the trip, *Choose Life at Yale* has been busy planning JFA's arrival on our campus next semester, organizing our presence at the March for Life in Washington, and debating various pro-choice groups on campus. I am currently finishing Dr. Christopher Kaczor's *The Ethics of Abortion*, recommended to me by JFA leader Trent Horn, which is the strongest philosophical defense of the pro-life position I've ever read and has given me myriad new arguments to use in speaking about the abortion issue.

I would be remiss if I didn't also mention the emotional aspect of the trip: both the intensity of JFA's volunteers and the emotional responses we observed on campus were startling. I left feeling deeply moved by the commitment of JFA to the cause—and I also left with a new level of empathy for those who reacted so violently to the graphic images, for we had clearly sparked a nerve with countless people who had realized that the unborn child is not an abstraction; it is a real thing. It was understandable why people reacted so angrily, even if their anger was misplaced.

Going forward, I feel not only more intellectually prepared, but I have a deeper understanding of all sides of the issue and how best to approach people who, in many different ways, have been impacted by the horrors of abortion. JFA was instrumental in this—and I thank everyone for their continued work on behalf of the unborn. JFA impacts people every day, and they certainly impacted this pro-lifer yearning to make a difference.

LETTER TO MR. CHRISTOPHER BUCKLEY

(March 20, 1012)

Dear Mr. Buckley,

The culture of life is under attack at Yale. Every day, the members of Choose life at Yale—our campus pro-life organization—must make intellectual battle with the liberal pro-choice mentality that pervades this campus. And making strides we are—before the year is over, we will have debated the campus pro-choice groups in a formal debate, we will have held a pro-life demonstration and vigil in the middle of campus, and we will have hosted countless pro-life ethicists and philosophers for discussions and seminars. The conversation is changing.

But we need your help. If conservatism and a culture of life is going to be rebuilt and defended on this campus, we need the resources to do it—and they are running short. Your generous donation will help ensure the fight does not end, and the engagement continues. Any amount would be tremendously appreciated. We'd also love to have you back on campus sometime soon!

If you can help, please send us your contribution to: CLAY, P.O. Box, New Haven, CT 06520. Feel free also to get in touch with me anytime at (347) 563-2250 or *john.arouti@gmail.com*.

Thanks so much for your time, Mr. Buckley, and thank you for all you do for conservatism.

Looking forward to being in touch.

Yours truly,

John Aroutiounian, CLAY Member

ABORTION IN IRELAND

(First Things, June 24, 2013)

THE "NIGHT OF the Big Wind" is still the stuff of folklore in Ireland. On January 6, 1839, an unexpected hurricane slammed into the Emerald Isle from the North Atlantic, decimating neighborhoods from County Mayo to Dublin and becoming the worst storm ever recorded in Irish history. Waves were said to have crashed *over* Ireland's towering Cliffs of Moher in County Clare. Perhaps most striking was the weather pattern in the run-up to the storm: an unexpectedly strong snowfall on January 5 followed by a warm front on the Epiphany, colliding with a second cold front that would produce the first of the hurricane-force winds.

The present political uproar over abortion law in Ireland"one of only three western European nations, together with Poland and Malta, which continue to ban the practice"seems to have arrived with similar ferocity. The warning signs, however, are decades-old.

Ireland has been "abortion-free," as pro-life group *Youth Defence* calls it, for as long as anyone can remember. The illegality of abortion has been codified in some form since 1861, and in 1983 the Constitution of Ireland was explicitly amended by the public to guarantee the equal right to life of the mother and the unborn child. The measure passed with sixty-seven percent of the vote in a decade when abortion restrictions were being repealed all around the world.

Since then, global abortion rights organizations have aggressively targeted the island nation. The Irish Family Planning Association (IFPA), associated with the International Planned Parenthood Federation, violated Irish law repeatedly in the 1990s" most recently advising women to *hide* their abortions from authorities, putting women's lives in danger in the event of postoperative complications.

And several thousand women receive assistance each year to seek abortions overseas in Great Britain, though the proportion of Irish women who receive abortions is dwarfed by the abortion rate in the United Kingdom and the Unites States.

Meanwhile, Ireland has maintained one of the lowest maternal mortality rates in the world. It is safer to be an expectant mother in pro-life Ireland than pro-choice America or Britain. Ireland's experience contradicts the "legal abortion makes pregnancy safer" logic, which perhaps explains why the pro-abortion movement has had its eyes trained on Ireland for so long. Ireland is an example of a healthcare system where the rights of both the baby and the mother are upheld equally" to the detriment of no one.

The next chapter of the abortion debate unfolded in 1992, when the Irish Supreme Court ruled that women had the right to an abortion if the mother's life was imperiled by the pregnancy. Known as the "X case," the decision sparked an ongoing debate about how to interpret the legislative mandate from the court, with successive governments reluctant to touch the issue for fear of upsetting the public.

The attack on pro-life Ireland resumed with a vengeance in 2005, when three women accused Ireland of violating their basic rights under the European Convention on Human Rights by prohibiting abortion. *A, B and C v. Ireland,* as the case was known, was a major pro-life victory. In its ruling, the European Court of Human Rights *threw out* the notion that abortion was a fundamental human right.

The latest uproar, which threatens to finally overthrow the pro-life consensus in Ireland, stems from the case of Savita Halappanavar, an Indian woman who miscarried and died of sepsis during her pregnancy in Galway. The case has become the rallying cry of abortion rights supporters, who maintain (along with Savita's husband) that her OB/GYN, Dr. Katherine Astbury, refused to provide her with a life-saving abortion. In response, Prime Minister Enda

Kenny has proposed a bill that would "clarify" the abortion statute in Ireland, making a clear exception in the constitutional ban for cases of maternal health and including an unrelated provision allowing for suicide as a reason for seeking terminating the pregnancy.

The problem is that the legislation is *redundant* at best and a Trojan horse at worst. Abortion is already permitted when the attending physician deems the pregnancy a threat to the mother's life. In fact, once the diagnosis of life-threatening sepsis came, an abortion was planned by Dr. Astbury. The problem was that the diagnosis came a day too late. As Eilis O'Hanlon of the *Independent* summarized, "It is clear that Savita died because she had severe sepsis which was not properly treated; an earlier abortion may have saved her life, but the reason she did not get one was because doctors failed to ascertain that her life was in danger."

This hasn't stopped Kenny, who continues to insist he is a pro-life politician working to bring "clarity" to the law. Never mind that the organization representing Ireland's doctors *feels that the law is unnecessary,* and never mind that countless medical experts have testified that abortion can compound the risk for women contemplating suicide.

The result, whether Kenny intends it or not, will mean a fatal break in the Irish pro-life consensus. The suicide loophole, which allows a woman to have an abortion if she receives the approval of three doctors, will quickly be exploited when information spreads regarding who the doctors sympathetic to the pro-choice cause are (see the similar case of New Zealand). And, within no time at all, Ireland will have *de facto* abortion on demand.

But as opposition has grown, Kenny has hunkered down"realizing that the legislation has become a referendum on his government. He's forbidden members of his party, Fine Gael, from voting their conscience on the bill, slated for a vote this summer. All the while, public opinion has held *remarkably steady* on the basic question of abortion. As of mid-2013 only thirty-nine percent of those polled supported abortion on demand, indicating little movement since 1983.

Despite this, today a majority of the Irish public supports Kenny's bill, swayed by the "Savita case" not to mention other factors chipping away at the pro-life position for years, like the eroding influence of the Roman Catholic Church. What the public fails to see, however, is that the bill is only the first front in a long-planned, well-coordinated storm.

A TIME FOR CHOOSING

(*Yale Daily News, September 9, 2013*)

YOU'VE ARRIVED AT Yale, and the ecstasy of opportunities at every turn—lifelong friendships, caffeinated upperclassmen offering you candy and begging you to join their club, a million combinations of possible majors and futures—probably hasn't begun to wear off yet. It's easy to get here and to buy the claim conveyed by the barrage of messages seeping from every nook and cranny between the cobblestones: "We've never had it so good"—as a former president once framed it in the speech that lifted him from relative obscurity in 1964.

It's easy to feel this way now. But circumstances can change rapidly in a few months, when you discover that not all paths lead to growth or fulfillment. Many activities at Yale are wastes of time—how else to describe hours spent in organizations compiling data, running errands or sitting through dull meetings? Certainly no activity is all pleasure, and immense amounts of hard work go into organizations about which students feel passionately. But if you detect tasks becoming chores akin to busywork—or that the best rationale for continuing is the hope that what you're doing is a means to a higher position where you'll be doing almost the same thing—it's a sure sign to stop. If your involvement is not bringing you closer to excellence—whether moral, physical, otherwise intellectual—it's a waste of time. Activities pursued as means to ends usually fall flat by sophomore year.

Back in the '60s, the Gipper's address went on to challenge the Johnson administration's narrative of progress. It's a political tool that national contenders have frequently used to get the nation to re-evaluate its standing. In between all the bright lights and dizzying signposts saying, "Do this!" or "Follow us!" it's often difficult to find the time to ask: Where am I, and where are we, going? Neither entire countries nor single individuals fully know the answer. Hearts, minds and circumstances change. But this is why planning is important—so that an unexpected change does not knock you off your feet.

It's also because, contrary to the spirit of levity floating you might associate with early college life, almost every decision is significant. And many more choices than we care to realize are really moral choices—full of dramatic consequences for what life at Yale and beyond will look like.

The American university is supposed to be, in the words of Yale Professor Seyla Benhabib GRD '77, a "collegium." Originating from classical civilization, the collegium is a community of learning—driven by intellectual inquiry, not by profit. It's an important model for governing boards to remember, but also for students. We are here to develop a moral system and an understanding of place. We are not simply here to reap profits and move on. It's time to make decisions—or at least determine how we'll make them—about what we believe and how we'll live. Life will throw enough ambiguities at us later.

These four years are a time for creativity, for developing our moral and civic characters. Some activities and commitments—and indeed, some people—lend themselves more to these goals than others. Music, sport, debate, community volunteering and religious devotion are all ways to bring us closer to a form of excellence. Sitting on councils and committees that serve an ill-defined purpose does not.

You just got here. The time for intellectual experimentation is now. And it's absurd to know what you want to do or to expect loyalty of friends with whom trust hasn't yet been established. It's a process, and it should be. But it's a plan you should start developing now, because your closest friends should help develop mutual excellence together. Will the friends you make here answer your 3 a.m. phone call in five or 10 years' time? True friendship requires trust, trust requires authenticity, and authenticity requires effort—because man is too self-interested for this to really be an effortless process.

No one leaves Yale a fully developed woman or man. We're too comfortable here to have fully figured out how we are going to live. And growth is a lifelong process. But you need a plan. Living as a skeptic in a world that requires constant moral choices means you'll be pushed into choices you didn't want to make. To perpetuate putting off those choices, and to ignore the realities of the moral decisions surrounding us, will eventually turn you into an aimless bureaucrat at best—and, at worst, will leave you saddled with regrets for what life at Yale could have been.

THE PRICE OF EMOTIONAL POVERTY

(*Yale Daily News, October 7, 2013*)

If you only have five minutes today and are reading this column, put it down and look up Robert F. Kennedy's speech at the University of Kansas on March 18, 1968, instead.

Not only is it one of the most beautiful and soaring works of oratory presented on the national stage in recent memory, but it's also full of oft-neglected insights about the state of American social life, written during a time of unprecedented turmoil. Kennedy, in a far cry from what our political discourse has looked like recently, talks about the health of our "national soul" and the emotional challenges we encounter in confronting growing poverty and inequality. Why, he asks, does the Gross National Product data look great on paper while there is social instability everywhere?

"Even if we act to erase material poverty," he notes, "there is another greater task, it is to confront the poverty of satisfaction—purpose and dignity—that afflicts us all."

If this sounds like a bizarre thing to say, consider how far removed our political conversations are from this kind of thinking today. In a discourse largely dominated by a tug-of-war between factions arguing for a little more redistribution or a little less, too little thought is given to the resources beyond money that people need to flourish.

Poverty takes many forms. Its material form is the most obvious and calls for our most immediate attention. But its more deeply rooted form, that of emotional poverty or the "poverty of satisfaction," is subtler and much harder to get rid of. It can affect the rich and the poor just as harshly, and I have personally seen it both inside and outside Yale's walls. And to understand poverty in America, we must come to grips with both forms.

When the wealthy suffer from emotional poverty they usually have the resources and the community to either pull themselves of the situation or to find help. But to suffer from both intense emotional and material poverty leaves an individual with next to nothing. Endemic poverty perpetuates itself when people grow up without unconditional love, communities that care, schools that are safe to learn in, bedtime stories and much more.

I was lucky. I grew up in a home with two parents who loved unconditionally. We didn't have much money. My parents had immigrated from Armenia to New York the year before I was born, and while they were doctors there, it would take more than a decade before they could earn anything remotely close to an American doctor's salary. So for about the first ten years of my life, we lived in small apartments in Manhattan and my parents worked in pawnshops, at labs running dishwashers and as babysitters. They kept me clothed and fed while studying for exams and climbing their way up. Classic immigrant story. But they also stayed up with me until I finished my homework and took me to the park on weekends. We were a family, and it felt that way every day. Home was a very safe place, where I could feel loved and wanted.

There is no discussion of emotional poverty in today's political paradigm. It's just not built into the discourse. When was the last time you heard either political party talk about the poverty of love in their narratives? Traditionally, we have not believed that government is supposed to make people feel loved. But, as Robert Putnam argued in his book *Bowling Alone*, people are increasingly disassociating from community institutions like churches that have traditionally taken responsibility for emotional wellbeing. Because people don't have those social resources to turn to, the political rhetoric needs to start grasping these issues.

Both in rich and poor communities, Americans need more than material wealth. In communities with few materials resources, the problems go beyond economic stagnation—issues like physical violence and poor health have roots in emotional problems like vulnerability and loneliness. In wealthy communities like Yale, we may not struggle with lack of material resources, but we do have some of the same emotional hunger. Our insecurity is manifesting itself in our sex culture, in our disturbing lack of inner peace and in our inability to get beyond superficiality in many of our friendships.

With the issue of emotional poverty so widespread, government—an increasingly large source, for better or worse, of social authority—must begin to speak to these problems.

THE KNOWLEDGE OLIGARCHY

(*Yale Daily News, November 11, 2013*)

As THE COLD sets in and the applications at the admissions office arrive daily by the hundreds, my thoughts recently wandered to the months before that hectic time started for me at the beginning of senior year, when I first learned just how much effort other students had already put into their applications. The prospect of applying to Yale only entered my head in the summer before senior year, and when I told my counselor at school she almost snickered: "People start their applications to Yale in the eighth grade!

It was a fact that had never occurred to me—in the eighth grade, I was dealing with a family move to Kentucky from New York City, and college was the last thing on my mind. It would take more than two years to start thinking concretely about the vague jumble of schools beginning to float around in the ether as possible choices. Finding out that friends had been making moves directed at college admission for years was a startling, alarming realization.

It wasn't until getting here that I discovered many people had spent years being groomed for this at mini-Yales around the country—boarding schools, day schools and uber-competitive public high schools with strong histories of sending people to the Ivies. Freshmen arrived on campus, as I'd soon figure out myself, already conversant in "Yale language"—in other words, they had taken humanitarian trips around the world and could knowledgably complain about which airports were comfortable and which ones to avoid. Somebody I met had been to 77 countries. All this projected confidence, legitimacy, learnedness.

Welcome to Yale!

But I was fortunate in two major ways: I went to a very decent, suburban public high school and I'd spent years in speech and debate. Confidence (or at least the visible kind) wasn't a problem. I could match the loudest "section asshole" if I wanted to—even though everyone knows the more socially adept way to handle section is to time your comments carefully and seem less-than-confident, even if you really have a lot to say on a particular day, so as to avoid playing into the stereotype. Winning at Yale means being so good that you know when to seem smart and when that's actually going to do more harm than good.

But if you're wondering where this is going, here it is: Almost no one in the world thinks this much about projecting the right self-image, and those who do are here in highest concentration. The students groomed by family and society from a very young age know not just how to work well, but also how to represent oneself in an insecure, neurotic world that discourages overt displays of wealth or knowledge. You've got to know when certain statements fly and when they don't. And these nuances and subtleties of how to behave go far beyond what common sense provides. You have to be intimately aware of how people think and perceive others in the current cultural context.

We live in a knowledge oligarchy, where not only are very few aware of these accepted modes of behavior—making it very hard to act in the requisite way for success among the elite—but this knowledge is also very hard to transmit. You already need to have some to get to Yale in the first place, and it only becomes more of an important factor from there on. What about those who don't, and never figure out what exactly it is you have to know and be aware of to have a shot at reaching the upper boundaries of the American dream? Or is elite culture really as segmented, out of reach and self-perpetuating as ever?

This adds a very different dimension to the discussion about economic and social inequality in America. It's true that every once in a while an extremely adept individual will come from poverty, aided by natural talents, and get to the top of the food chain. But for every one of these individuals it seems as though there must be 10 who had a lot of help along the way—who were told, "Do this," "Don't do that," and who came to Yale with their vocabulary and awareness already trained for the social situation they were about to walk into. It's true for Yale, her fellow Ivies and for the many other hubs of elite culture in America today.

The knowledge oligarchy disproportionately favors the upper class, and it's a subtler kind of dominance because it exists between the lines of speech and behavior. But it's just another way that those in endemic poverty are systematically short-changed by a status quo whose bizarre ways they cannot even begin to comprehend.

LIGHTING UP IN THE DARK

(*Yale Daily News, January 22, 2014*)

THERE'S VERY LITTLE anyone can contribute to the marijuana legalization debate at this point. We know the numbers: The American Civil Liberties Union reports that over half of the drug arrests in 2010 were for pot, and of the 8.2 million arrests over the last decade, 88 percent were for possession only—many for very small amounts. We also know that enforcement, like that of many other crimes, is often racist: African Americans are three times as likely as whites to be arrested for pot use.

But we also know that this debate is, at its core, a rather unpredictable means-ends calculation: Is alleviating these clearly unjust incarceration rates justified when we consider the effect of further destigmatization and normalization of pot use on society? Do we really want another legal alcohol-like substance floating around (yes, yes, I know, it's an imperfect analogy for both sides) for people waiting to try?

Stop reading and take to Google if you want an answer to those questions. It's worth taking up instead, I think, the advice that President Obama gave to his daughters over the past weekend: "[Pot is] not something I encourage, and I've told my daughters I think it's a bad idea, a waste of time, not very healthy," the father of two said.

But the question is: Who cares about his advice?

Just a little over 50 years ago, as the country stood on the brink of several defining social movements, pot use was a rarity in America. Gallup reports that only 4 percent of adults said they had tried marijuana in 1969—there's bound to be some underreporting in that number, though the reality of a very dramatic increase in use in the intervening years remains the same.

Back then, everyday life was a little less mapped out than it is today: There were fewer suburbs, fewer cars and stoplights, fewer stores, fewer schools, fewer school activities, more space between neighbors, more open space in general. The list could go on, but the point is that life lacked much of the structure we know today—it was far more common in many places for kids to play, unattended and cellphone-less, in unnamed parcels of land than in public parks or on the concrete of sprawling suburban neighborhoods. You had to be more nimble and to proceed more with open eyes, because everything didn't have a sign on it. And while life was less structured, it was more compact—your neighbors knew you, and it was possible that the entire town, for better or for worse, knew you.

One of the big changes of the past 50 years has occurred in the manner in which people form communities, which has gone from being a matter of necessity in everyday life to a completely voluntary association. People now move to the communities they want to join, and even then they can withdraw at any time—an option not open to most in history.

What this also means is that parents are less aware of what their children are doing than ever before. Think about the infinite number of things you could do, in high school and now in college, without your parents being aware. Think of the effect your mother's worried face or her stifled tears could have on you when she found out about your transgressions. It matters less and less what President Obama—or any other parent in the country—thinks, as he's less likely to find out if his daughters are smoking pot than 50 years ago. And he's also less likely to influence their decision if he does find out.

Increasingly, the only person left to shape your want and desires is yourself, with family and community replaced by media and the microcultures of cliques and friend groups, who do not often have an individual's best interests at heart. There's less wisdom for young people today to draw from, because the structure is such that they often didn't receive any.

In short, it means that the forces shaping our wants and desires, many of which we don't control despite our myopic belief in our own autonomy, have grown more impersonal—and consequently, less responsible for our outcomes. All the while, life today is both more structured and the list of freedoms, drugs included, more dangerous. And the politicization of many of these freedoms makes autonomous decision making, as opposed to just accepting the narrative thrown at you, even more difficult.

Whether pot legalization is worth the cost today will inevitably be answered by state legalization projects over the next couple of years. But one thing remains clear: If legalization were happening 50 years ago, pot users would be better off.

OUR LANGUAGE EXCLUDES

(*Yale Daily News, February 5, 2014*)

YOU'RE LISTENING TO a talk—maybe it's a professor, a politician, a public speaker of some repute—and then it comes. Perhaps it's subtle at first, but then, all of a sudden, the speaker's laid it on you even faster than the last 14 times you've heard it: "You'll be most successful in life if you do what you love." They then go on to reflect about how lucky they are: Who else gets to wake up in the morning and be thrilled about going to work? And then, the clincher: As the next generation of "leaders," do as I do.

Not everyone has heard a version of this talk, though chances are pretty high if you go to Yale. That said, it's by no means restricted to those who've dabbled in (or soaked in) "elite culture." It's an increasingly common refrain for a few reasons. First, it's good to hear, especially when most people know (or, perhaps as it applies to Yale, have at least seen on TV) other Americans who feel alienated from their work while they struggle to make ends meet. Second, for the middle and upper classes, it's at least partially true: They have the resources to acquire the skills needed for a job they won't hate.

At Yale, this advice is often flouted. It's not bold to guess that most of the throngs of students currently going through interviews weren't born aspiring to spend their college summers crunching data for a consulting firm. But even for those who succumb, for whatever reason on the spectrum of legitimacy, most believe that the bit about doing what you love is true: Either you really love the high-pressure situations those jobs provide, or you'll do what you love after. Easy breezy.

Plenty of people talk about whether the "do what you love"

advice is good or bad. But the more interesting question is whether it's actually applicable to everyone.

In reality, only a privileged few can get away with loving their work all the time. For everyone else, a varying combination of personal satisfaction and the ability to put food on the table is much more likely. But it seems that the most pressing issue here involves how this language affects the inequality problem in America, particularly with the renewed focus on alleviating poverty.

Poverty, as I've seen it in my family and friends, is like a physical chain. We won't know how fast those who are perpetually poor can run, because they're never allowed to show the world without this unjust deadweight attached. Almost everyone, from President Obama to Paul Ryan, acknowledges this.

But unless you give in to some transhumanist, determinist belief that says everyone can be made—depending on the right combination of social variables—to experience equal levels of devotion, force of personality or desire to succeed, that's not the whole nine yards. We know what happens to the folks in the middle classes and above who are, descriptively speaking, average—they continue living, for the most part, their not-too-shabby lifestyles. We all know plenty of people in this category. What does "average" here mean? Take an example: I knew a guy who had everything you could ask for—a wonderful home, good friends, good schooling—but he had very little drive to do much more.

There's a distinction between poverty and ordinariness that our lexicon eschews. If you've been inculcated in the same culture as I've been, you might be thinking that talking about people this way is insensitive. But there's nothing wrong with not having all-consuming passions or ambitions. It feels that way because the culture we live in—of maximization—implies in many ways that anything below the maximum is worse.

But what happens to the poor who are "average"? Those who, even if society succeeds in providing opportunity ladders, simply don't climb up very far, if at all?

Even the desire to be productive and to push yourself forward comes from an arbitrary combination of nature and nurture, plus (if you believe in it) some free will. But the truly meek—those not able to get themselves onto the ladder, whether because of their will or because that's just how they were born—have no way out using the language so popular today.

Even if they don't inherit the earth in this life, people like this will always exist. Which means, for the determinists among us, we have to find ways of engineering their lives. Or perhaps a little more realistically, we've got to sober up and adjust our language of success and opportunity so that it doesn't rob them of the human dignity that they deserve just as much as you and I.

WHERE IS YOUR PRIDE, YALE?

(*Yale Daily News, April 2, 2014*)

YOU DON'T REALLY hear the word "pride" much in conversations in the dining halls. Sure, through late night conversations, we often know what makes our close friends proud or embarrassed.

But even though Yale is very much a community made up of a lot groups with distinct identities, it's rare to hear someone speak of their pride in belonging to that group.

So I decided to conduct a little study. I asked 10 good friends—people whose preferences, personalities and backgrounds I knew pretty well—to name five things that made them proud. No other instructions—not "the most proud," not "secretly proud," no specifics about whether they had to stick to certain categories. Just whatever came to mind that they were willing to share.

When finished, I had results from people of different genders, races, nationalities, sexual orientations, levels of religiosity and socioeconomic backgrounds. Being Yalies certainly counted against maximal diversity but I wasn't exactly planning to publish the results in a psychology journal. Moreover, their proximity to me as friends meant I knew certain things about all of them that studies and reports usually don't provide. All 10 are very trustworthy, principled, thoughtful, kind and altruistic.

The results? First, the obvious: We're all proud of ourselves in one way or another. Some are proud of being able to successfully lead others, and in the ways they've improved as people. We're proud of being independent, of sticking to our principles, of getting fancy jobs, of doing excellent work, of meeting our parents' expectations, of being cosmopolitan, of looking good, of going to Yale. One friend was proud of making the English national swim team, after five hours of daily training and a two-hour subway commute. Another was proud to be someone who friends trusted to lean on in moments of need: "It's really important to me to be a person who others feel is there for them."

But then it becomes more complicated. A handful of interviewees mentioned they were proud of their family: of parents that were hardworking, self-sacrificing and honest, of a sibling trying hard, of "home" for everything and everyone it represents, for "my grandfather, a 13-year old Italian immigrant who didn't know a word of English and who spent all of his working years in a factory earning and saving money for his family." A handful also mentioned friends for their accomplishments and important moments they've shared together.

And now we get to the more unusual sources of pride. "I'm proud of my country," a friend said. "I think America gets a bad rap at Yale. We make mistakes—of hubris and of ignorance—but there really is no greater force for good in the world than America." Another said her "connection to all of the people who came before me" gave her a strong sense of identity. Fewer still said faith; one friend was proud of the missionaries involved in relief work worldwide, and another of people who keep their Catholic faith alive and stick to its principles (even in a difficult environment, as Yale can often be). Only two people mentioned the military, and both came from military backgrounds.

So here come the sweeping generalizations. A sizeable chunk of people only mentioned things related to themselves or those immediately around them. But this didn't signify selfishness at all: People are increasingly proud of fewer kinds of things, because community, faith and nation can seem close or irrelevant based on what you choose to believe and how strong of a connection you feel. Dislocation or alienation from these categories is common, and it often limits the experience of pride to the immediate. You put your pride in things that you feel a part of or that are close to you. Whether America, for instance, feels close to you depends both on you and the circumstances you grew up in. This raises interesting questions of policy and leadership. For example, how would the fact that a leader never had a close friend or neighbor in the military while young impact her judgment? It's one of many questions people wanting to go into leadership should be self-conscious about.

A final observation: Pride is, in many ways, a luxury. It helps anchor identity, establish life priorities and can provide a sense of transcendence. And not everyone is lucky to have role models in people or larger institutions that make them feel proud. For those that do, diversity in pride should be cherished and developed. It starts with the inner self, for a firm sense of basic dignity.

But to feel—no, to be—part of something larger, it's got to end outside of it.

SALMON, NOT PINK

(*Yale Daily News, April 17, 2014*)

TWO WINTERS AGO, I stood on the beach in a remote part of western Costa Rica, after having somehow managed to convince my poor parents—all they wanted was one relaxing week to shake off the exhaustion of their 8-to-8 hospital work schedules—to forsake a less adventurous vacation and rent a little bungalow on the edge of a tiny coastal village.

If you were a local resident (or even a tourist, for that matter), the sight of this guy standing on the beach would have seemed bizarrely out of place. Clad in seersucker shorts and a polo from a Vineyard Vines sale, I looked out at the shimmering bay as the obvious question hit: "Who are you?"

The answer, in that moment of handicapping self-consciousness only possible in a setting vastly different from what you're used to, wasn't obvious then and it isn't now. I wasn't the extremely awkward, slightly foreign, vested elementary school kid who would sprint home after school. Nor was I the middle-schooler in Kentucky who came from New York and started to pick up, slowly, all the social cues. But, now a sophomore at Yale, I also knew that wearing a salmon (not pink) polo and seersucker shorts didn't make me an East Coast yuppie on the inside any more than it made that girl I'd pass on Old Campus every day (wearing some variant of blue scales and red feathers) Lady Gaga.

Go ahead, psychoanalyze. It's not a hard case. After growing up in an Armenian immigrant household where every day felt like a climb for everyone involved, you say, you probably wanted validation, and turned to the clothing of the WASP elect (even though this has become so cliché that the WASP elect are now scrambling to diversify their wardrobes). Or, perhaps, you wanted to stand out when you went home, wearing "I go to Yale" because it was too obnoxious to say it aloud. Or, you just liked pink.

All these explanations are probably somewhat true. Yale is full of middle and upper middle class kids who resemble young, fit, hungry dogs: They've tasted meat for the first time, and their eyes have a crazed intensity about them. Go to the next J.P. Morgan information session, or stop by the News, if you really don't know what I'm talking about (or, for that matter, read through Yale College Council election histories since time immemorial).

But as these questions of success and identity clash, weird things start to happen—and the effects certainly aren't limited to any class. People start to become their "hyper-selves," and soon it feels like campus is drowning under the influence of its own individuality. People become all kinds of archetypes: the bubbly (often wealthy) guy with the great hair in all the photos, the Yale Political Union hack, the YCC bureaucrat, the radical activist, the conservative crusader, the Gaga, the jock. You could go on. As colleges like Yale become ever more diverse and international, these archetypes take on all sorts of new variations, but the fundamentals stay relatively constant. None of these categories are bad in themselves (debatable, I know), but they all present the possibility of their own pink polo moments.

When these moments happen, if personal experience is any guide, another hard question can sometimes present itself: Which is the bigger joke—that my self has been narrowed into this specific identity that only represents a small part of who I actually am, or that I'll have to pretend to be the same person I was before I left?

Look, some people don't end up asking themselves these questions. Some feel like their developed identities represent them very well, and that's fine. I remember my personal surprise at seeing how comfortable a group of students I was on a summer trip with felt in their suede shoes, pants and jewelry. It wasn't showy masquerading as understated, it was just understated. Ostentatiousness in America really is, more often than not, insecurity or class-consciousness in disguise.

Everyone has heard the cliché that you should be yourself, because everyone else is taken. But what do you do when you're already taken? Everywhere you look, personal lives are individualized and planned: parenthood, relationships, even relaxation. This makes the urge to distinguish yourself on established, tangible terms very strong, and it suggests something deeply wrong with American university life. It leads to inadvertent close-mindedness, and it phases out a deeper connection to intangibles.

HOW (NOT) TO SAY HELLO

(*Yale Daily News, September 9, 2014*)

IT HAPPENS WITH enough frequency to make you wonder. You're on the street, in a dining hall or going to class, and you say "Hi" to someone—only to get a deer-in-the-headlights look or, even more bizarre, a reciprocal "Hey" that's uttered without eye contact. It's like greeting a zombie. Sometimes it's accidental, but often it's tacitly assumed to be a normal way of greeting an acquaintance. Well, it's not. It's rude and highly abnormal.

For those wondering, I'm not a freshman from the Midwest in the throes of withdrawal because everyone on the East Coast is impersonal. I grew up in New York City, where a smile or an unwarranted greeting can get you assaulted. But that's a city. Yale is, ostensibly, a community. And there's no reason we should be morphing into neurotic characters from Woody Allen films so early in life.

Many students arrive at Yale on day one already carrying emotional baggage. It's to be expected that bringing together a large chunk of high school overachievers on one campus results in a pooling of intelligence—and a pooling of predictably similar neuroses. But Yale life, with its toxic brew of pressuring forces, heightens those issues. A sizeable number of students arrive on campus already susceptible to stress and anxiety. When the Yale avalanche hits, or an unexpected event catches them off guard, their vulnerability reaches a critical point.

On the very different question of character, objectively bad personality traits—like impatience, condescension, even deceit—aren't as easily suppressed here as they are in other communities. At Yale, these qualities can run rampant because they are often rewarded: Friends lend their tacit acceptance to groupthink and narrow-mindedness, or allow one another to get away with white lies that cover up for missing commitments. It's a four-year exercise in low to mid-level personal manipulation, just to keep the machine running smoothly. Even if people come through Yale's gates unexposed to these maneuvers, they learn the tricks of the trade pretty soon.

But I suppose the question then becomes: So what? Maybe most Yalies' ability to connect with people outside this life-on-steroids bubble isn't improving, but it's pretty easy to go through post-Yale life never having to leave the bubble. This goes almost without saying for people from elite and upper-middle class backgrounds. But it can also be true for people from low-income backgrounds.

Families and friends, often the only links to the communities left behind, recede into the background as internships, fellowships and exciting job prospects take priority. Summers, and then years, fill up. You're not the same, and it increasingly feels like they aren't either.

Faculty and staff are just as susceptible to the perverse incentive structure rewarding self-interested behavior. Professors are not encouraged to foster meaningful relationships with students. They tend to, on the whole, exhibit excessive self-confidence (often necessary for climbing the extremely political and cutthroat academic ladder), condescension and a particularly self-righteous brand of political liberalism. Maybe it's a survival mechanism, but it doesn't make for the best model of academic freedom. Outliers in the faculty are out there, but they're increasingly hard to find. Yale and its sister institutions have done a great job of exporting their most recognizable cultural product: academic self-assuredness.

All this raises the question of whether places like Yale should exist, or whether, as William Deresiewicz insists, Ivy League students would be better off attending public universities. That might be healthier for students, but his argument downplays the role brands have come to play in people's beliefs about education and future earnings potential. The "best" school will always be the one that will make a student the most money—and that's not likely to change.

There's no "what we should do" part of this column. Once people are in this culture, it's nearly impossible to go back. All I ask is that students spend some time living with people whose lives are ordered differently, instead of studying or rationalizing others' beliefs from afar. It might help mitigate our problems. And just try, please try, to look people in the eye when saying hello.

UNIVERSAL RIGHTS MATTER

(*Yale Daily News, October 7, 2014*)

Multiculturalism and pluralism are in the news a lot these days. The reasons are mixed: Sometimes, it's clear that we're not working hard enough to make room for beliefs and identities different from our own; at other times, critics note that we can't allow toleranceto override violations of what we believe are universal individual rights.

It's a tricky balance, and it's hard work on both the policy level and the human level. And it gets harder outside of places like Yale, where—frankly—most people believe nearly the same things. Here, inclusion and respect are the closest things we have to universal dogmas.

Multiculturalism in practice takes on many forms. Armenia, for instance, is sandwiched between Eastern Europe and the Middle East. Yazidis, Kurds, Jews, Iranians, Russians and other groups have all lived peacefully as minority groups in the small mountainous republic. For their part, Armenians have also lived peacefully for centuries as minorities in Eastern European and Middle Eastern lands, despite vast differences in faith and culture.

That's not the whole story, of course. History and political realities cause tensions. But where integration has succeeded, the similarities are common: melting language barriers, non-interference with the customs of minority groups and more anti-discrimination legislation regarding jobs and access to government institutions.

In America, our fluid ethnic and religious identity is both a model for the world and a challenge to navigate. But our reality has slowly come to more accurately resemble the commitment to individual rights and human dignity laid out at the founding—ideas that had been brewing for centuries, despite frequent hypocrisy in deeds. And the Obama administration's global human rights agenda rests on using influence to empower cultures and peoples around the world to move away from conflict-stricken (and, in many cases, colonial) pasts. The eradication of preventable diseases, the defense of women's rights, and building adequate supply infrastructures around are all top priorities.

Regardless of how you view the past, Western countries today are uniquely able to fulfill that role. Accusations of imperialism help remind us to respect cultural differences, but they can be unhelpful when considering the scope of human suffering and Western organizations' financial capacity for change. It also means the U.S. and other countries need to make some awkward decisions and judgments about cultural practices or beliefs they don't hold—but that may seriously threaten what we believe are universal human rights.

This past Thursday, activist Jaha Dukureh and women's rights group Equality Now met with representatives from the White House and several federal agencies in D.C. to raise awareness about female genital mutilation, in which a woman's sexual organs are mutilated or completely amputated. Dukureh's petition on change.org has garnered over 200,000 signatures, yet the issue is unknown to many Americans.

Earlier this summer, President Obama spoke frankly about the FGM epidemic in parts of Africa, the Middle East, and around the world: "I think that's a tradition that is barbaric and should be eliminated. Violence towards women—I don't care for that tradition. I'm not interested in it. It needs to be eliminated." That's powerful language, but it's not enough: While FGM is illegal in the U.S., unknown numbers of girls travel abroad every year with their families to undergo the procedure often under brutal conditions. Governments need joint initiatives to work with cultural groups to discourage this medically (and religiously) unnecessary practice, American doctors need guidelines for reporting and health agencies need new surveys to determine how many people are affected. One study conducted by Newsweek in 2000 found that 228,000 girls in the U.S. "lived with or were at risk of undergoing FGM."

The FGM example, and others like it, makes clear that we can't afford to be silent about human rights abuses just because they happen overseas. It's not practical, because modern travel ensures that these abuses end up on our shores anyway. Nor is it morally responsible, when we're often the only ones who can do something. That's "we" in both a macro and micro sense: At Yale, more international service trips could focus on developing young women leaders abroad, instead of one-time infrastructure projects. Women in countless places still can't conceive of the idea that they might run their societies someday. Getting this idea to them means a better future for them as individuals and their entire societies. Yalies can help make that happen.

The next few generations have the opportunity to finally get rid of some of the world's ugliest diseases and social practices. But first, we've got to remember that human dignity always comes first—and to have the courage to act.

WASTING YALE'S GIFT

(*Yale Daily News, October 21, 2014*)

ONE OF THE more memorable conversations I've had in the last few months began with the usual sharing of upcoming summer plans with a Yale friend. I mentioned I'd be spending two weeks living in a monastery in Jerusalem before a summer internship began. As (mostly) a joke, I added that I might just stay there and join the monks for good. It'd be a liberating break from the rat race of college life and beyond. Her response: "Talk about a waste of a Yale education!"

I thought she was completely wrong. And yet it can be difficult to go through Yale and not end up catching yourself judging, in the back of your mind, those who don't put their education "to good use," whatever you understand that term to mean. Far from just a benign conversation starter, the "What did you do this summer?" question is loaded with expectations. The interrogator is waiting to be dazzled.

But while on the topic of what constitutes a good use of our four years here and what constitutes a waste of time and effort, let's do a bit of soul-searching. It's a question many freshmen are in the midst of trying to answer right now.

I don't know how many Yale freshmen were student council presidents in high school, though I'm told the number is disproportionately high. Fine. For these students, who are already familiar with what an elected student body does, the college versions are pretty similar, if on a slightly larger scale.

The limitations—we are, after all, just students in a huge corporate institution with a brand and image to maintain—are also similar. And yet, large numbers of freshmen pursue positions in student government, apparently ready to consign college life to a sort of high school 2.0. Many will find out, sooner or later, that only one person out of the hundreds who want it will end up being president—and then they'll either settle for a lesser role or quit altogether, hours wasted in committee meetings discussing toilet paper or dining hall cereal options.

I don't want to belittle the work that administrative committees or the student council do. The typical Yale College Council insider will tick off the list of accomplishments in recent years. But that response misses the point. Many changes could have been implemented without the bureaucratic black hole of the college and class council apparatuses, which often acts as a rubber stamp rather than a brain trust of innovative ideas. But there's a deeper point to be made. There are more pressing demands on a student's time than student government or its counterparts. By this I mean either more pressing moral responsibilities to serve other communities or an obligation to invest time not into an organization's day-to-day operations but into one's personal ethical growth.

It is too easy to treat life as a continuation of high school. A leadership post in college, a string of glossy internships, a polished seat at a top graduate school, a cushy job. LinkedIn is teeming with these profiles.

Is anything wrong with this setup? Most will agree that an unexamined life is not worth living, but a life of examination isn't necessarily incompatible with this. It's more about the motivations, I think, than the outcomes. Some iteration of the life description above could very well be a productive, interesting, meaningful one. But if you believe in something like the importance of learning how to lead the good life, of discovering truth, a high school 2.0 life doesn't provide it.

I'll cut the philosophizing and get to the punch line: In all likelihood, you can spend the next four years doing something much more valuable than student government. Your Yale degree, for better of worse, will get you far, so take some liberties you otherwise wouldn't. Communities next door and far away could really use your help. And you need yourself to spend these years creating the manual you'll refer back to for the rest of your life. Many overcompensate for not having a deep sense of who they are and what they believe by just continuing to climb until an existential crisis hits.

And you won't have time to start putting together your life manual if you're at committee meetings by day and sending out survey emails by night.

COLUMBIA LAW SCHOOL APPLICATION ASSIGNMENT

(Spring of 2016)

I HAVE RECEIVED two tickets for violations over my life. The first was a moving violation ticket issued in May of 2011, my senior year of high school, outside of Salt Lake City. A friend and I were on a sightseeing trip across Utah. As I drove, we passed two police cars parked on the right edge of the highway. I continued to drive in the right lane at normal speed while passing the cars. One of the two police vehicles quickly stopped us to issue a ticket for violating Utah's "move over" law, which stipulates motorists must move into a farther lane upon passing a parked police car in order to protect officers from being hit by vehicles. I paid the ticket as soon a I returned home. As of 2015, many states, including Utah, were continuing campaigns to inform drivers about the law, as many continued violating it unwittingly. I certainly will not be in that position again.

The second was a subway violation ticket issued in New York City in December of 2012. Three years ago, in the winter of my sophomore year at Yale following a four-day succession of finals, I found myself leaping into the subway en route to Grand Central Terminal. Large suitcase in tow, I raced to make the A train audibly pulling into the station. As per Murphy's Law, the bag could not squeeze past the turnstile. When someone walking out opened the service gate, I ran through, grateful for the lifeline, only to be stopped by a police officer emerging from an unmarked door: I hadn't swiped the MetroCard. I walked away, dejected, ten minutes later. The train was gone, and I'd been slapped with a $100 ticket for "jumping the turnstile," though no jumping had been involved. I sent in the money, as with a parking ticket, and forgot about it until my eye caught a *Daily News* headline in 2014: "Fare evasion arrests surge in recent years." Many who are stopped for the reason I was can't just board the next train. The New York Police Department is authorized to treat "turnstile jumping" as a misdemeanor—a crime—instead of a parking-type violation. A police officer can arrest the offender at will, though the New York District Attorney's office found that arrests had increased sixty-nine percent from 2008 to 2013 and that being African American, Latino, or simply failing to present identification all significantly increased the probability of arrest and jail time: for every white arrest, there are five Latino arrests, and eight African American arrests. I appeared to be white, I had a driver's license, and I had no criminal history. With this privilege, a careless act comes and goes—without it, school enrollment, employment prospects, and an entire future may instantly disappear is an avalanche of trouble, with little to no means to escape. The immense difference, which manifests itself all the more powerfully in criminal arrests and prosecutions, rises far above a question of inequality: it is, as Ta-Nehisi Coates describes, one of the many "cosmic injustices" that animate daily life in America and that disproportionally target minorities and the poor.

CHAPTER III

Love, Faith, and Virtue

---

1. *Middle School and High School Years*

LETTER TO A TEACHER [RE: MS. ORLANDO]

(P.S. 187, New York City, December 17, 2006)

Dear Ms. Orlando,

Oh my goodness, where to start! Let me start off by apologizing for not staying in touch with you for such a long while. It has been, to say the least, an incredibly hectic and exciting time in our first 6 months in Lexington, Kentucky. So much has happened! It would take tens of letters for me to convey all that has happened and all that has occurred in such a short period of time…so I better start now.

Let me start off by saying that the school system is wonderful. I daresay, better than that of New York's. Many times over. There is a huge array of extracurricular activities for students——I myself am part of the Morton Middle School Academic Team (in which the team goes around to different schools and answers a series of trivia questions in a Jeopardy-style setting, with buzzers}, Speech Team, Student Council, and Student Technology Leadership Program (called STLP), where I am part of the daily morning school news broadcast. (One other aspect worth noting——the Student Council is does not have an election-based system; any person who is truly interested in helping the school can attend.)

In terms of hard-core academics, the Literacy (which is called Language Arts) content is about the same, as goes with Social Studies. We have a great Life/Physical/Earth Science teacher. And math comes in many levels, from Algebra Part 2, to Algebra 1, to Advanced Geometry, to Algebra 2. The math curriculum is very vigorous. I am currently in Advanced Geometry, and was very surprised to see the intensity of the math curriculum——light years ahead of the New York system. We also have 2 to 3 electives per semester, including Economics, Tech Ed, Career Development, Performing Arts, Family and Consumer Science, Physical Education, and Art. There are basketball, volleyball, and football teams, and there is a huge track field out back. All students are required to take either Spanish or French as a Foreign Language, as part of a two-year program. We have a very dedicated principal and assistant principal (the principal's name is Jock Gum!). One interesting downside, though—no recess during lunch!

Anyway, school has taken up a very large portion of my time, aside from tennis lessons and family time. All the kids are very nice and I've found lots of new friends.

In mid-November, I was part of a 3-day delegation which went to Frankfort, the state capital, for an in-government conference, in which we were able to literally "take over" the state legislature and decide upon whether to pass or send down student-created bills and measures-sitting in the state legislature chambers! During the visit, I had the honor of being named "Outstanding Speaker"——and award which about 10 of the 900 attending received.

I hope all is well in New York, and that everyone at P.S./I.S. 187 are doing well.

Despite the many activities that I take part in, I often find myself reminiscing about my old school, friends, teacher. and relatives. I want to take this opportunity to thank you kindly on the glowing recommendation that you wrote on my behalf several months ago——1 was truly humbled. I constantly remember all my favorite teachers at 187—-you are always remembered and thought of, Ms. Orlando. Thank you for being such an important part of my life at 187, where I spent 8 years of my education.

Please send my regards to all at Hudson Cliffs, and a very Merry Christmas and a joyous New Year to you.

Please write back soon!

Love, John

MY PERSONAL WRITING IDIOSYNCRASIES

(*AP English Assignment, October 26, 2009*)

My mother walked into my room the other day. "No," I said. She persisted. "But you haven't even considered how…"

"No," I said again. It was final. Perhaps I was being unreasonable. My parents and I had been feuding about whether or not to relocate my desk, currently situated against the window in my room. I have a magnificent view of my street, so beautiful now in the abundance of autumn. I watch runners struggle going up my tedious hill. "They asked for it," I think to myself. I watch dog owners stroll along, marveling at the beauty of the tree-lined lane. "Oh look," my mind quips, "There goes the man who cursed at my mother after his dog lunged at her." The view from my window is truly a very beautiful one. Every now and then, when I'm churning all the goo in my mind, trying to find a satisfactory way to write an essay for AP English, I open the window. Crisp autumn air comes streaming in. Other times it's moist spring air, vibrant and refreshing.

And other times, as I sit at my desk, typing away at my laptop, I glance outside and see rain. Dark, gloomy, pouring rain. And I feel safe. It's like that feeling you get when you're looking out an airplane window after you've completed the initial ascent, and you realize that the only thing stopping you from being sucked out of the plane and hurled towards a certain death is a thin (but surely very durable) plastic barrier. You begin to establish a relationship with the window—a relationship built on trust. You have no *choice* but to trust it. In a similar fashion, as I swirl my chair around and look outside, observing the scary exterior unfold, I begin to trust my window. It's keeping me and my thoughts from the coldness, wetness, and dreariness of the outside. For without the window, my thoughts would surely perish, forgotten amidst the clamor of the howling rainstorm. My thoughts and I are grateful. And I feel safe. I continue writing.

So I was clearly displeased when my parents proposed moving my desk, that prime writing location, across my room to border a wall. A wall. A dull, green wall. Their reasoning? The draft coming through from the little crevices on the sides of the window was blowing on me and making me sick.

Let me make one thing clear: there is no draft. I got sick because everyone else at school was. In all me years writing at this desk, in my favorite writing position (legs crossed Indian-style on the swirly chair, a position absolutely indispensible for writing anything having as much as a shot at being considered decent writing), I have never felt a draft or a breeze come from that window.

Nothing. And the window sure didn't start letting air in overnight. And even if it did, how is this my fault? Why the assault on my years of acquaintance with this writing location? I proposed simply installing new, airtight windows. That proposal didn't fly.

But after a long brawl, it was determined that the desk would remain untouched. I know teenagers often say that their parents "don't understand," whatever that means. And I find much of that entire argument shallow and unspecific. But here was a very specific case of parents clearly demonstrating a blatant disregard for their child's academic and emotional needs. They simply didn't understand.

I hate change. Maybe "hate" is too strong a word, but I generally dislike movement or fluidity in life. As soon as I heard "change" come out of then-Senator Barack Obama's mouth, I knew I had to go looking for another candidate to support. No candidate advocating a radical shift in policy on *anything* –domestic issues, foreign issues, or otherwise—would have my backing. And I have generally been this way my entire life, especially when it comes to writing. I run my hands through my hair ("Stop that," my father says). I swirl around my chair. I bring a cup of tea up to my room and slowly drink. I write my opinion column for the school newspaper, I check up on the latest news.

"Obama's approval hits new low," the headline reads. "Hah!" I think. "How about that for some real change?" Maybe change isn't that bad. I go downstairs to have another talk with my parents about that one writing desk they once wanted to move.

U.S. SENATE PAGE SCHOOL ASSIGNMENT ESSAY

(February 22, 2010)

EVERYONE NEEDS A protector, and the telephone in Rooms 28 serves as mine—my lifeline to the world, my comforter in times of stress, and a pleasant (if sometimes distant) reminder that the world is larger than the two-block stretch to the Hart Building and back.

Just the look of the white slim-line, with its dangling spiral cord, multi-colored buttons, light-up screen and little sticker, "EMERGENCY AT WEBSTER HALL CALL 4-0911," reassures you that it can connect you to someone dear and close or someone to help in times of danger.

Except when lights-out arrives. What follows is a painful task: removing the phone jack from the handset, pressing the orange ("salmon-colored," as once described) "Rls" button, and knowing that you have indeed just "released" yourself from the world. Darkness then penetrates every corner of the room, with the faint glow of lights outside shining in and casting shadows here and there. To make matters worse, the telephone handset must be put out outside the heavy wooden door until morning. The door feels almost heavier at night, somehow even more sturdy and stationary than usual.

The telephone in my room is going to be my friend. We are going to become very amiable companions, and I anticipate relying on it many times to save me in times of stress. It already has. Grab the handset, begin dialing the soft, grey buttons, and know that relief is just a few dial tones away.

I retreat to my desk, which—to my surprise—feels relatively comfortable. With all my books laid out on the upper shelf and my order of things on the desk (binders to the left, stationary next, newspapers to the far right without exception), fleeing to it when the phone is gone provides some therapeutic end-of-day relief. There is something to be said for writing letters at a desk, and I have come to enjoy the task during my tenure at the page dorm. Hours may be spent writing away in this manner, if not disturbed by the occasional shots of air freshener from the paranormal automated air freshener contraption. Every so often (I unsuccessfully attempted several times to count the intervals between shots), a sharp pop resonates from two corners of the room. If you're standing close enough, a light drizzle of artificial cherry scent trickles down and burns your eyes. The whole episode is annoying, nor for the sound or the unpleasant drizzle nearly as much as the fact that someone thought us so smelly that we needed periodic scent-releasers to keep our rooms smelling fresh.

These are the defining objects in room twenty-eight. Some relaxing, some degrading, some with no personality or meaning whatsoever. At the end of the day, the dorm room provides a much-needed getaway that few other locations in Washington, D.C. can (I reckon perhaps a spa might do the trick, but I haven't been able to locate one near Webster Hall yet). The room relaxes and calms the best a taxpayer-financed room can. The carpet (usually the first sign that you're not in the Senate, since most of a Page's day is spent staring at the carpet floor) is soft and welcoming. The bunk beds are familiar and warm, the wood giving off a faint glow under the lights. Those lights, too, convey a certain quaint, oddly inviting sadness. If the white, boring, unadorned walls could talk, they would probably tell depressing stories of pages long past –exhausted, much like us—going through the same daily premature early morning wake-up routine. And during the day, they would muse and await tired bodies to return and seek their company again.

A GREAT TEACHER [RE: MRS. BARBOUR]

(Henry Clay High School Academy, October 26, 2010)

IT IS OFTEN noted that there exists a substantive difference between a "teacher" and an "educator." It is relatively easy to be a teacher—that is, to help facilitate the transfer of material from some medium into a student's mind. A person can accomplish the task just as easily as a computer or disk can. To be an educator, however—to spark a love of learning and teach in a way that transcends the walls of school—is an art form far from the simple mechanics of teaching. Ashley Barbour is the embodiment of that art which is education.

In Mrs. Barbour's classroom, a student does not simply learn about the workings of our civic government or study the politics of other societies. Students are immersed in culture, dialogue, and multimedia presentations that give meaning to the words on the textbook page. Her lessons are punctuated with personal anecdotes which always connect to the issue being studied, and no comment or story from students ever goes unappreciated. Mrs. Barbour's openness to a frank exchange of ideas, beliefs, and personal experiences fosters independence of thought and creates an atmosphere where students can grow, learning how to think analytically and examine issues and events from a worldview different than their own.

"I am indebted," Alexander the Great once acknowledged, "To my father for living, but to my teacher for living well." Mrs. Barbour's approach is not only a successful method for teaching course material, but her class is effectively a guide for etiquette and behavior for adolescent students on the cusp of adulthood. It is ironic that our educational system today rests on the notion that student must, upon walking into a classroom, respect the teacher—regardless of whether respect is shown in return. It is ironic because this expectation is applied when young adults are at the peak of their "rebelliousness" anti-authoritarianism. Learning so often does not take place in the classroom because teachers assume they will be treated with deference without showing any semblance of outward respect or acknowledgment in return. It is, at first glance, stunning how Ashley Barbour seemingly effortlessly manages to command the respect of her students. This is rooted in her insistence upon treating each of her students as an adult, and fostering a relationship of mutual understanding. Condescension is not found in her practice. In insisting upon this mutual respect, Mrs. Barbour teaches her students to respect others by first respecting themselves—for, as she is keenly aware, lack of self-esteem is often the root of indecent behavior. Mrs. Barbour is a source of inspiration and support for countless students, and I am proud to include myself with that affiliation. She educates her students not simply for an upcoming AP test or college course, but for a lifetime of continued intellectual and emotional growth.

J. S. RUMBAUGH HISTORICAL ORATION CONTEST

(*February 25, 2011*)

THE MORNING WAS cold. The citizens? Frightened. The world was waiting. It was April 19, 1775, the dawn haze still plainly visible in a sea of sunlight in the sleepy town of Concorcd, Massachusetts. The farmers were few, determined to make a stand. The redcoats were plentiful, determined to crush the mere thought of a rebellion. Neither side could ever possibly predict what would come next.

Oh, that shot. That shot heard 'round the world. The shot that started a war, framed a message, and created America. We talk about it today with a great sense of awe and wonderment, amazed that such a small handful of men (*minutemen*, as they called themselves) could muster the courage to start what would be known as the defeat of an empire. But what really was this shot? How did it happen? And what was the result?

British troops had occupied Boston since 1768, as a reactionary measure brought upon by the boisterous American backlash to the passage of the so-called "Intolerable Acts," which, among other things, closed the Port of Boston, forced citizens to give their homes for the quartering of British soldiers upon request, and consolidated control of the Massachusetts government under Britain. Outside of Boston, tensions ran even higher. Citizen militias had gathered supplies for defense in the event of a possible British strike. Thomas Gage, General and Governor of Massachusetts Bay, received orders on April 14 from Secretary of State William Legge to dismantle the citizen threat, who were known to be storing weapons in Concord. The mission was to be carried out on April 19. Little did he know that a surprise of glorious proportions was to follow.

The night of April 18, 1775—the night before a battle that would forever remain emblazoned in human history—served as a shining prelude to the fugue of the years that would follow. Samuel Adams and John Hancock, soon to-be revolutionary leaders, had received word of the British threat from sources in London and had fled from Boston to Lexington by April 8. On the night of April 18, Dr. Joseph Warren informed William Dawes and Paul Revere that the troops would be making the assault by the following morning. Upon seeing two lights flicker at the top of the Old North Church, indicating the British would be crossing the Charles River en route to Lexington and Concord, Revere, Dawes, and Dr. Samuel Prescott, American heroes all, led the mission to inform the citizens of Greater Boston about the impending British threat on their security, carrying out the entire perilous evening journey on horseback. Their actions inspired a nation to rise to the occasion, their mission depicted so vividly in Longfellow's *The Midnight Ride of Paul Revere.*

Lexington and Concord knew that the British would soon be

at their doorsteps, but the real danger-of a long, hard, drawn-out war—was still very imminent. It was more than imminent. It was fate. But America didn't know that. The citizens of Massachusetts didn't know that. Yet. All of this began to change as the radiating beams of sunlight began to shine in the wee hours of the following morning.

The militiamen of the towns of Lexington and Concord were as prepared as they could be to defend their little town and the arsenal they possessed. At Lexington Green, thirty-eight Americans, grossly outnumbered by six hundred British troops, made the first stand. The British pressed onward to Concord, determined to seize the supplies and squelch rebellion. Four hundred and fifty Americans stood in their way that time, prohibiting the redcoats from crossing the Old North Bridge-the gateway to Concord. What transpired then is rather unclear. Which side fired the first shot is but a mystery. What is known is this—as "the embattled farmers stood," and fired "the shot heard 'round the world," as we remember it today.

The British won that battle. The American line of defense was penetrated and the British stormed the city, set fire to the courthouse, and confiscated the arms. Redcoats on their return march to the Boston area were the targets of frequent guerilla firing coming from American militias. As the struggle wound to a close, ninety-three Americans had died, gone missing, or been wounded. On the British side, casualties amounted to two hundred and seventy-three. The colonies now knew what was to come. Fate had been realized. The war had begun.

The battles at Lexington and Concord set off the shot heard world over. Americans lined up to join the militia forces, which numbered at least fifteen thousand by the following day. The actions of the minutemen became the impetus for the creation of the Continental Army, established by the Continental Congress only about two months following the battles. British public opinion began to swing, as ships carried the message of the American cause overseas. In the words of John Adams, who had seen the battlefields, "the Die was cast, the Rubicon crossed."

The American Revolution did not officially start until more than one year following "the shot heard 'round the world." The war that followed would last another seven years. One wonders, though, whether it all would have happened had it not been for the individuals on that other side of the Old North Bridge at Concord. We don't know. But we do know this—their actions that day served as a shining call to arms in defense of their freedoms. This message remains as radiant and influential today is inspiring Americans' hopes and dreams as it did when it inspired a nation to stand up for its most basic, God-given right—freedom.

MAN OF BATTLE, MAN OF PEACE

(Spring of 2011)

THE STORY OF the American Revolution and its heroic, visionary military leader George Washington, is one of the most often-told accounts of American history. We are told, if not for the brave valor of General Washington and his men in the dark years of the Revolution, the colonies—our nation—would not have achieved independence from the mighty British Empire. The interpretation is, no doubt, accurate, but it does not come close to telling the entire story. Why is George Washington so highly venerated—as a general and as a statesman—in American society?

The answer might lie in the events following the Revolutionary War—troubling times for the upstart nation. The fledgling colonies, fresh out of a costly and hard-fought war for independence, had been driven nearly to the point of bankruptcy. The dollar was worth little, and the Continental Congress had been unable to pay the troops of the Continental Army their salaries in the aftermath of the war. There was evident anger and dismay among the troops, who had sacrificed their livelihoods for the war effort and had received little to no compensation in return. The officers had even heard that the government was going broke—which wasn't entirely false—and that the compensation might never come.

It did not take long for tensions to escalate. Following the decisive victory of the Continental Army over General George Cornwallis' men at Yorktown, General Washington's men returned to the Hudson Valley to monitor the British garrison at New York City. On March 10, 1783, an anonymous letter began making the rounds amongst the officers of Washington's main camp at Newburgh, New York. The letter stated the soldiers' complaints and announced a meeting of officers the following day; everything about the move signaled the possibility of mutiny. The disgruntled men had also notified Congress of their grievances in writing. The men feared that when the war finally ended, they would "grow old in poverty, wretchedness and contempt," unpaid and disrespected. Congress did little to allay these fears.

At this critical juncture, everything the men had fought for was under attack. Under attack from within. The nation had survived the war with Britain, but a mutiny of its troops and an ensuing coup could be the new nation's death knell, depriving it of its last remaining strength and creating international vulnerability. The officers of the Newburgh Conspiracy seemed determined, out of desperation, to accomplish with relatively few men what the entire British army could not do.

Enter George Washington. Having realized the unrest in his army, he ordered that the meeting be instead held on March 15th. As the meeting opened, conversation began about the soldiers' grievances against the American government. Suddenly, General

Washington walked into the room, to the astonishment of his officers. What followed was one of the most breathtaking moments in early American history. Washington begged his officers not to "lessen the dignity and sully the glory you have hitherto maintained" by seeking violent means. He then produced a letter from a Virginia congressman, which explained Congress' financial difficulties. He began to read, but quickly started to stumble over the words, unable to make out the writing. He paused and removed a pair of glasses from his pocket. Few of the men had seen the spectacles before. "Gentlemen," he announced, "You will permit me to put on my spectacles, for I have not only grown gray but almost blind in the service of my country."

The audience of soldiers were reportedly moved to tears seeing the deteriorating health of their leader as a result of many years of battle. If Washington was not angry at Congress, they had far less right to be. As the general finished the letter and left the room, resolutions were immediately made by the officers expressing a reaffirmation of faith in their nation and government. And the so-called mutiny effectively collapsed, cementing henceforth the role of Congress in control of the armed forces, with the President acting as Commander-in-Chief. The soldiers' pay, by the way, eventually came.

George Washington's actions at Newburgh established the general as distinguished in battle and distinguished in peace. This was politics truly at its best—a unifying force which sought to remind citizens with justifiably angry tempers of their common interests. This model, unfortunately, seems to have become lost in today's political dialogue. Anger and bitter, personal partisanship threaten disunion, and some have even gone so far as to suggest rebellion. The current state of American politics beckons for this type of Washingtonian leadership—leadership which the politicians in office today, beginning with the President and running the gamut of elected officials—have failed to provide.

It is ironic, then, that the city which bears George Washington's name functions very much devoid of the spirit of its founder. Compromise and respect have taken a backseat to the fiery rhetoric of hotheads on the Hill. It is easy, yes, to rail about the broken system, as so many do. Fixing it has proven a more difficult challenge. It is time we looked back more than two hundred years, and remembered how the leaders who so adroitly navigated 'the uncharted waters facing a new nation led it with conviction and insistence upon respect. Looking back to George Washington, man of battle but more importantly man of peace, is the best way forward.

NATIONAL HONOR SOCIETY CLUB SPEECH

(*April 21, 2011*)

Good evening, everyone. You know, life is very interesting. I don't know if this has happened to you, but often times, I think back to things I've said to people before—maybe a year ago, or two years ago—and I say to myself, "Gosh, John, what you said then was absolute crap. Just total nonsense. Which is good I guess, because it means we're growing as individuals, becoming smarter, realizing the things we said and thought before aren't really how things actually are. So I guess it's good. But I say that because, in case anything I say tonight comes across as stupidity to you, it probably is. It's just that I don't know it yet.

I'm supposed to talk to you about leadership tonight. Not quite sure why Hayes picked me, I've been President of a couple clubs, Governor of KYA, but really those titles aren't what leadership is about. So I thought of how I was going to say something half-decent tonight; something at least a little meaningful that might stick with somebody in the room. Who am I to talk? Who are we to talk? We're only a year older than you all. We certainly don't have an innate wisdom that comes with walking into your first senior class. But I guess, from some of the experience with leadership we've had, we can offer you some advice. So this is what I can say about leadership.

For me, leadership begins with empathy. It begins with understanding the people you come in contact with, their views, how where they come from in life impacts who they are. If you are able to empathize with someone, understand them, you are much better equipped to lead them. It continues with vision and dedication to a cause.

And it does not matter what that cause may be. If you're passionate about it, if you feel the impact your work has towards the betterment of others is significant, don't let anyone tell you it's not a worthwhile cause. Maybe you're passionate about the environment and keeping our school clean. Maybe you're passionate about working on AIDS prevention and awareness. Maybe you're politically passionate. Maybe you feel called to be a pro-life advocate. Or a pro-choice advocate. Whatever you choose to do, that is service. In whatever you choose to do, I only ask you to empathize with those you work with, and with those you work against. Really try to understand them. Feel how they feel. True leaders excite others by tapping into the good in all of us. Leaders mess up, just like everyone else, but they acknowledge their mistakes and emerge stronger than ever.

Because honestly, how many of you would be here if you didn't get the benefit of being able to put "National Honor Society" on your college application? If it was just a community service club, with nothing in return? Probably very few. I don't know if I would be here last year. But let me tell you something—if all that this club is going to be for you is signing this book, attending the meetings, and logging hours spent hating what you were doing to fulfill the community service requirement, do yourself a favor and quit now.

Trust me, you'll have plenty more to put on your college application. Stay in this club only because you care. Make yourself believe in the community service you do. Find something you're passionate about. Believe in something. If you don't believe in something, as the corny old phrase goes, you're bound to fall for anything.

And, if you've already forgotten everything I've said, at least maybe remember for a little while this last wish I have for you as leaders: I personally hope and pray that each and every one of you—every one of us—goes out into the world and does really well—in school, in our jobs, whatever.

But what's even more important is that we all go out into the world and do good.

HENRY CLAY HIGH SCHOOL ACADEMY GRADUATION DAY ADDRESS

(June 4, 2011)

So, FOLKS, WE made it. After four years of work, four years of study, four years of playing our hearts out on the field, of writing our hearts out on paper, we made it. After four years of love and anger, friendship and animosity—of laughing harder than we ever have, and of crying pretty hard too, we made it. It took a lot to get here: lots of sleepless nights, sweaty days. And the whole experience was punctuated by all kinds of moments: happy ones as well as sad ones, and moments of great achievement but also great embarrassment. You know, I remember walking into the connector building on a rainy day once, books in hand—took a step forward into a puddle and WHAM—I was on the floor, books everywhere. It was just about as school was starting, and this big group of people behind me were laughing hysterically—most of them were girls. But just as memorable was my first ever speech team trophy, or when I was elected Governor at the Kentucky Youth Assembly.

For you, it's probably something else—maybe it's the first ever touchdown you made, or your first tennis win. Your first basketball shot, your first performance, your first real friendship, or your first kiss—that you'll remember for quite a while. Or maybe it's something totally different. Whatever you take away from high school, today—as we all graduate *together*—know that today, you made it. Carry the energy and the passion you've built up and go conquer the world, class of 2011. Whether you're going to college, whether you're entering the workforce—let the force always be with you, and don't let anything or anyone hold you back.

Thank you, Henry Clay. Thank you to the educators and mentors who have made this day possible. Thank you to our parents, who've been with us from day one and stand with us today as we enter adulthood.

Henry Clay, it has been an honor to serve you as Student Body President. This might be the last time we are altogether, but let us use this day as a starting point—and let us never give up fighting for our dreams. As Eleanor Roosevelt said, "The future belongs to those who believe in the beauty of their dreams." So let us always stand up for what we believe in, stand up for our friends and families, and stand up today and every day to make not only ourselves better—but to make this world a more compassionate, welcoming, better place. And now, with diplomas in hand, let's go show the world what it means to be a Blue Devil. Thank you.

HENRY CLAY HIGH SCHOOL ACADEMY GRADUATION DAY PERFORMANCE

(June 4, 2011)

SO IN THINKING how best to commemorate this day, thought that each academy teacher has played a huge role. After all, as much as this is a celebration of us, it's just as much a celebration of the people who helped us get here. So what could be more appropriate to commemorate all our teachers than a little serenade or I suppose it's a poem I wrote—perhaps you could call it a rap song? Not really my element, bear with me.

Academy 11, looks like we're about done.
But yeah, over the past four years, there's been some fun.

Freshman year we had Ms. Barbour, she knows government like no other;
And Mista Lentz, who loves Star Wars more than I love my motha.
Don't forget Ms. Logsdon, she was green to the core.
Five years from now she's gonna be the next Al Gore.

Then came Mr. Holloway, a better teacher I've no had;
And then Ms. Haggerty, just me breathing made her mad;
Mr. Ratliff was a sweetheart, who showed me chemistry;
And junior year we had Matt Logsdon, who taught us English wonderfully.

Mr. Pope, of all my teachers, you're number one on the list.
But tonight I've got a confession to make—I'm a communist.

And this year, Mr. Reynolds' class, where in English
we immersed.
I wonder why he assigned me all the play characters who
always died first. (sigh)

But now Ms. Workman, you like our momma.
Helpin' us get through all our Academy Drama.
You jumpstarted our futures, you always knew what
to do.
I wouldn't be going where I am for college if it wasn't
for you.

But I know what you gonna say—that you only facilitate.
But now's not the time for modesty, Ms. Workman,
cuz you frickin great!
So give it up for Ms. Workman, this is all because of her.
Happy retirement Ms. Workman, you the world's eight
great wonder.

YALE APPLICATION ESSAY

(*Spring of 2010*)

I WISH I had an algorithm for life. An equation, or a method, or something I could use to tie together everything I've done and the choices I've made. I wish I had a cute, generic little story I could use on a college application that could glue all the pieces—perhaps something like how I use a Rubik's Cube as an analogy, or how playing the harp transcends my material existence, or how observing a spear of grass for hours taught me to put everything into context. But I don't. I hate Rubik's Cubes, the only time I've been near a harp is when I went to Ireland this summer (where they're kind of unavoidable), and Whitman was the least favorite part of my summer reading (though I have a feeling I'll come to appreciate him down the road).

I found three words, etched on a steel plate in an Irish craft shop in Dublin, that I think provide the only working explanation of who I really am. I was doing some shopping for friends as the two-week student exchange program last summer came to a close, when I saw the Irish-made sign. *Amor Vincit Omnia*, it read. Having taken Latin throughout high school, I was familiar with the phrase. It had always inspired me. But seeing it etched on a steel plate, simply but starkly, was stunning. I asked the shopkeeper how much the plate cost, but the answer, I already knew, wouldn't really matter.

"Love conquers all" is about the only way I feel I can quantify my life. I have never followed a formula or an algorithm for the things I have done. I did not get involved with Student Government, Speech, Debate, Academic Team, or found two clubs of my own as part of an elaborate plan to "look good on paper." I did not start my own newspaper when I was ten, or apply to be a "Kid Reporter" for *TIME for Kids* Magazine as a means to some sort of collegiate end eight years down the road. It was because I loved those things—to write, to read, to research. And I certainly did not spend five months in Washington as a Senate Page, which involved going to sleep at midnight and waking up at 5 a.m. every weekday morning under duress, so I could put it on my resume. No, and even if my parents had known that all this might be beneficial down the road, they wouldn't have insisted anyway. My parents have never made me do anything I did not want to do. Ever. I wasn't pushed into getting good grades, nor was I castigated if I did not. No. *Amor Vincit Omnia.*

I love everything I do, and I fully invest myself emotionally into the people and the activities I love. I used to not be this way. I used to hate the emotional baggage that came with loving someone or something so much that it hurt. But stumbling upon a quote from Mother Teresa once, I realized just how flawed that approach was. "I have found the paradox," she says, "That if you love until it hurts, there can be no more hurt, only more love." I bought two steel plates. One for myself, and one for my best friend, a guy whom I love more than he will ever know—the person who, along with Mother Teresa (though I know he would reject the juxtaposition), breathed new life into my belief that giving your all to the people and the issues most dear is the only formula one ever needs. I would not have met him if not for the Senate Page Program. When I visited Quinton in Utah this summer, he shocked me (as he is fond of doing) with his tenderness and amazing heart. He hung the plate right above his bed. As soon as I flew home, I hung mine in the exact same place.

I love *Amor Vincit Omnia*. I love it so much because it never stops holding true.

Love conquers all, and it does it again and again. Love conquers me every single day.

SUESS!

(2010)

Dear Kid,

You're alone. And I know that it's rough.
Living a street life is bound to be tough.

I can't say that I've lived it. My experience it's not.
But I can say I've been through a similar spot.

It's not easy, I know, to be on the streets.
To have folks who ignore who you are underneath.

And I'm sure you're distracted. I know I would be,
If drugs and the "gang life" were my community.

So you ask, "What's to become of me?"
Will I end up a beggar? A loner? Another meaningless flea?"

That's what we fear; to end up a speck on a wall.
A life with no meaning, no substance at all.

But the fear that's the worst fear there's around
Is not being able to love, and finding no love to be found.

I say this perhaps like I seem to know all. But that's not it,
  don't you see?
The only reason I know this is because that happened to me.

We don't have time for details, but believe me it's true.
And I simply didn't know what I could do.

And then I realized...your heart beats 100,000 times a day!
Can you believe it? It's a fact! I was just blown away!

So isn't it best to make the 100,000 times count?
Don't be afraid to love, and you'll marvel at the amount...

...of love you will gain from people who'll say
They never expected to be loved in that way.

And this love will take you over mountains and lakes.
Away from the world of crime and no breaks.

I promise you that, and if it doesn't work you can sue.
I'll settle by giving all my love to you.

And if you ever need more, come straight to me.
The reserves of love are endless, you see.

You are brave, you are tough, you are strong, you are proud.
Now just take your love and go dazzle the crowd!

And don't you ever forget:
Love conquers all, and it hasn't failed once yet.

Sending my love from a loving Kentuckian.
Yours truly, John Aroutiounian

PEER EVALUATION FOR ANNA GHNOULY FOR DARTMOUTH COLLEGE

(*December 17, 2010*)

HOW LONG HAVE YOU KNOWN THIS CANDIDATE AND IN WHAT CONTEXT?

I had the privilege of meeting Anna while working as a United States Senate Page during the Spring 2010 term, which ran from January 24 through June 4, 2010. The Senate Page environment might be likened to the reality television show *Survivor*. Students attend school and work in each other's company, and free time is almost entirely spent together due to the program's strict regulations for leaving the Senate Page Residence Hall. The school curriculum is rigorous, especially given the time constraints, and the work schedule is equally so, with the workday running anywhere from ten to sixteen hours. This sheltered environment lent itself, however, to truly getting a sense of who the twenty-nine other individuals were and left little doubt as to the character of each. It was in this context that I met Anna, who left an indelible mark on me and many of the Pages who were fortunate to be touched by her spirit. Since leaving Washington, we have met three times and continue to speak to each other often.

WHAT ARE THE FIRST WORDS THAT COME TO YOUR MIND THAT DESCRIBE THIS CANDIDATE?

Loving, self-sacrificing, intellectually curious, humble, strong-willed, good-natured, determined, caring, funny, brave, open-minded.

STATEMENT

It is with a heavy hand that I write my friend Anna Ghnouly's peer evaluation, knowing that however many glittering adjectives I use, personal anecdotes I give, or unique words that I come up with to add to the list above before I put the letter in the mail, I will still be frustrated when I look over the final version—knowing that I have not been able to do justice to her glowing character and unbridled spirit. That having been said, I shall try my absolute best.

Anna and I became acquainted early on in Washington, where we were often on the same shift at work, providing clerical support for Senators and staff from our perch on the Senate rostrum. It took a very brief time for me to see Anna's principled work ethic and affable personality. Whenever we were off duty during the workday, I would observe her completing homework or, as the semester progressed, helping a friend in need with an assignment or personal issue. But, as I quickly learned, her evident studiousness and friendly demeanor conveyed only a tiny portion of her character.

The Page Program had its share of ups and downs, but having Anna as a friend meant having a shoulder to lean on whenever the need arose. She could have several hours of homework to finish in one evening, but if a friend was in need of her attention, she would put it all away for as long as necessary to help comfort or discuss whatever issue arose.

But despite her academic rigor and sharp personal skills, she refused praise with an intransigent humility that never ceased to amaze me. Anna is, in addition to the attributes aforementioned, an avid dancer, linguist, athlete (accomplished in women's crew and Bikram yoga), and humanitarian. She has taken several humanitarian trips throughout the world, including one to Cambodia. Most recently, she spent a month of her last summer in Tanzania, providing assistance to schoolchildren as part of an organized group effort. While in Tanzania, she climbed atop Mount Kilimanjaro. I am in awe of her bravery! But, I must say, not even that feat touched me the way what she did following her trip did. Upon returning, she sent me a letter with a rock from the top of Kilimanjaro. The letter read, "Place the rock on your desk as a motivator because climbing Kili was the hardest thing I've ever done in my life. When I didn't think I could make it, I proved myself wrong." Reading the letter and holding that rock, which now goes with me wherever I go, gave me goose bumps. I am holding it right now, hoping some spiritual force will help me enumerate all the reasons why Anna deserves Dartmouth.

But make no mistake—Dartmouth deserves Anna just as much as she does it. I have met no one who better upholds Dartmouth's motto, *Vox clamantis in deserto*. In a brutal high school world, driven by grades, shallow desires, fads, and fashion, Anna pierces through it all and displays genuineness, vitality and brightness of human spirit I have yet to find in another individual. She is a voice of humanity in the wilderness, and I urge you to help continue to kindle her spirit at your institution.

The day marking the end of the Page Program was among the most difficult days of my life, and not because of the joy that the work brought or the unrestricted access to the Capitol and its personalities (Senators, Congressmen, and occasionally the President) it provided. It was so difficult because the extraordinary people with whom I had spent every day for the past five months—Anna chief among them—would no longer be a daily, physical presence in my life. When friends and family ask about what the Page experience was like, I always reply that the opportunities and the exposure were wonderful, but the people made it life-changing. Whenever I tell people this, Anna Ghnouly is always who I am referencing.

On that final day of the program, Anna was awarded several prestigious awards by the United States Senate Page School, including awards for being the top student in three of her classes. To put that into context, the Page School only offers four classes per student. Anna was, unequivocally, the highest-achieving student in the entire Page class, respected by all her peers for her ethic, her kindness, and her geniality.

I am honored that Anna has opened her life to me, and I am thankful every day for her friendship. You might have noticed that Anna and I are both applying to Dartmouth. In fact, we have written each other's peer evaluations. It would, no doubt, be convenient to make the assumption that this was some sort of friendly quid pro quo—an effort to write glowing words about each other with the hope that the admissions committee would not notice. Let me dispel such notion. If I am not offered admission at Dartmouth, I'd like to think, for the sake of my own self-confidence, that the committee made a mistake in rejecting my application. If Anna is not offered admission, I will be convinced that the committee sorely erred in its decision making.

I urge you to accept Anna Ghnouly's application to Dartmouth, and I am certain that you will soon see this '15 student touch the lives of countless other members of her class and school. I offer as testament of her character the impact she has forever made on my life. And I have no doubt that regardless of which college Anna attends, it will not be long before she ranks amongst its most notable alumni. It is the choice of the Dartmouth admissions committee, then, whether your institution will be able to claim her as your own.

[Editor's Note: *John was offered position at Dartmouth but chose Yale.*]

2. *College Years*

REFLECTION, OVER THE ATLANTIC

(*Handwritten on AirBerlin paper bag, April 21, 2012*)

OUR SUCCESS IS not and cannot be defined by what we, as individuals, create—for whatever it is that we create (reputation, legacy, history, ideology, cities of stone [edifices]) will undoubtedly & invariably, fade away or fall in the end. Rather, our success as people is defined by how well we provide for the continuity—the passing on—of wisdom and knowledge of truth to those who come after us. Part and parcel with this is respecting, honoring and building upon the collective human inheritance passed down to us. It is through this careful and caring passing down of inheritance…

that we succeed in our fleeting roles on this Earth. Some might say this is remarkably boring or anti-individual; on the contrary, how one chooses to teach and pass down the message—the beauty of the words and ideas, or the brilliance of the framing of concepts or the depth of sharing of experience leaves enormous room for the expression of the individual. But this is permissible insofar as the individual does not seek self-gratification, but rather strives for communion in understanding with his Maker and fulfills his duty as a link—a *necessary* link—in the chain of the continuity of human wisdom. Each link—and thus, each individual—is crucial. And when our link fails, disorientation further down the chain ensues, often with severely damaging results. This view on our role as individuals—a fundamentally humble one, though affirming the individual's uniqueness and importance—is the most consistent, healthy way of living one's life.

One is constantly a learner and a teacher, his mind always open but his heart resolute. This attitude is to be preferred over a bottom-up one because it works better, yes; but more importantly, because it is true.

EMBRACING INSIGNIFICANCE

(October 6, 2012)

THE ONLY DREAM I remember from my nap last night, necessitated by the all-nighter the day before, is running after a train—ticket and luggage in hand, though fully conscious of the fact that I had already missed it. When I woke up, it was 9:28. My train to Boston was leaving at 9:33. It's funny how cruelly life mocks us sometimes.

I had begun napping at 4:30, thinking it impossible that I should sleep longer than a couple hours. I had even asked for two wake-up calls from friends. But my body just wouldn't have it. Now, Saturday morning at 5 a.m., I find myself at the Boston airport, waiting for my plane to Nantucket. I ended up taking a cab from New Haven instead, paying an ungodly amount, and getting absolutely no sleep (again) on airport chairs instead of the hotel I had planned on staying at for the night. What's more, I slept through an afternoon's worth of extracurriculars at Yale, falling yet a bit more behind. Two midterms, for which I have not yet begun to study, loom next week. A large paper and an exam follow the week after. Then, it's back home to help my parents move before a few days to recuperate and catch up on hundreds of pages of reading before the untold travails November will bring.

Of course, none of this is a big deal. My Yale responsibilities remain intact, if in need of some clean up; I'm on the way to a new journalism project; I will somehow find a way to eek out sufficient grades on my exams, throwing in some more sleepless nights on the way. The best college advice I ever got was to schedule your life to accommodate your most productive hours—if those happened to be 3 and 4 in the morning, so be it.

If you've managed to keep reading thus far, today's *News* must be particularly dry, for some variant of the aforementioned description of a Yale student's life is, with slight alterations, a fixture of these pages. From the poignant work of Marina Keegan to Teo Soares, lamentations and paeans to Yale life are nothing news. We all know that the truth is that we're not as busy as we think, that we can miss the next five consecutive events scheduled on our iCal with really negligible impact on the arc of life (even if—no, *especially* if any of those events involve an encounter with a celebrity or politician), and that even our most pressing commitments at Yale would not seem nearly as pressing if we weren't within the confines of New Haven.

I have had more than a fair share of conversations with friends who all say the same thing—they aren't ready to commit to a major activity:

—If you've found your thing, great—but if you haven't, keep open to the world of possibilities—focus on friends—and don't give in to idea that your success here will be measured by Everything is TOO Big a deal

—Can't get attached to anything—it's because Yale demands submission THEN it's curious that the ones who submit to one cause—do the best

—Can't do that. Ideologically arrogant. And it's arrogant—to demand so much of people so young. It's just wrong.

—So will keep at it. FRIENDS...who knew that the best way to network would be to actually care about people? WHO KNEW?!?

Charles Hill once said that college used to be a place people came to try to be men—in this "trying" they often failed. Today's Yale tolerates failure less and less. More unforgiving, more deadlines. That's why students suffer from blepharospasm, that's why so many are sad and depressed, that's also why so men leave Yale exhausted nihilists who don't quite know what to do next after succumbing to structures that—quite unreasonably—demanded their total submission.

Enjoy being, for now, largely insignificant. Try many things, try breaking into significance.

Different from suspension of judgment—but finding vocations is not like finding a value system.

Not about experimentation—exactly because experimentation is not always good that we have to be careful. This is a time to expand, not shrink, horizons. That's the whole idea behind a liberal arts education.

CONTROVERSIAL THEOLOGIAN DISCUSSES FORGIVENESS

(*Yale Daily News, October 19, 2012*)

Margaret Farley GRD '73, a Divinity School professor and member of the Sisters of Mercy whose writings on sexual ethics drew the ire of the Vatican this summer, spoke about her beliefs before a crowd of over 100 Thursday evening.

Farley's book, "Just Love: A Framework for Christian Sexual Ethics," sparked controversy after its publication because it presented a theological defense of homosexuality, masturbation and sex outside of marriage. During her lecture, entitled "Forgiveness in the Service of Justice," Farley discussed the need to emphasize forgiveness in modern social justice movements. Though her talk did not directly address the criticism she received from the Vatican, audience members in the St. Thomas More Chapel asked Farley how she dealt with the Church's condemnation of her values.

The Vatican's Congregation for the Doctrine of the Faith, the body responsible for clarifying issues related to Church doctrine, has called Farley's interpretation a "defective understanding of natural law" that may cause "grave harm to the faithful," alleging that she is ignoring centuries of teaching on topics related to sexuality.

"I respect the beliefs of the church though I don't agree with them," Farley told the News after her lecture. "I haven't been trying to argue for or against Church doctrine. Rather, I have taught in an educational setting for 40 years, and that's the role of a professional ethicist: to help people think things through."

Farley defended her book during the question and answer portion of her talk, maintaining that her aim was never to spark antagonism with the Church. Still, Farley faulted the Vatican for failing to adopt substantive changes to its procedure for revising doctrine in the wake of the Second Vatican Council, which was intended to reform the Church and consider its place in the modern world in the 1960s.

During the talk itself, Farley divided her consideration of forgiveness and its practical implications into three parts, focusing on Biblical text, the meaning of forgiveness and the relationship between the concepts of forgiveness, justice and resistance.

"Biblical text asks something of the Roman Catholic Church that it doesn't understand," Farley said. "The message of forgiveness, in essence, constitutes the Christian message in its entirety."

Farley rejected the notion of passivity in response to injustice, bringing up the truth commissions that existed in Argentina, Chile and South Africa in the latter half of the 20th century as examples of how injustice could be reconciled through mediums that facilitated forgiveness—an approach she described as integral to moving away from large-scale conflict.

Audience members interviewed had mixed reactions to the talk.

Father Bob Beloin, Yale's Catholic chaplain, defended his decision to host Farley's lecture at St. Thomas More, adding that he invited Farley to the church three years ago, before the controversy surrounding her new book erupted.

"When [the controversy] began, we found no reason to rescind the invitation because she was never officially silenced by the Church," he said. "I have a profound appreciation for the personal integrity and scholarship of Margaret Farley."

Father Joe Donnelly, who travelled from Southbury, Conn. to hear Farley speak, said her poise was "measured, focused and full of faith."

But Kelly Schumann '15, who attended the lecture, agreed with some of the criticisms that have been made of Farley's teaching, adding that she felt Farley's talk relied too heavily on non-Biblical sources, including the Quran and the poetry of Emily Dickinson.

St. Thomas More parishioner Isabel Marin '12 said she feels Farley's talk was unnecessarily argumentative.

"I definitely felt there was an implied spirit of attack on the church," Marin said. "I found this odd, given she never claimed to believe anything the church disagreed with. She seems to be going out of her way to attack it."

Farley's book was published in 2008.

THE STORM HAS ARRIVED

(*Yale Daily News, November 2, 2012*)

AMID THE DISARMING shock of having so little to do on Monday, as I watched the winds getting stronger from my room and heard the occasional scream as students flouting the curfew encountered various flying objects outside, I decided to do something I hadn't in a while: read the entirety of the YDN opinion page. Therein I found many anxieties common to Yalies, ranging from concern about post-graduation employment to the importance of spending time with family amid our oh-so-busy lives to the typical Yale jeremiad against conservatism. Facebook was also a continuing aggregate of student sentiment. Friends posted songs of thanks to Yale for keeping us safe and paeans to our truly brave dining hall staff—many of whom drove home as the storm bore down on the Connecticut coast.

It's true. Yale knows how to handle these situations well. Never have I been so comforted at receiving so many emails from Linda Koch Lorimer in the span of a day.

But there's also been a creeping feeling growing inside of me, predating this storm. It's been growing the more I read angst-ridden columns, the more I talk to friends, the more I wonder about what my own life will look like. Indeed, this other storm—which seems to have made landfall a long time ago, even if unnoticed—threatens to do much more damage to the Yale student body than Hurricane Sandy.

It has become clear how obscenely narrow most students' realities at Yale are. Many of us burn through our four years with our post-graduation lives always in the front of our brains. We spend so little time contemplating things just for their own sake, and we forget how to enjoy activities and people who don't seem to matter in the context of our extremely limited criteria for success. We proceed to shake our heads (er, respectfully disagree) at those who differ politically.

Every Yalie acknowledges these problems, but rarely do we do anything about them. We pause, we reflect for a moment and then we move on.

What if we designated a month of the upcoming summer to roam the foothills of Nepal with a friend—and not for the purpose of teaching English to Nepalese schoolchildren? Or, for the religious, made a pilgrimage to a holy site? We could propose a vacation idea to our families. We could find that student we've always disagreed with and start a conversation about his views, rather than disagreeing from afar.

Reflection is great, but we should act on our observations and self-critiques after we make them.

Complacency here is so easy to come across. The continuous treadmill that is life at Yale, with all its conveniences, makes following ambition and seeking achievement too easy. We are as far removed as we will ever be from the nasty, brutish and short world beyond. What we often fail to see is that in this faux world in which we live, embracing insignificance—even just a little—would make us far more mature. It would help us understand what it means when people drive through a hurricane just so our unrealistic state of being can be maintained.

Some of my best friends tell me they feel uninspired by their activities, that they had fallen in love with an academic interest and that they can't seem to commit to anyone amid the boom-and-bust cycles of their romantic relationships. Friendship seems to come naturally here, but is a person who you see on a biweekly basis for a one-hour time slot a friend? Has their loyalty, empathy, or respect for you been tested? Has yours?

Yale was once idealized as a place dedicated to making its students invested in things: in each other, in ideas. It used to teach and foster friendship, love and virtue—and in doing so, to prepare people for the real world, even if they got to live in an artificial one for a while. All this is certainly gone, and the University doesn't even profess to teach these things amid the prevailing skepticism of the day.

But Yale students are still smart, and—even if they don't realize it—notice in bits and pieces that this place's thinking has changed, and for the worse. They feel it in their everyday lives.

It's now up to us to teach ourselves what this university won't: contemplation and virtue. Yale's hollow marble can't protect us from our own immaturity, superficiality and inaction.

WHEN THE POWER GOES OFF

(*Yale Daily News, April 4, 2013*)

I WENT HOME to New York City over Easter weekend to see my parents and to do what we do as a family only once a year—go to church. If you're at Holy Cross Church of Armenia any other weekend, there are (maybe) 10 parishioners in the pews. But this weekend, the holiest of the Christian calendar, there's hardly an empty seat in the building. Everyone looks at each other nervously for cues on when to stand and sit, since most haven't been since the same time last year. Yet every year, they come back.

I met a friend in the city later that day for dinner. As she and I perused the eclectic shops and restaurants, we came upon a façade that looked completely anachronistic. "St. Stanislaus Polish Catholic Church," the display board read, adjacent to a huge bust of Pope John Paul II. We went in to have a look. She immediately crossed herself thrice—repeating the gesture as we left.

"You know, I don't really believe anything the church teaches," she said. "But tonight, after I get drunk, I'm probably going to stumble over to Easter Vigil at 4 a.m."

This entire episode shocked me almost as much as another here at Yale, when a friend—surely one of the most passionate, ardent atheists on campus freshman year—was caught (by me) at Slifka, with a kippah on his head. "I thought you hated this stuff!"

"I'm keeping an open mind," he replied, without a trace of the tenacity with which he defended and evangelized atheism freshman year.

The metanarrative of the prodigal son spans millennia, taking on 20th century forms in the lives and works of Edith Stein, Evelyn Waugh, C.S. Lewis and Oscar Wilde. Lewis recalled his conversion to Christianity as an experience in which he was "kicking, struggling, resentful, and darting his eyes in every direction for a chance to escape." In the end, he felt compelled to submit to what—whether he liked it or not—he deemed to be the truth. Leah Libresco '11 converted to Catholicism from atheism after years of intense debates with friends from the Yale Political Union.

Religion is lost on a great many Yale students, for whom religious practice is a childhood activity one compartmentalizes in college, if not abandoning it completely. Few have the deep, serious discussions about how to live, partly because the implications of these discussions are way too real. We intensely hunger for truth but don't know, don't have the time or don't have the bravery to start looking.

Religion is powerful because of God. Social justice is a noble cause, and lifelong self-improvement should be in the back of everyone's mind. But being part of a community center can do that for you. For those who think that this is all religion offers, you're only getting the frosting on the cake. Tastes good, looks good, feels good—but it ain't the cake. It is the externality of divinity from the meekness and banality of life that makes it powerful. It is this externality that reminds us, when we grow blind by routine, that good and evil are everywhere around and inside of us.

When the power goes out, as it's bound to do at some point in every individual's life, the distractions with which we foolishly placate ourselves and justify the significance of our existence fade away.

Serenity is hard to come by, but religion isn't just another balm. Some days you feel good, some days you don't, but religion teaches you to take everyone as they come and to live authentically—because God is going nowhere. As another convert, English poet Gerard Manley Hopkins, put it, He "plays in ten thousand places, / Lovely in limbs, and lovely in eyes not his."

So Yale, please start talking again. Talk long hours into the night. And sure, you'll still do your homework, you'll still run 10 clubs, you'll still go to Toad's—but do a little bit of forward thinking, too, so that you're a little less scared when the lights go out. Ask yourself, when you go to church once a year, why you bother showing up at all. Are you selling yourself short?

And finally, while you still can, look, as Hopkins says, just a little closer, "into the features of men's faces." Is there anything there?

DEATH WITH DECENCY

(*Yale Daily News, April 11, 2013*)

When the apartheid government of South Africa banned Shirley Jackson's famous short story "The Lottery" only a few years following the end of World War II, the novelist was proud: "They, at least, understood the story," her husband recalled her saying. Her admonition that blindly followed routine can cause unrecognized injustice led people from small towns across America to cancel their subscriptions to The New Yorker in droves. They hadn't understood. She was, after all, insulting their morality—their basic ability to distinguish between good and bad. Of course people could distinguish between their base instincts and justice, they thought. In Jackson's fictional town, a selected person is annually sacrificed at the altar of the community. But can tradition actually ever be so vile? Can evil really be carried out unconsciously in places that feel so safe?

This week brought the sad news of the death of former Prime Minister Margaret Thatcher, and the tragic, untimely suicide of American pastor Rick Warren's son. The former was 87; the latter, 27. As responses to the news came in, I felt that sick pang in the stomach that accompanied finishing "The Lottery" for the first time. It's a feeling I can only recall on two other occasions: when televised crowds gathered in front of the White House, chanting "USA" over the killing of Osama bin Laden, and when the news first broke of protests at funerals of soldiers. Here were examples of the celebration of death—joy from others' pain. Here were functioning members of society reverting to perhaps one of the most primordial emotions characteristic to man: the desire to see someone suffer or be stomped into the ground in exchange for their perceived misdeeds. Perhaps we refuse to pick up the stones ourselves, like Shirley Jackson's characters or the societies that still condone stoning as a means of punishment—but are we any more consistent or morally upstanding if we're standing in the sidelines, cheering death on? How are we any better than the audiences at gladiatorial exhibitions?

Man is more than the sum of his parts. He is more than his biological tendencies. It is no surprise that when we see or hear about humans acting in ways corresponding to their animal-like instincts, we often get the very disconcerting sense that what is being done is actually inhuman—for it is the gap between that animal self and who we are that constitutes our nature as human beings, distinct from other animals.

This is precisely why the death penalty, a relic of our primordial past, is quickly being dispensed with. It is why infanticide, in all its forms, will also eventually disappear. But we haven't adequately stomped out the phenomenon of celebrating the deaths and sufferings of others. I was reminded of this every time I heard a friend say, just this week, that they were "dancing in the streets" when they heard Baroness Thatcher had died. I was reminded of it every time I saw pictures of young people in England drinking on the day of her death. I shuddered when I read that many people were mocking the beliefs of Rick Warren while he grieved for his son. And I did not know what to say when I heard a student say he was happier at Thatcher's death than bin Laden's. How can death ever be anything but a time to grieve? If the death involved someone with injustice in his or her past, whatever your locus for measuring injustice might be, is the cause for grief not even greater? Ought we do nothing other than mourn that, on the occasion of their death, there is so little to celebrate about how they lived?

Distance fosters alienation. Media, which creates social distance, only adds to alienation. It is easy, then, to come to think of those we hate as symbols, as ideas and not as people. They become merely the channels of our frustration, of our hate and anger. We do not come to terms with ourselves or our station in life, and we continue to cultivate a very inhuman seed in our hearts that allows us to ignore the humanity of people whose actions we disagree with or cannot comprehend. In celebrating the deaths of those we judge to have carried out evil, we add to alienation, to disconnection, to a loss of empathy in ourselves and in civil society at large. In fact, we make carrying out evil all the more routine.

After all, the lottery happens every year.

FINDING GOLD IN THE DARK

(*The Logos, Yale's Undergraduate Magazine of Christian Thought, Fall of 2013*)

HOW GOOD WRITERS must have had it three hundred years ago. How wonderful it must have felt to pen books and essays regarding emotion with abandon, unafraid—or, at least, less so—of the damning critique of unoriginality. Having your thoughts labeled "cliché" is in many ways more stinging than the charge of plagiarism: in the latter instance, you are accused of foolishly stealing something good and proudly calling it your own; in the former, you are accused of proudly calling something your own and foolishly thinking it was good. But everything has become cliché. As someone somewhere has surely already noted, even the realization that most of your mental output is flimflam that people "in touch" with reality came across on the Internet ages ago is itself a cliché.

As a consequence, countless young men and women considering themselves in that number of "in touch" literati have seemingly concluded that they have nothing new—nothing personally meaningful beyond what's already been said—to say about love, let alone a smorgasbord of other anchors of human sentimentality and behavior. Indeed, it is at least largely a consequence of the information onslaught of the last several decades that we "come across" more and more, yet know less and less. To talk of love in the context of loyalty, responsibility, and any sense of permanence in college is so embarrassing nowadays, so childish—few think themselves apt to make any sort of contribution to such a discussion, and scoff at others who try.

Abandoning, even temporarily, the notion of finding personal meaningfulness within timeless aspects of the human condition is not only destructive and contrary to the dignity of the individual, but a direct affront to the spirit of Christian purpose. Confining (out of respect to St. Valentine) our discussion to love, a languishing hope in finding something uniquely beautiful in our relationships with others leads to the confusing (and often fruitless) endeavor involving "finding your own meaning." Because we aren't aimless blobs of jelly floating around in the universe, and were created with dignity and express purpose, the search for meaning in those who reject the universality of purpose in each individual takes all sorts of twists and turns. Countless friends have told me about their experiences dabbling in all sorts of religions, taking up new causes, and retrofitting personal relationships with illusory meanings that weren't there before. Many things can attempt to fill, if not completely, the void left by a rejection of purpose. For some, a pet issue—environmentalism, sexual liberation, you name it—essentially becomes their church, complete with dogma, rigid adherents, and a salvation narrative.

Over Christmas Break, I spent a week traversing Costa Rica. The country is absolutely beautiful, and its people are happy—though large swaths of the capital city, San Jose, are in shambles. On our last evening there, my family was recommended a restaurant in a hotel located in the heart of town called the *Grano de Oro,* or "the grain of gold." As the taxi rolled up to the entrance, the sight of the surroundings were miserable—blocks upon blocks stank of urban decay and desolation.

And then we walked into the hotel, and it was as if we'd entered into the "Play it again, Sam!" scene from *Casablanca*. Velvet walls. Beautiful grandfather clocks. A medieval courtyard, laced with lights and gentle music caressing the guests enjoying their meals. It was a relic from times past—a "grain of gold," indeed.

How do we create our own grains of gold, amid the prevailing darkness and narcissistic delusion at Yale? It certainly doesn't help when we find out what goes on in WLH during off-hours, as Nathan Harden's *Sex and God at Yale* recently exposed. The concept of a relationship is scary and difficult—as it *should* be. Relationships involve commitment, effort, and continual self-confrontation and improvement.

All the more reason to go out on a limb. To be—ironically—countercultural. Today, living on the edge is not random sex with the first person you manage to reel in from Toad's—it's courtship and self-giving. It's showing "need love," to borrow C.S. Lewis' term, but it's also showing "gift love." We love because we need to feel it back, but we must also love purely for the sake of giving. True love reflects the concept of *agape*—Koine Greek for Christ's love of man, and man's reciprocal love of Christ through his deeds and love of others. In no greater form can this be expressed between individuals than through practicing self-sacrificing love, where the adventure of the evening is not the new sex move but the latest act of charity—more shocking and lasting than the impression that the former can provide. It is freedom redefined, shifting the idea from "freedom to" to "freedom from," if we may borrow the social theorist Isaiah Berlin's framing. More properly understood, true freedom lies not in availing oneself of whatever he wants to indulge an appetite, but in liberation from the strains of the appetite through the discovery of a higher good.

Everything is betting against you. The medicalization of sex (and, consequently, morality) provides the intellectual background to the "free sex" movement, and the peer pressure provides the social background. Given this background, people convince themselves that the mutual taking found in a one-night stand is harmless. In this atmosphere, individuals are bound to make all sorts of mistakes, to be gripped by all kinds of lust, and to prescribe the name "love" to what is nothing more than a set of raging hormones. The Yale student, contrary to what may be his own belief, is no Augustine, and even he fell into similar traps many times over. The key is to always call mistakes by their true name. The moment a mistake is no longer recognized as such, and sin is "accounted for," the individual is on his way into more trouble.

Are Leon Kass and the *New York Times'* Alex Williams right about the "end of courtship"? This Valentine's Day, and in the weeks, months, and years ahead, you have the power to be countercultural. Too retro? No. Rad.

RESCUING HEROISM

(*Yale Daily News, October 28, 2013*)

MY FAITH TEACHES me that I can be a saint, if I will it. It teaches that you can be a saint, too. But that's a hard thing to believe.

It's easy to doubt our own potential to be heroic. There's a saying by Nathaniel Hawthorne that goes, "A hero cannot be a hero unless in a heroic world." I wonder if he's right. And if so, does my doubt come from living in a decidedly nonheroic world?

If you're getting ready to call my bluff, don't worry. I'll do it. This isn't going to rapidly devolve into a tired, conservative philippic against the failure of the modern age and a clarion call to return to classical virtue. Actually, heroes are everywhere today. They're starting nonprofits for forgotten causes, abandoning their livelihoods for dangerous projects overseas and they're proving themselves every day on the battlefield in our armed forces. I remember being little and hearing about the man who jumped in front of a moving subway train to save a rider who had fallen onto the tracks. These aren't random acts—people of faith and of science (and quite a few of both) will tell you that an inclination towards heroism is programmed into our minds, and it's not going away.

But Hawthorne's observation isn't entirely wrong: We live in a time that doesn't make heroism readily accessible. The generations that came before us in the 20th century all had inescapable tests —of strength, of character—that they knew they would have to confront. We know about them through family stories and great novels. The characters who grappled with questions of faith, identity and loyalty against the backdrop of the world wars became the stuff of legends. After them came the Vietnam War and the social movements of the '60s and '70s, with their moral demands of young people on and off the battlefield. Those who acted with courage and bravery were noted, honored and remembered. People were asked to take stands in trying times, and they did.

The modern "rebel without a cause" wants to be as extraordinary, but it's not nearly as clear how.

We don't need war to summon our creative, or heroic, attributes. Opportunities are everywhere: in community service, in our families and especially in our friendships, where just loving unconditionally can be a heroic act in a world where expressing brokenness is awkward and taboo. A lesser-known Hawthorne expression goes, "The greatest obstacle to being heroic is the doubt whether one may not be going to prove one's self a fool;

the truest heroism is to resist the doubt." He's on point. One of my best friends at Yale—she's since graduated and joined the Marines—heard about a distant friend of a friend in a bad place in life and drove, that very same night, hundreds of miles to help. I was flabbergasted when I heard. While I was still reeling, she was already driving.

Our culture isn't set up in a way that engenders heroic thinking. Heroism is driven chiefly by a sense of duty, a reactionary feeling that we have an obligation toward someone in need. Members of our generation structure our lives around choices, not duties. Take Yale life. It starts with the little things, like how we talk about the projects and activities we devote our time to. "What I'm most interested in is..." or "I really could not care less about..." are some of the operative phrases we've all used. That Yale gives us so many choices is a testament to how lucky we are to be here. But that so many activities we do are based on our own free choice, and that we stick around only because we want to, is a sign of a problem.

It translates into relationships with people, too. It's easy to get a meal with a friend you see once every few months. It's a staple of life at Yale. But it's much harder to really invest time in getting to know someone and watching their personality unfold in different settings over the course of years. To see friends in the context of a single conversation is important, but what's more important is to see their loyalty tested in trying situations. In a world centered on options, opportunities to show true character don't occur frequently.

No, we don't need a war to understand that we should cultivate loyalty, duty and depth in our relations with the people and the projects we are close to. Heroism, if we still want it, demands a sense of obligation toward others. But do we want heroism? Is our apathetic, if peaceful lull worth it, if it comes at the cost of losing the virtues that make life worth living? But more fundamentally: Do we want to be more than simply what we want to be?

THE BEARDED MAN AND ME

(Yale Daily News, December 2, 2013)

COMING HOME IS always a mixed bag frequently full of boisterous relatives, warm nights on the couch with parents and time to reflect while briefly outside of the college rat race mentality. But it's a mixed bag because it also means lying in bed, staring at the ceiling and thinking, "How many more days like this will I have?" What if Metro North derails tomorrow or there's a gunman on campus—and the thin balloon of invincibility is popped? What if something happens to my parents? Who will I call to feel safe? Not just comforted, but safe.

Gratitude for each day is an ideal, at least in my own case, very inconsistently practiced. But the gratitude that rushes in at home during nights like those isn't just plain gratitude. It comes with a generous burst of dread. Dread because precious moments are so short, and once you realize you're in the middle of one, even shorter. I'd give a lot to take this awareness away and to live in the moment again the way kids do, when the "big picture" meant Arthur at 4 p.m., not thinking about internships, plans for after graduation, marriage, and the possibility of being alone.

But being at Yale, you've got to put this wistful mood aside. There are papers to write and goals to make. You shelve your vulnerability far away and focus on running the race; when you need a break (but can't have one long enough when each day feels shorter and shorter, daylight savings time or not), it's off to Toad's we go. Pause, rewind, repeat. Each time, we get a little more impatient and a little harder on the inside.

But on the thirtieth time you encounter the bearded man who paces up and down Chapel Street, occasionally asking for money, something happens. You're sitting in Starbucks with a professor, and the bearded man comes in. The professor says, "Hey man! Want some coffee?" He stops to say he's doing just fine, a cup of coffee would be great, thanks. He asks who I am. "Oh, just one of my students!" When he leaves, the professor explains that he's a regular at his church. And no matter how little the man has, he always puts something in the collection basket. I bring the conversation back to where it was—some obscure book theme that now seems pathetically trivial—hoping he doesn't notice as I pretend to look at the British Art Museum display and wipe the moisture from the corner of my eye.

And then there's the day full of missteps, when you come back to your room and your ritualistic online news browsing is interrupted by wandering thoughts about that unpleasant look from someone in section, the friend you've neglected, the grandmother you haven't called in a month. You catch yourself, and you think, "No! No time for these thoughts! Save it for break." And then, on Facebook, that picture of the pope kissing a terrifyingly disfigured man pops up. He is huddled in the pope's embrace. The cynic, the rat racer on your left shoulder smirks: "What a great PR stunt!" But then you keep looking. The man looks awful. It's the type of thing that might make you cross the street if you saw it in person.

And then you realize—you just thought of him as a "thing." The balloon of invincibility is popped. You're glad your roommate isn't home, because your shirt quickly becomes damp from drying your eyes and you don't want him to think you were doing anything involving bodily fluids—especially crying. And in that moment, you love the pope, a better man than you can ever imagine you'll be.

In these moments, and countless others like it, our feelings are exposed to everyone—and most of all, to ourselves. What's unsettling in all these moments is the possibility that not everything is a construct, that maybe there are things, including untapped energies within us, that point to the transcendent—that maybe some meaning was, and is, and will always be there long after we're gone. It's almost as if, even in our world, we're still haunted, to paraphrase Flannery O'Connor, by the suspicion that we're here for an actual reason, and that reason is equally true for all of us, whether or not we believe in it.

The thanks we give on Thanksgiving comes and goes. It's already mostly gone, in fact. But we're still here, operating in our broken world as our broken selves. But our lives are filled with moments like these when, if we only stop to listen, the ineffable person inside is asking, however faintly: "Remember me?"

FULL PLATES, EMPTY HEARTS

(*Yale Daily News, February 19, 2014*)

It was the last meeting of my philosophy class's discussion section, and the TA was waxing nostalgic. As she said her goodbyes, she dispensed the customary closing platitude: "I hope that, if this class has taught you anything, it's to question everything." Five years ago, when I stuck a "Question Everything" pin on my backpack and drove to high school, it would have sounded like good advice. But this time around, I couldn't wait to walk out the door.

Most in college today are old enough to be able to look at photos of their young selves existing in a previous age of fashion and respond with some combination of chuckling and cringing. It's also possible to do that with thoughts—previously held opinions or worries that seem careless or trivial today. It's usually a good thing, a sign of growing up.

This was the case, for a while, with "question everything."

Teenagers are prone to love this motto. They use it with their parents, with their teachers (sometimes to their face), and they use it internally when considering the ideas they read or hear about. Every easy target—everything that sounds "stupid," by whatever criteria used, gets an eye roll and a list of obnoxious, incredulous questions. Sometimes it's merited, but usually it's not.

I was, for the most part, no different. Most of what people said that I didn't immediately agree with was clearly because of fatal flaws in their reasoning. There was no time for that which wasn't useful or didn't feel right.

But something goes unrealized when you go around "questioning everything." You're rarely turning the critical eye inward. What ends up happening is that you do whatever you want, living in the present moment, and regarding everything else with doubt.

The present is the most selfish of times, more so than the past—which is gone and therefore useless—and more so than the future, which invites all sorts of considerations and can't be used now. But the present is here: We consume it like a car consumes gas, only we're continually running for about eighty years or so. We're burning through every minute, every step, everything we eat, read, every person we talk to. And to question everything is the ultimate way to live in the present and the present alone—because, sold as noble skepticism, it's a license to live free of being tied to something that directs us away from mere consumption.

A country, much like a person, is only as great as the stories it tells itself about itself. The stories aren't always completely true and they're usually more than a little self-serving. But often, the story provides a background to check against when things go awry—take the American commitment to equality in political rhetoric compared with the history of slavery. It was because the ideal existed in the first place that gave us something to compare the reality to. It allowed for the point at which people started saying, "Wait. We're not who we say we are."

It works with people, too. We all know we believe things about ourselves that aren't wholly accurate, even if we wish they were. But they're probably at least somewhat true, and we seek to make our realities conform better to the ideal. Sure, without the reflective aspect, both countries and people can lapse into ignorant chest thumping: patriotism becomes nationalism and self-respect becomes narcissism. But without the ultimate belief in the story, all we have are our whims and desires of the moment.

It has become so hard to identify with any situation not your own. Maybe it was always like this, but it seems like so much of our existence nowadays is spent doing things that allow us to see reflections of ourselves—the clubs we join, the people we associate with, the technology we use.

"But we all volunteer!" you say. "Every summer! And we all have friends with different beliefs than us!" Yet I wonder if this is usually a case of feeling or just observing and using for our own sake.

Most will never feel living on a dollar a day, even if they know what it means. Religion's another case. I remember hearing an exchange between two friends, where one said he was religious, and explained what that meant for his beliefs about the world and his place in it. The other said, with astonishment, "You actually believe that?"

People in the West, in the fifty years since what you believed could determine life or death, have become experts at living life with a constant mirror held up to themselves while everything else is "problematic." Now, whether or not we smash it might be the difference between significant human connection and lonely, self-absorbed obscurity.

THE CHRISTIAN CENTURY AHEAD

(*Yale Daily News, March 26, 2014*)

SEEING PAUL RUDNICK'S "Valhalla," a senior project being staged this week at Yale, will have you trying to stifle bouts of laughter as you think about the show on your walk back from the Whitney Theater. The irreverent play explores the role of faith in our lives, perceptions of homosexuality across classes and the tension between searching for beauty and fulfilling obligations.

A pretty tragic story when you step back to think about it a bit, "Valhalla" raises unsettling questions about how people arrive at conclusions about what they want and who they are, and about how family and societal conceptions can help or hurt the process. It's scary to weigh the possibility that the values and ideals we tell ourselves we most want may not exist as we imagine them—like Valhalla itself, a heaven of sorts in Norse mythology.

On a more concrete level, it's startling to think about the dramatic expansion of social rights in the Americas and Europe—and increasingly, in other parts of the world—in the past fifty years. Though often socially turbulent, the years since the Vietnam War have broadly featured more attention to general welfare in thought and deed than at any point in history. Pictures, messages and friends in many places—our broad media exposure to people of many backgrounds—affect the scope of public empathy, helping to shape political outcomes. It's the non-commercial side of the "Oprah effect"—take the oft-mentioned example of how her show and others like it have played a key role in public acceptance of gay rights. Proximity breeds empathy.

This isn't limited to any one issue. Anywhere and anytime people have a case for more freedom and compassion, there's a better chance now than ever that their movement will take off. If you temporarily suspend partisan biases, this was basically the idea behind President George Bush's Freedom Agenda, and much of that rhetoric and policy remains consistent with President Barack Obama's administration.

In this sense, we're living in the most authentically Christian time ever—think Sermon on the Mount, though certainly many of its themes are found in other world religions. The world being "smaller" means people have more occasions to understand and feel for each other. It's a structural change, and technology has a lot to do with it. The gnostic impulse has got to be resisted here—we'll never have heaven on earth. But no one can ignore the ways in which our society today is giving people the opportunity to believe that there is meaningful life possible in the material world—to escape living the Gnostic heresy.

Even identity politics, often decried in the U.S. (and sometimes on Yale's campus) as a force working against cultural and political unity, has its roots in this new reality. In fact, it's an outgrowth of people's longing for community, which is as strong as ever. But what's more is that globalization makes the urge to put oneself on the map stronger, because it's easier to get lost nowadays in questions of personal identity if you don't. Religion and culture aren't going anywhere, and big, pluralistic societies should do everything they can—from providing vouchers for parochial schools to supporting cultural groups—to help free association flourish in America. Far from being fracturing, these forces help to unite, in that they remind people of all stripes of the values that bring Americans together under one flag. National culture being less monolithic than it used to be doesn't mean that national identity will die.

None of this is necessarily here to stay forever—freedom to communicate could once again decline at any moment. Countries around the world remind us all the time, for example, that censorship works, and that which we have has to be defended. And what is often thought of as conservative skepticism about many of these societal changes is understandable and often very valid. The fact that there are many more voices saying very different, contradictory things means that people will have to be more careful when taking cues about what they believe from what they see and read. The 1950s are over. This means that, more than ever, family and meaningful person-to-person contact is essential for avoiding immoral decisions, establishing counterpoints to opinions from far away.

It's somewhat ironic that we live in a time where it's easier to be "true to yourself" than ever before, but likely harder to establish what that really means outside of our immediate desires and personal goals. But the years ahead give us the ideal opportunity to take a world more ready to see neighborly love and empathy and to develop it, through community, into reflections—however imperfect—of our own Valhallas.

FOR AN END TO COLUMNS

(*Yale Daily News, December 4, 2014*)

IF YOU'VE BEEN on Wikipedia at any point this week—and of course you have—then you'll know. It's asking for your money. That huge tab blares right in your face every so often as part of Wikipedia's fundraising drives. Its pitch is brilliant for what it says (they need the money because they don't sell ad space) just as much as for what it doesn't say (your life would really be different without it).

The proliferation of Wikipedia, other "free access, free content" sites and now smartphones will continue to revolutionize the way people around the world access information. You can educate yourself in ways that would otherwise have been impossible—or at least required quite a bit more cost and effort. You won't likely learn "how to think" from the Internet alone, but the democratization of knowledge remains a colossal change in the way we get our facts.

The effect isn't limited to encyclopedias. It also applies to news. Newspapers, magazines, television stations and even "public intellectuals" essentially amassed thought monopolies until about two decades ago. The information and ideas that were in print or on television were what you consumed. Contrarians who felt something wasn't quite right could seek out alternatives, but it took time and concerted effort—or a trip to the library, at least.

The bottom line is that organizations that had a lot of unquestioned authority now have to compete for it—and they often can't. A few that were big enough, like *The New York Times*, had the resources and the manpower to buy time to adjust in the last 10 years, and they might ride out the wave, but not without more cuts in newsroom staff (a new round of departures at the Times is happening this week).

My prediction is that, in the next 10 years, the glitzy magazines so many Yalies will soon want to work for in their careers will start experiencing the same fate. The smaller ones won't survive. The reason is simple: People don't care to listen to (much less pay for) the perspectives that the people who work at the *New Yorker* publish just because they work at the *New Yorker*. Some people would call this new impatience ignorance. But it's just a result of bringing much more rigorous competition to journalism. Fancy publications still hire some of the best writers who will still produce some of the best journalism, but the people who are just hanging on because of the organization's institutional heft will be getting early retirement offers sooner or later. Reporters who write stories about Pope Francis' "breakthrough announcement" that evolution is not contested by the Church need to get different beats or go back to school. Or just read a history book. Spoiler: It's not news.

Columns, for their part, are on their way out—especially print columns where the author can't link to other sites and sources. Editorials these days are more about conversation that the reader can access and read. YDN-style pieces without this feature, still retained by some major news organizations, will continue to be phased out, though they'll definitely continue to thrive on college campuses—where amateurs like us will take full advantage and maybe learn something in the process. It's definitely an opportunity that teaches the writer far more than it ever teaches or informs the readers, who have to be the subjects of naïve, poorly thought-out or sensationalist pieces.

We should embrace the end of columns and the end of news "authorities" in general. Every single person alive can deliver breaking news today, and though organizations that can hire trained, brilliant journalists can and absolutely must remain, those people take up a fraction of those currently employed. I'm hoping this eventually means CNN bites the dust too, since breaking news can now be reported by anyone with a smartphone and paid pundits' commentary can't be tolerated by anyone.

The new information and journalism world is full of risks. There's much more talent out there, and much more trash. The only safeguard against turning into a master conspiracy theorist online—or just a badly informed citizen—is education and civic engagement, which can involve the Internet but which ultimately requires person-to-person interaction.

Maybe I'm naïve, but I'm excited for the end of columns. I'm excited for bad talent being weeded out and new voices that never had a chance to rise. Money, fame and all the rest are still disproportionately large obstacles to people with great ideas who don't have the means. But the Internet has made it just a little easier.

But for all those who—for whatever inexplicable reason—have continued to read and comment on this stuff, it's taught this amateurish columnist a ton. I'll always be grateful.

CHAPTER IV
Identity

WILL WE REMEMBER?

(*Yale Daily News, April 24, 2013*)

My grandmother once observed that my birthday, April 23rd, is wedged every year between two rather unfortunate dates—Vladimir Lenin's birthday, and today, Armenian Genocide Remembrance Day. For me, the latter has made for a sobering change of tone each year from the happy day that came before it, but—like a death in the family—it doesn't hit you right away.

Of course, every year I'd sign petitions demanding that the President issue a statement joining a wide swath of nations and 43 American states in recognizing the Armenian Genocide. At home, we'd watch an old PBS documentary about the genocide. But how does one wrap his head around 1.5 million people having been murdered? What kind of a framework can a person —a child, no less—apply to make sense of it? How can a kid realize that, were he alive in what is now eastern Turkey in 1917, he'd likely be an orphan, his mother raped and murdered?

It is not very different from trying, in vain, to make sense of the Holocaust. Theodore Adorno might have put it best when he remarked that to try "to write a poem after Auschwitz is barbaric."

How can one live after the Shoah? How can one make sense of existence?

But I am, perhaps frightfully, beginning to comprehend what it was. This year, when I attended a commemoration ceremony at an Armenian church in Trumbull, Conn., I heard a rendition of poet Paruyr Sevak's "The Unsilenceable Belfry." Wheelbarrows became caskets, he wrote. In the evening, I heard an old Armenian church hymn for the first time: "Mother, where are you?" The beautiful, haunting chorus sang of Christ pleading for his mother during the crucifixion. That Sunday night, for the first time, I could cry about the genocide.

When German statesman Willy Brandt went to Warsaw in 1970, he visited a memorial marking the Warsaw Ghetto Uprising to lay a wreath. Then, suddenly, he knelt. He didn't have to, but he did, and the entire world saw.

Here, the Armenian Genocide is different, because no Turkish head of state has ever knelt at a monument of the genocide. The Turkish government denies that an event amounting to anything close to genocide took place. Anti-Armenian sentiment extends to the present day, as well. Documentary clips about the Armenian Genocide on YouTube are often followed by all kinds of comments with ethnic slurs.

Obviously, these sentiments don't express the sentiments of nearly all Turkish people. But a strong, anti-Armenian cultural strain, buttressed by resurgent Turkish nationalism, definitely thrives in modern Turkey. And it makes days like today all the more painful, because it begs the question of how to heal an open wound that will not close. How do we remember the dead when few others will—in fact, when some will actually falsify history, directly opposing most historians of the period, to claim that the names of the dead are mere fiction. But the primary source documents are all there for people to see.

The late ambassador Henry Morgenthau, Sr., called the Armenian Genocide a "campaign of race extermination." In justifying the beginning of the Holocaust, Hitler asked a group of Nazis whether anyone remembered the Armenians.

But in the end, this is much more than a historical dispute—because it's not really a dispute at all, except for those on the radical fringe. It's a cultural struggle to forgive the crimes of those who didn't acknowledge (and whose descendants still don't) that they have anything for which to be forgiven.

The theologian Reinhold Niebuhr DIV 1914 once published a book called "The Irony of American History," but the book is really littered with ironies of every kind. One particularly poignant one is that of Christ himself—that a man utterly mocked, condemned and crucified next to two lowly prisoners is resurrected, and that in doing so he pays for the mistakes of a world that doesn't even acknowledge its sin. For the past hundred years, the Armenian people have been living this irony: trying to look the unrepentant in the eye and forgive. But it is hard, and the wound is not nearly closed.

Whether we will remember is an open question. I will, haunted by the faces of the genocides of the twentieth century. And tonight, I'll accompany my friends to the Women's Table, where we'll remember together. We will forget politics, and we will remember the child marched into the desert by the Ottomans, stripped of a family and a home, crying out for his mother. And we will try—we will try our very hardest—to forgive.

"LUYS" FOUNDATION MOTIVATION LETTER

(Spring of 2014)

It would almost feel trivial to call my Armenian heritage my "identity," because it is far more than a voluntary association that anchors character. It is, beginning with when I could think for myself, a crucial component of how I see the world—from interactions with individuals to relationships with ideas. It is a source of happiness and love and a reminder of responsibility and purpose. There is no "choice" to be Armenian just like there is no choosing your blood type.

But an individual can decide for himself how much that reality is going to impact his life. As an undergraduate at Yale University, I founded an Armenian club to bring students and faculty together in a large campus where it's easy to feel alone as an Armenian. I hope to go on to law school—a platform that will provide both the opportunity to have a career in the field I am most passionate about and to continue giving back to the Armenian world by raising awareness outside and continuing to influence change inside.

Hearing about Luys for the first time, not too long ago, was a definite "too good-to-be-true" moment. The program combines an intellectual network of Armenians around the world with the opportunity to travel to Armenia and put words into action. This has been exactly the sort of network I have been looking for—young people who are deeply committed to a long-term relationship in sustaining and continuing to build Armenia and the larger Armenian community around the world. I fully intend to put the skills I am learning at Yale to use in helping the community—whether this means consulting on business and nonprofit development, teaching or mentoring students in philosophy or political science, or helping young people see careers in law later down the road. I already have in mind programs for helping expose the world of knowledge and opportunity to more Armenian youth, and to better integrate the world's leading institutions with a wealth of talent that needs to be cultivated for use in Armenia. Whether the future involves these projects, or others, my future will be intricately linked with the Armenian world.

DEACONS' TRAINING PROGRAM IN JERUSALEM APPLICATION ESSAY

(April of 2014)

"INTIMATIONS OF IMMORTALITY from Recollections of Early Childhood" may be William Wordsworth's most insightful—and devastating—work of poetry. The English Romantic poet begins with an account of what may be called his own fall from grace: *There was a time when meadow, grove, and stream, / The earth, and every common sight, / To me did seem Apparelled in celestial light, / The glory and the freshness of a dream. / It is not now as it hath been of yore; / Turn wheresoe'er I may, By night or day, / The things which I have seen I now can see no more.* As children, we are born with the capacity to envision the world beyond its material borders. Nature and time are infused with meaning, and imagination allows us—before we have learned much of anything—to begin to grasp the moral dimensions of the universe we inhabit.

But this inner awe is not a static characteristic. It is malleable, subject to the stories and teachings it is exposed to as children grow up and have to reckon with the sinful world as it is, from rough schoolyard interactions with bullies to deaths in the family. As a child of immigrant parents growing up in a New York neighborhood ethnically diverse and lacking a large Armenian community, Holy Cross Church helped keep this inner knowledge of another world alive when the material world around me presented countless difficulties. Some of my earliest memories—the ones that explain why Holy Cross has remained the parish I return to after all these years—are of standing in front of the icon of *Charkhapan Soorp Asdvadzadzin* and praying for God's help, of shuddering in the pews before Communion as a voice from the balcony above sang "Der Voghormia" with a haunting beauty convincing me that the angels' tears were deluging Heaven at that very moment, and of staring out into the incense-filled church while holding the Holy Cross as an altar boy. I can never forget the darkness of the church on the evening of Holy Thursday, followed soon by the joy of Easter Sunday. These days are among the most meaningful of the year.

Time passed, grandparents passed away, and my family—my parents and I—moved to Kentucky, where there was no Armenian Church community. Our Armenian language, spoken at home, remained the only daily link with what we had left behind. A teenager by this time, I entered a period when I truly could "see no more," as Wordsworth says. I did well academically and socially—but I became cognizant as I moved through high school that some key internal part was being left undeveloped. One day, for seemingly no other reason than the movement of the Holy Spirit, I drove myself to the closest Catholic Church after school and prayed. It was my first time back in a church in a couple years.

I was accepted to Yale the year following, where I met wonderful friends whose Christian conviction—in a university known for its modern secularism—astounded and inspired me. As I pursued my studies in both the History and Ethics, Politics & Economics (EP&E) majors, I took classes on church history and theology from the beginning onward. I started attending Catholic Mass with my friends more and more regularly, but the *badarak* always lingered in my thoughts. Soon, with my parents back in New York, I started commuting to the city for services at Holy Cross. I make my best attempt to assist at the parish as much as I can. I also found the Armenian Apostolic parish in nearby Trumbull, CT, where I occasionally attend services when I cannot return home. Also by a movement of grace, I began to sense a desire to understand the Divine Liturgy line-by-line and to study the history of the Oriental Orthodox communion.

With each passing month, I feel my knowledge growing. The Armenian Church is a gift of endless depth for the Armenian people, and we have both a spiritual and comm responsibility towards it. The Deacons' Training Program would, for me, represent a unique opportunity to deepen my understanding of the Liturgy for a lifetime serving the Church. As I enter my last undergraduate year and must discern among vocations and fields, the program could come at no better time.

The role of altar servers and others who know the Liturgy is, as I've observed, crucial for both the *badarak* and for educating fellow parishioners. Personally, it is also a very special way to deepen my relationship with Christ. But my parish in particular, as St. Nersess is likely aware, needs help. It has an old and storied legacy among the Armenian churches in the Eastern Diocese, but the number of parishioners in the pews every week is small—and notably absent is a significant number of young people. As an altar server with the experience that the Deacons' Training Program in Jerusalem will afford, I plan on not only serving a greater, more liturgically educated role in church services, but in working more closely with the resources of the parish to reengage the Armenian community in the area. The Armenians of New York are not gone—many may have moved to the suburbs, but many also remain in the city. The responsibility for reengagement lies most directly with those who recognize it and want to do something about it.

If accepted, I hope and pray that the program helps me to connect more fully with the Armenian Apostolic Church as a whole and to assist my parish in particular. And, on a very personal level, I know that it will continue to nurture me to do that which Wordsworth says is lost with the closing of childhood: to see more fully.

THE LAST MAN

AVOIDING CHECKMATE IN 2,000 YEARS OF ARMENIAN GRAND STRATEGY

(*Grand Strategy II, Yale University, Fall of 2014*)

TWO MEN, ONE Israeli and the other Palestinian, are screaming loudly at each other as police cars arrive. The scene is unfolding just within Zion Gate as I walk into the Old City of Jerusalem, on my way back from prayers on Mount Zion with a group of seminary students. I see a fist fly out of the corner of my eye as we quickly walk past, trying not to notice or be noticed. We climb up the winding streets of Jerusalem's Armenian Quarter with our black cloaks flapping against the wind—the priests are leading the procession, easily distinguished from the novices by their hooded cloaks and the heavy metal crosses around their necks. As the monastery compound comes into full view, everything feels safe once more. The street sign to the left reads "Armenian Orthodox Patriarchate Street" in English, Hebrew, and Arabic. *How in the world,* I wonder as the heavy gate guarding the walled compound shuts closed, *have the Armenians survived for so long in the middle of all this?*

Later that evening, I asked a priest a question that I was sure would have some sort of root theological answer. The Armenian Orthodox Church, if one pays attention, uses a very distinct rendering of the cross in its imagery. It is decorated with vines on each corner, and the lines radiating out from where the vertical and horizontal planks meet are usually concave, as opposed to linear. But it can't properly be called a "crucifix," as in the Roman Catholic Church, because it's missing an important feature: Jesus. I wanted to know why Armenian crosses didn't ordinarily depict Christ on the cross. We spoke in Armenian. "There is a theological answer," the priest told me over tea and baklava. "The cross being empty symbolizes Christ's victory over death. But that's not quite the full answer. Armenians have always lived and worked in places where they were in the minority. A more discreet cross is less likely to be noticed and less likely to offend a neighbor." It was a surprising answer, as immediately deflating as it was ultimately revealing. *It certainly answered the question,* I thought. In fact, it answered more than one.

Departure

It's difficult to find an Armenian who doesn't love quotes about Armenia. They're particularly fond of one uttered by the California writer William Saroyan, which I found hanging on a wall inside St. Nersess Armenian Seminary in New Rochelle, New York, on the night of June 24th, before a group of deacons-in-training left for Jerusalem:

> I should like to see any power of the world destroy this race, this small tribe of unimportant people, whose wars have all been fought and lost, whose structures have crumbled, literature is unread, music is unheard, and prayers are no more answered. Go ahead, destroy Armenia. See if you can do it. Send them into the desert without bread or water. Burn their homes and churches. Then see if they will not laugh, sing and pray again. For when two of them meet anywhere in the world, see if they will not create a New Armenia.

Not exactly sanguine, I thought, but certainly defiant. It was the kind of quote that gained cultural cachet in the aftermath of the Armenian Genocide, when over one million Armenians living in Ottoman Turkey were killed in politically, ethnically and religiously motivated extermination campaigns. But the quote helped, at least, to rationalize being in New Rochelle that evening with twelve other college students—with varying degrees of Armenian speaking ability, appearance, and cultural or historical knowledge—whom I had never met before. The following morning, our group left for Tel Aviv for a two-week intensive program in Armenian religious education. From there, I would leave the group and depart for Armenia proper for a month-long cooperative research project with the Armenian government and the Luys Foundation, an NGO focused on economic development in rural towns. In Armenia, I would seek to understand popular perceptions of the country's current geopolitical and economic situation, particularly as it attempts to move beyond its Soviet past and to carve out a separate niche in the conduct of international relations, with the shadow of Russia constantly looming. My hope was to return in August with a better understanding of how the Armenian people understood their role in the world, and how historical memory shaped national consciousness in a way that had implications for the practice of grand strategy. I also hoped to deduce whether any of the principles underlying Armenia's relations with its political surroundings were applicable to other small countries operating in close proximity to large, ambitious states which try to dictate how its neighbors and satellites should act.

The flight to Tel Aviv, incidentally, connected through Moscow, and the company taking us there was Aeroflot. The Russian national carrier has changed the flag on its planes' tails since the Soviet days, but it has curiously retained the iconic "winged hammer and sickle" logo on its doors, seats, and napkins. Our plane was named the "Anton Chekhov." The flight attendants, all female and all dressed in blinding blood orange outfits, were stereotypically Russian down to the last: tall, imposing, and severe, whether you spoke to them in English or Russian (I tried both). Perhaps this just happened to be the profile of the employees on this particular flight, but it would not be too surprising, I thought, if Aeroflot's human resources department actually selected for these traits. It was an airline with amenities on par with most others, but a distinctly Russian facade that retained more than a few resemblances to the old Soviet, quasi-imperial aesthetic. But no one seemed to mind, from the flight attendants to the Russian man setting beside me. It seemed, in fact, to be just what they wanted and expected.

After a brief stop in Moscow's Sheremetyevo International Airport, complete with a glistening new terminal for international arrivals, we were off to Tel Aviv. According to the flight map, we flew over the Black Sea, Turkey, and over the Mediterranean—Aeroflot has been avoiding flying over Syria since a surface-to-air missile narrowly missed one of its planes in April 2013.

The Shadow of History

The Syrian Civil War, and the subsequent rise of ISIS, has by now displaced millions and permanently uprooted entire ethnic and religious populations. More than 100,000 Armenians lived in Syria prior to the outbreak, concentrated in Aleppo and in several cities in the northwest, where some towns had Armenian majorities. Some of those communities easily predated the Crusades. Most have been abandoned now, yet stories constantly come in through Armenian and diaspora news media of families who remain. Interspersed with the conflicting news reports, it is not uncommon to hear references at Armenian dinner tables to ancient Armenia. At its height in the century before Christ, the Kingdom of Armenia encompassed parts of present day Syria, Iran, Israel, Turkey, Lebanon, and Iraq, as well as a wide swath of the Caucasus. But Armenia as a sprawling empire has been the historical exception, and the nation—perhaps because it has always operated in a geopolitical crossroads, perhaps for other reasons—has never proven itself adept at maintaining a large degree of political power. By 69 BC, King Tigranes the Great (*Tigran Metz* in Armenian) had expanded the borders of the independent kingdom to include Jerusalem,

Damascus, modern-day Armenia, and quite a bit of what was in between. By the time of the Roman Emperor Augustus a few decades later, the kingdom had lost much of its possessions and had become a Roman client state. "Tigran," however, remains one of the most popular boys' names in the country today.

The kingdom, reduced to a buffer state for the Roman Empire, soon became a stomping ground for battles between the Romans and the Parthian Empire. It would remain in limbo, as first the two sides and then others contended for influence, until 428 AD. In the meantime, Christianity swept through the Levant and reached the Caucasus, becoming the state religion of Armenia in 301 A.D. when the king converted to Christianity. The Edict of Milan, which provided for tolerance for Christians in the Roman Empire, would not be issued until 313. It is therefore still common to hear Armenians say that theirs was the first Christian country in the world, and that their church predates the Roman Church. While the official separation of the Armenian Orthodox Church took place at the Council of Chalcedon over a minor Christological dispute in 451, its fierce independence was by then already a mainstay for over a century. The church's contact with Western Christianity would remain limited until the Crusades.

In the centuries to come, Armenia would be divided among the Persians, the Byzantines, the Umayyad Caliphate, the Mongols, the Mamluks, the Ottomans, and then he Soviets, periodically gaining independence—as in the case of the medieval Bagratid Kingdom of Armenia from 884 to 1045, when it fell to the Seljuk Empire, and the Crusader-allied Armenian Kingdom of Cilicia (in present day Turkey and Syria) from 1198-1375. But perhaps the shortest-lived was the First Republic of Armenia, the first recognized state since the Kingdom of Cilicia which emerged in the aftermath of the Armenian Genocide in 1918—and which ceased to exist shortly thereafter when the Soviet Red Army marched into the capital, Yerevan, in 1920.

Each period in Armenia's history is rife with political drama, but the grand strategic theme is constant: in most instances, under various empires' control, Armenia managed to swiftly marshal military, political, and/or economic resources to secure the freedom to trade and worship. In the case of Persian Armenia, for example, a combination of factors including the high status of Armenian nobles among the Persian nobility (there was frequent intermarriage) and the military insurrection led by general Vardan Mamikonian resulted in the Nvarsak Treaty of 484, stopping Persian efforts to convert Armenians to Zoroastrianism. In the Ottoman Empire, the Millet system provided for a separate Armenian legal system under Ottoman rule. In each case, partial autonomy was achieved through a combination of force and diplomacy, two critical factors in the foreign affairs of any peoples. But the third element is perhaps more emblematic of the Armenian legacy in international conduct: a significant degree of accommodation.

The Murder That Split a Church

A few months before sitting in the plane headed for Tel Aviv, I found myself talking to a friend in the reception area of Holy Cross Armenian Church in the Washington Heights neighborhood of Manhattan, a mostly Puerto Rican and Dominican neighborhood that still bears the marks of a previous wave of immigration: a few Irish pubs on Broadway, Yeshiva University, a Greek Orthodox church, and Holy Cross. She was telling me about a recent trip she took to the Holy Land with a group of young professionals and a priest, and I made a mental note to do some digging of my own to see how a trip to Jerusalem might be possible. She was new to the parish, so I told her about how there had once been a large Armenian community in the area, how this was why my parents had chosen to live in the neighborhood twenty years ago, how the Divine Liturgy (Mass) goes on every week—despite there sometimes being no more than five people in attendance. "Do you know the story?" I asked her, gesturing towards the altar. "Of course," she replied. "Everyone knows the story."

To the right of the altar is buried Archbishop Leon Tourian, the primate of the Armenian Church in America from 1931-1933. Tourian had arrived at the parish on December 24, 1933, to lead the celebration of a Christmas eve service. As he processed up the middle aisle towards the altar, a group of men surrounded him and stabbed him repeatedly with butcher knives, fleeing the scene immediately afterward. He was dead in minutes, lying on the ground as screams continued to emanate from the congregation.

Several months before, Archbishop Tourian had been in Chicago to deliver a speech, and he had noticed flying among the crowd the flag of the First Republic of Armenia on a banner. He ordered the flag removed, and exhorted those gathered to repress their patriotic sympathies while Armenia remained a part of the Soviet Union, so that the Church would not suffer further political retribution. It did not need mentioning that the USSR was hostile to churches everywhere; many in America in the 1920s and 1930s were well aware that Joseph Stalin was in the midst of an anticlerical and antireligious campaign that saw priests murdered by the thousands and religious property confiscated and destroyed. Those in the Armenian diaspora, whether they were from Armenia proper or lands in the Middle East with ancient Armenian populations, would likely have had a heightened awareness regarding these events. But the Armenian Church under Soviet rule, unlike the Russian Orthodox Church and the Catholic Church in the Soviet Union, managed to avoid a great deal of the damage. This was in part because of the political pressure exerted by the community in the diaspora and—critically—because it did not resist a degree of Soviet encroachment. Soviet leaders recognized that purging the Church entirely might cause a split in the diaspora that would be politically disadvantageous to the Kremlin, and Church leaders understood the need to appease the regime. In World War II, the

Primate of the Church encouraged Armenians to enlist in Stalin's army, and by the 1950s it was well known that the KGB vetted priests.

Archbishop Tourian, then, tried to do his part to assist efforts at accommodating the regime, a notable feature of Armenian grand strategy since at least the time of Persian Armenia. Yet a growing minority movement was becoming convinced that Church policy amounted to collaborating with evil, especially in light of the brutality inflicted upon churches by the Soviet regime in the 1930s. Once Tourian had made his position clear, the situation was ready to explode. The group of men who surrounded and killed him a few months later were all found to be members of the Armenian Revolutionary Federation, or "Dashnags," who were agitating for an independent state.

The assassination's ripple effects are still being felt today: after that evening in 1933, the Armenian Church split into two political factions with the same theology and liturgy. The supporters of accommodation, the majority of Armenians worldwide, remained loyal to the Apostolic See located in Armenia proper, then under Soviet rule. Those opposed, however, soon organized and declared their loyalty to the Apostolic See of Cilicia in exile, located in Lebanon, which was free of Soviet influence. To this day, the split remains in parishes across the United States and the world. Whether the Church in Armenia would be alive to tell the story had it not cooperated with the Soviet government, however, remains an open question. So does, Dashnags today will quickly note, the possibility that the Church—in ways large or small—might have helped to support the "evil empire."

Into the Walled City

The Aeroflot plane landed. It was nighttime in Tel Aviv, and a priest was waiting to whisk us away to Jerusalem. Keeping a monastery alive and functioning through several rounds of daily prayers, it turned out, was only the bare minimum requirement for the priests in Jerusalem. With a population of less than 2,000 laypeople and clergy to tend to the upkeep of one sixth of the territory within Old Jerusalem, multitasking was a must. In the 1940s, I was told, the population was over 40,000. Those who remain today find work, and life in general, difficult among the intense ethnic and religious clashes that are constantly just over the horizon. The clergy and the laity speak Armenian, in addition to Hebrew, Arabic, and English or Russian—and the See of Jerusalem has proven quite adept at keeping relations good with both the Jewish and Arab populations clustered together in the area. There are frequent visits by Israeli cabinet ministers to the monastery compound to meet with the Armenian Patriarch of Jerusalem, and the See also maintains good relations with the Kingdom of Jordan, which donated land on its western border for the construction of a major new church that opened last month.

Over the next two weeks, we became integrated into the schedule of the monastery. The wakeup call came at six every morning, when all the seminarians and priests would process into St. James Cathedral for Morning Prayer. Two hours later, classes for the seminary students would commence, and our group would begin the day's travel itinerary. This was one of our luxuries as visitors. The other, of course, was that we were only there for two weeks, while they continued work every day, without fail. At noon, it was back to the cathedral for prayer, more classes, and then back again to the cathedral at five. Every evening, while everyone else studied and slept, two seminarians would head out to the Church of the Holy Sepulcher for the routine all-night vigil. Each Sunday, the entire clerical population of the monastery would process to the Holy Sepulcher for Mass. The cathedral, one of the holiest in Christendom, is maintained jointly by the Greek, Armenian, and Latin churches. I asked a priest what would happen if, by chance, the seminarians just didn't go out one night.

"It can't happen," he said. "The Greeks and the Latins are very political. If we don't go, it's a sign of weakness. We will lose our rights to celebrate in the cathedral. Next thing you know, we will go the way of the Georgians." He was referring to the Georgian Orthodox Church, which had significant holdings in the Holy Land but was squeezed out over time because of political and financial wrangling. His tone seemed a bit paranoid, but the concern was palpable. Perhaps they owed their outliving the Georgians to that very attitude of constant vigilance.

And so, the seminarians, along with the priests, work. They run an operation inside the monastery walls, and they also celebrate Masses regularly in several locations scattered around the Holy Land, including the Church of the Holy Sepulcher and the Church of the Nativity in Bethlehem, inside the West Bank. A few decades ago, they would often make the trip from the Old City to Bethlehem on foot. The security situation doesn't permit that kind of freedom anymore. And these seminarians are among the youngest in the world, ranging from 14 to 24, drawn from the remaining Armenian communities in the Middle East and Armenia proper. While the younger students go to regular academic classes by day, the older students continue higher-level religious instruction, on the road to becoming priests, monks, and bishops. Returning home on vacation only becomes an option after completing the fourth year. It is a level of commitment almost inconceivable to an American student of the same age. I asked one of the younger seminarians if he intended to stay when he obtained his diploma: "Of course," he responded without a lick of self-consciousness or doubt, "I am going to become a *Vardabed*." At age 14, he was near proficient in four languages, and completely set on becoming a celibate bishop.

This discipline and the recognition of the need for constant vigilance—in essence, a perpetual "crisis mode" of living—are at the heart of why Armenians retain so much real estate, both physical and spiritual, in the Holy Land today. It also helps to explain why, when faced with matters relating to internal affairs, the seemingly spotless ship begins to show blemishes. Within the confines of the monastery compound are housed the priests and the seminarians. But outnumbering them both is a large population of Armenian laypeople who are either descendants of the ancient Armenian community in Jerusalem, descendants of refugees who sought the safety of the monastery in the waning days of the Ottoman Empire's extermination campaigns, or recent immigrants from Armenia who have come in search of work. Relations between the clergy and the laity are very poor, with both sides accusing the other of acting in bad faith. They are also, as I found out, very eager to tell their side of the story to whoever will listen. The priests complain that the people do not attend church or support the monastery's religious mission—the compound is, after all, one of the few in the world where laity live with cloistered priests and monks. The people, for their part, complain that the priests are self-concerned and not interested in providing pastoral support for the community. Several young people I spoke to do not know whether they will continue living in Jerusalem once they have the resources to leave. Many of the adults work for the monastery in various support roles, but they complain of low pay and of being squeezed out themselves amid the area's ethnic favoritism. The only school within the compound for Armenian children is in need of critical updates, as it still uses the education system of the British mandate era—one of the reasons why Armenian students, many of them quite bright, find it difficult to secure placements in Israeli universities. Still, quite a few do.

I remember awaking, a few minutes after six, on the final day in Jerusalem to head to *Taboor*, the Morning Prayer service. I donned my cloak, and walked up the already hot steps across what felt like a barren, stone-covered Eden. But I was taken by my thoughts—either that, or still not fully awake—and I made a premature right turn. I kept going until, directly in front ahead, stood a tree covered with dazzling violet flowers. Attention restored, I turned around from the dead end and ran to join the seminarians, who had already begun.

Homeland

It is not necessary to set foot on Armenian land to feel as though you have arrived. A few minutes after the plane took off, and Tel Aviv faded from view, the aisle was crowded with passengers. No word about the sign being turned off and people were already unfastening their belts, getting out their food and liquor, and talking to their neighbors. The party plane to Yerevan was airborne.

One can't help but surmise that this restlessness and seemingly absolute sense of individual autonomy contributes to the internal squabbles, as seen in Jerusalem. As soon as we had arrived at the airport, we were funneled into the line to purchase a visa (for Americans, no advance arrangements are needed).

"You're from America, eh?" asked the customs officer. *Ayo,* I responded, and asked if she had been there. She hadn't, adding wistfully, *Es yerkire yerkir chi!*—"This country isn't a country!" Amongst Armenians living there now, it's a popular expression that's meant to convey dissatisfaction with the economy, with politics, with everything. But it isn't exactly what you want a customs officer telling visitors upon arrival. Those very same qualities that seem to help Armenians survive and thrive in the minority amidst foreign populations—indeed, Armenians in the Ottoman Empire had a reputation for success in trade—might be working against them at home. It's a tempting, if incomplete, diagnosis, seemingly confirmed every time you enter a cab and say "Barev" to the driver—"Hello" in Armenian. Extremely inexpensive cabs have proliferated in Yerevan following the 2009 recession, which cut deeply into Armenia's growth rate, among the highest in the region during the early 2000s. To a tee, each driver picked up on my accent, which lacked the intonations and the slang common nowadays in Yerevan. What would follow was usually a barrage of questions: *What brings you back here? Where are you from? Ah, New York—I have a cousin in New York!—is it as nice as they say?* And then, most importantly, *Do you like Armenia?* Each time, I would say that it's impossible not to like: the immense natural and historic beauty, the food, the warmth of people. They would always agree, usually swelling with pride that an Armenian from the diaspora approved of the motherland. And then a rant would begin: *Our president is corrupt. Azerbaijan is planning a new attack. Putin is on our side. Putin is not on our side. Is the United States going to help? It's impossible to make money in this country. The government is run by thieves. You can't trust anyone.* I would sit and listen, doing my best to be agreeable until we arrived at the destination. On three separate rides, I remember there being no meter and I asked the driver how much to pay. "However much you want!" I have yet to hear that response in any other country.

In 2007, the Armenian economy was still booming, and the World Bank published a report entitled, "The Caucasian Tiger: Sustaining Economic Growth in Armenia." Citing the "stellar growth" in Armenia over the past decade, fueled by macroeconomic stability and market reforms, the policy experts presented a series of proposals for safeguarding the rise of the economy. But the report certainly did not take into account the global financial crisis of 2009, which had severe repercussions for growth in the Armenian economy. The cranes that had popped up across the skyline of Yerevan ground to a halt, and the real estate boom froze. Many of these unfinished projects are still there, just as they were left in 2009.

With its very high literacy rate in Armenian, Russian, and increasingly English, Armenians with the resources to leave are doing so in high numbers, though the government refuses to release comprehensive figures. Most, especially from depressed provinces, are heading to Russia, where blue-collar jobs are still relatively plentiful and where the possibility of economic mobility still exists. The few who can afford to relocate to France or the United States do, without looking back. In the meantime, foreign investment, especially from wealthy Armenians in large diaspora communities located in Russia, the United States, France, and Argentina, has also slowed, in part due to the meltdown and also because of "donor fatigue." Donors have grown weary of interference from the Armenian government, which, in its domestic affairs, is perceived as wildly corrupt and largely inept. The corruption is hard to deny. A group of wealthy businessmen, dubbed "the oligarchs," have erected obnoxious, sprawling estates in various provinces outside the capital with the government's blessing, while pensions, as one of my older relatives told me, "will buy you enough food for a weekend." This daily reality comes on top of stories of new offenses and conspiracies, some true and others undeniably exaggerated. Many lead all the way back to the 1999 shootings of the Parliament Speaker and Prime Minister inside the Armenian National Assembly, an event that shocked the consciousness of post-Soviet, modern Armenian society and inaugurated a new era of cynicism that today is back with a vengeance.

Moving the Lonely King Around

The Armenian chess champion Garry Kasparov is considered by many to be the greatest chess player of all time. Using various statistical methods, he usually clocks in first or second, behind Bobby Fischer or 2014 breakout champion Magnus Carlsen. It would seem like a stroke of luck, until you notice that there is another Armenian, Levon Aronian, on the global top ten list. On November 28, 2014, a 13 year old California boy, Samuel Sevian, became the youngest ever person to be designated a chess "Grandmaster" by the World Chess Federation. For such a small country, could this still only be a matter of coincidence?

On May 23, 2014, *The New Republic* ran a piece entitled, "Armenia Is an International Superpower—at Chess." The article detailed the unlikely odds of Armenia's rise to chess prominence and described how the isolated country in 2011 introduced national, mandatory chess instruction during primary school, the only country in the world to have instituted such a requirement. But Armenian chess aptitude, evident in players like Kasparov and Sevian, predated the 2011 education mandate. "For a country so hopelessly unable to master the world's geo-political realities," the writer exclaimed, "it is a cradle of strategy, precision and expert outmanoeuvering. It soars ahead in its aptitude at chess." Expert observations were brought up in support of the phenomenon:

> "Of the bits I've seen of the Armenian model, I was impressed with how incredibly good their children were at visualising things," remarks the *Telegraph's* chess columnist and head of charity Chess in Schools and Communities Malcolm Pein. "I saw, I think it was a class of what we call here Year Fours, who could literally move pieces around in their head along a chessboard. A lot of children can do that, but they were incredibly good at it."

It's difficult to say what, precisely, makes Armenian children so good at chess, but the proof is in the lists of top players around the world. It may also help explain why, when it comes to the practice of foreign policy, Armenia is not quite as and clueless as the piece in *The New Republic* would have it.

Though talk to any Armenian and they will tell you how much they love their land, the geostrategic position of the country is hardly enviable. Landlocked and surrounded by outright hostile neighbors to the east (Azerbaijan) and to the west (Turkey), the country maintains necessarily cordial relations with the volatile governments of Georgia to the north and Iran to the south—risking utter isolation if it fails to do so ("I remember," another close relative in Yerevan tells me, "when really the only way to get into or out of Armenia was by plane."). It has also thus far managed—in a feat that wasn't accomplished in Georgia and Ukraine, leading to disastrous instability and loss of life—to maintain good relations with both Russia and the West. This comes, at least in part, from a clear sense among top-ranking Armenian diplomats that Armenia is the king fleeing checkmate on a chessboard, with most of its defenses gone (in Armenia's case, it should be admitted that the defenses never really existed in the first place). In Yerevan, I interviewed several leading officials in both the Armenian foreign and diaspora ministries on the condition that their remarks remain off the record. What was unmistakable in each interview, however, was the degree to which their thinking operated according to the awareness of the need for a constant readiness to mobilize. This sense of crisis and vigilance, so valuable to Armenians throughout time and place, seems to be playing a direct role in the execution of a nuanced foreign policy with respect to the large players both in the region and globally.

The Soviet Union under Joseph Stalin, as Vladislav Zubok and others have noted, worked to minimize dissent directed at the Kremlin through a "divide-and-conquer" strategy that created ethnic minority enclaves within the various member states of the USSR. When the Soviet Union collapsed, several regional conflicts erupted. One such conflict was the Nagorno-Karabakh (NKR) War fought between Armenia and Azerbaijan in the early 1990s over a small, majority-Armenian enclave in Azerbaijan that had lobbied Moscow for union with Armenia since the 1940s—only to be turned down each time. The conflict, still vividly regarded as the worst time for Armenia in recent memory, was accompanied by power and food shortages in Armenia proper. Azerbaijani civilians fled the breakaway province amid directed violence, and Armenians in Baku were the subjects of ethnic pogroms. As bilateral relations deteriorated, Turkey—a close ally of Azerbaijan—closed its border with Armenia, and it remains closed today. Russia sold arms to both sides in the conflict, though the eventual result was an Armenian military victory that led to a European-negotiated armistice in force until now. In recent years, border violence has become more frequent, as an Azerbaijan flush with oil revenue seeks to reclaim what it views as stolen land. On November 13th, an Armenian military helicopter was shot down over Karabakh, leading to two military deaths.

If the shooting was a provocation, Armenia has not responded. Cognizant of the difficulty that would be involved in pulling off another 1994-style victory, Armenia has become heavily invested in the peace process, while sticking firmly to its territorial claims. The policy seems to be working, as Azerbaijan appears to have been the aggressor in the November attacks and the international community roundly criticized the unwarranted escalation. Armenia's calculation seems to be working, as representatives for several major negotiating countries involved in the Organization for Security and Cooperation in Europe's Minsk Group—the working committee responsible for attempting to resolve the decades-long crisis—privately told me in Yerevan that Azerbaijan's continued demand for a total return of Nagorno-Karabakh was now seen as untenable. Russia, for its part, continues to sell arms to both the Armenian-backed government in NKR and to Baku, and it certainly retains an interest in instability in the region, which guarantees Armenia's dependence on Moscow for military and political aid. Additionally, Russia continues to use Armenia in order to retain a military base in the Caucasus, a privilege that has grown harder to come by in the wake of Georgia's and Ukraine's moves westward. Given the set of conflicting interests, the Azerbaijani powder keg, and the unwillingness for a new war, Armenian diplomats understand that maintaining the current stalemate is the best option as far as the NKR issue is concerned. Throughout much of 2013, news reports surfaced that Russia was pressuring the Armenian president, Serzh Sargsyan, to sign on to the new Eurasian Economic Union (EEU) championed by Vladimir Putin. To the surprise of both some Armenian observers and the European Union delegation stationed in Yerevan, Sargsyan agreed the following year, and it will be one of the official member states when the EEU formally debuts in 2015. Sources I spoke to who are close to the President admitted that, in the days prior to the decision, they had little indication as to which way he would swing.

Most recent news reports would seem to suggest that Armenia is swinging firmly in Russia's direction, but the surprise EEU move came five years after Armenia entered the European Union's Eastern Partnership, an initiative dedicated to increasing talks aimed at bolstering trade and travel arrangements with the post-Soviet states of Eastern Europe. Moreover, 2013 saw the opening of the European Union Center in Armenia, the EU's "communication hub" in Yerevan. With economically strong and politically active diaspora communities in Russia, as well as France and the United States, Armenia's foreign policy has always taken an "all hands on deck" approach that sought to incorporate ties with all the countries in which there was a substantial Armenian presence. In the case of Russia and the United States, both also happen to be intensely engaged in the regions of the Caucasus and the northern Middle East at present.

While relations with Moscow are currently strong and seem to be getting stronger, Armenia's diaspora community in France and the United States—which historically comes mostly from the Middle East and Turkey and has no affinity for Russia or Soviet-era policies—is an important counterweight adding balance to the Armenian government's approach while lobbying on behalf of the country in the West. Its main political arm in the U.S., the Armenian National Committee of America (ANCA), helps to lead a Congressional pro-Armenia caucus with over 150 members. This concerted lobbying effort has led to visibility—in 2012, Hillary Clinton made the first official visit of a U.S. Secretary of State to Armenia in decades—and it has also led to political clout. Following the outbreak of war in NKR in 1992, the U.S. Congress banned Azerbaijan from receiving federal aid. Azerbaijan became the only post-Soviet bloc country to be slapped with such a ban. Azeri and Turkish lobbying efforts have since caught up, but the "Armenian lobby" retains considerable influence among U.S. policymakers. In France, another center of the Armenian diaspora, the community is also politically organized: French president Francois Hollande announced in October that he would be attending the 100th anniversary commemoration of the Armenian Genocide in Yerevan next year, seen in part as a gesture aimed at wooing the large population of Armenian-French voters. "Water," writes Sun Tzu, "shapes its course according to the nature of the ground over which it flows." As the ground under Armenia continues to shift, it seeks to avoid checkmate by shifting the emphasis on ties from one ally to the other. The difficulty lies in shifting only so much as to accomplish the aims without losing any friends.

The Turkish Question

At one point during my research in Yerevan, which took me to many government offices, libraries, and border towns, I was asked to accompany a group of Armenian high school students on a service trip to Yeghegnadzor, a small town near the western border with Turkey. The trip was organized by the Luys Foundation, which matches Armenian students living in the diaspora who spend part of their summers in Armenia with mentees throughout the country. The collaborative groups then spend two weeks at a time learning the principles of economic development in various projects around the country and implementing small-scale assistance and revitalization projects. I obliged.

Many of the students, like Armenian kids everywhere, had high hopes: they wanted to go to Harvard, Yale, Columbia. Several asked me to help them with their English, and I promised to read their college applications when the time came. Over those two weeks, we got to know Yeghegnadzor—a model, in many ways, of cities across Armenia. Its economy depressed and its infrastructure poor, people are leaving for Russia in droves. The town park and city center, quite vibrant when built in the Soviet era, had fallen into decay. The scenery is incredible—I was reminded of the rugged hills of Utah, except with ancient churches scattered throughout the landscape—and though the region doesn't have anything close to a functioning tourism authority, a steady trickle of Europeans and Americans who are diligent enough to come on their own arrive daily. Our project was to put on a regional arts festival that serves as one of the city's only major draws, and it ended up drawing several thousand visitors. But Yeghegnadzor, and other towns like it, are still suffering from the shutdown of the western border with Turkey two decades ago, and the recent economic downturn has only made things worse. I asked our host if she plans to leave: "When I am able to," she said.

Because it's a border town, Yeghegnadzor is always preparing. I awoke one morning to the sounds of military drums and marching—the local unit, stationed on the border, was rehearsing for a military parade in a few days. The possibility of conflict is always present in the Armenian consciousness—and when conflict has come before, the people have not hesitated to "fight a damn good war," as one American official in Armenia told me. But with the movement of goods and people so heavily and artificially curtailed, it's unclear how long military preparedness and morale in battle will continue to trump an outright deficiency in resources.

Turkey is a regional player with large ambitions. A century ago, its predecessor, the Ottoman Empire, viewed the large Armenian population within its borders as a threat to these ambitions, and an extermination campaign began. Today, the Armenian threat to a reemerging Turkey is small, but it continues to be a nagging presence on its eastern border with a history of antagonizing both Turkey and its ally, Azerbaijan. Since Turkey's closing of the border crossings with Armenia in 1992 over the NRK war, relations have deteriorated further. In 2009, Turkey and Armenia—after negotiations with the E.U. and the United States, buoyed by a last-minute push made by Hillary Clinton—signed unprecedented protocols to normalize bilateral relations and reopen the border, pending ratification. The ratification, however, never came. In Turkey, public opinion turned against ratification amid incendiary statements surrounding the fact that the protocols left the Armenian "occupation" of NKR unaddressed. Armenia, amid backlash that the documents glossed over the issue of Turkish culpability in the Armenian Genocide (and wary of submitting the protocols for parliamentary ratification if Turkey was not going to), suspended the process. It was a tactical move, but the failure to reach an agreement was another in a long string of disappointing efforts at opening the logjam. Armenian officials still insist publicly and privately that there was no other choice, given the change of climate in Turkey. Whether or not this is indeed true, the mutual blame game means the diplomatic freeze will continue. Armenia's perplexing relationship with Turkey, despite intense efforts by Western diplomats, shows no signs of improving. Armenia has, time and time again, succeeding in martialing political resources to avoid checkmate—which, currently, would entail a deal that would force it to give up control of NKR or put aside its demand for Genocide recognition. But, without reinforcements, a king can only run around avoiding checkmate on a chessboard for so long.

The 20th Century: Memories That Linger

As far as Armenian foreign affairs are concerned, two critical twentieth century historical realities spill directly into the present: the Armenian Genocide and the events of the Soviet era. No Armenian child grows up without being exposed to the narrative of the Genocide—how people were marched into the desert, how Hitler allegedly cited its passage from international memory as proof that he could carry out a similar campaign against the Jews, how the Turkish government still denies blame. In Armenia, where the reality of Turkish animus is more acutely felt, this narrative can bend toward hatred, something I noticed as a relatively common feature of citizens' views, whether they were old or young. This kind of singular hatred in public and private commentary is a relatively new phenomenon for Armenians, who have existed among peoples of different religious and ethnic backgrounds for millennia. It is, as I perceived it in Yerevan and elsewhere, one of the leading threats to the success of Armenian grand strategy going forward, as its emotionally charged nature threatens to plant a permanent hereditary hatred that would work against one of Armenians' core survival skills: accommodation.

On the issue of Armenian Genocide recognition and the closing of the wound—the perception of an injustice not accounted for—in the global Armenian consciousness, Armenia today finds that it doesn't control the outcome. It is one place where Armenian strategic vision simply can't compete with the outsize role Turkey plays in the world. The historical reality of the Genocide has long been settled, with the International Association of Genocide Scholars unanimously affirming its historical veracity, along with twenty-two countries (including France and Russia) and forty-three U.S. states in formal declarations. Holocaust survivor and scholar Elie Wiesel has long championed the issue in the United States. Yet the United States has never formally issued recognition. To understand how difficult an issue it is for politicians to dance around, it is worth noting that Senators Barack Obama and Hillary Clinton, while running for president, offered full-throated statements in support of recognition. Once in office, the administration called it a "dangerous door" to walk through for what it could mean for U.S.-Turkey relations. In Turkey, it is a national taboo: alleging that the Genocide took place may get you slapped with the crime of "insulting Turkishness," according to changes made in 2005 to the penal code. It's only slightly been tweaked since then. American historian Stephen Kinzer frames the status of Genocide recognition in Turkey in stark terms:

> The [Erdogan] regime has also stood by as ultra-nationalist ideas have spread alarmingly in the Turkish body politic. These ideas far exceed patriotic pride, going so far as to insist that "nation" and "Turkishness" are abstractions so central to life that anyone who seems to violate traditional meanings is a traitor. That category has broadened steadily from those who criticize the army or question Atatturk's legacy to anyone who speaks out for Kurdish rights, seeks more freedom for Christians or offers alternative views of the Armenian tragedy.

There are cracks in the pavement among certain sectors of the Turkish public, and Turkish president Erdogan in April offered qualified "condolences" to the descendants of Genocide victims for the first time. But the historical memory of the Genocide, unacknowledged by Turkey officially, has taken on a political dimension in both Armenia and Turkey and threatens to become a permanent roadblock in efforts toward diplomatic rapprochement. The Armenian grand strategy applied to this issue has thus far involved creating and maintaining pressure points in various corners of the world, in the hope that Turkish grandstanding collapses in the face of overwhelming historical evidence and political pressure. The reality, however, increasingly seems to be that change in Turkish opinion, if it is to happen, must happen from within Turkish society.

The other historical reality Armenia must more fully reckon with is how to deal with its Soviet past. How this historical relationship will play out in the years to come is as open a question as the direction of Genocide recognition in Turkey. Unlike the experiences of many Eastern European nations under Soviet rule or influence, it is more difficult to dismiss Armenia's time as a Soviet Socialist Republic as overwhelmingly negative. A simple walk through Yerevan reveals why: the Soviets built almost everything, from the sprawling squares, to many of the artistic venues, to the subway lines. Everyone to whom I posed the question of what quality of life was like under Soviet rule—from academics in the capital to villagers in Yeghegnadzor—described the 1960s, 70s, and early 80s as a golden era, of sorts. The academics said learning was more appreciated then. A villager told me that the poor were better treated then. "Now," he said, "we're nobody, and Armenia's nobody." While this narrative sets aside the brutality of the early Soviet period for Armenia and the rest of the USSR, and while it leaves unknown the fate of political dissidents under Soviet rule, it hints at an underlying truth about the Soviet Union that played to Armenians' strengths: it was a very diverse society, and Armenians have thrived while living in diversity. Now, according to this point of view, Armenia is closed, inward looking, and—consequently—self-destructing. This widely differs, it should be said, from how Armenians living in the diaspora think about the Soviet period: a time of political and religious repression, during which Armenia's links to its heroic Christian past were severed and whitewashed. The two views underscore a wide diversity of opinion amongst Armenians worldwide that have played to the country's political advantage.

As Russia moves to consolidate power over its satellite states, however, the legacy of Soviet involvement in Armenia may come under more intense scrutiny. On this historical issue, just as in the case of the Genocide issue, what has been a strength of Armenian grand strategy might be in need of a critical makeover. Unless the late Soviet era is contextualized and the national mood sobers in regard to Armenia's perceived prosperity during the last few decades of the Soviet Union, the result could be a series of political moves that make Armenia's still-successful foreign policy tightrope walk much more shaky. The last-minute decision to join Russia's

Eurasian Economic Union, for instance, may end up being one such botched move. But public opinion in Armenia isn't likely to change for as long as the economy continues to limp along, and Russia is perceived as the only strong ally Armenia can count on. It is a two-way cycle: the current situation reinforces public views, yet a change in public views will likely have to precede a change in the status quo.

These are realities of which Russia is all but certainly aware, and it tries hard to maintain the public image that it is Armenia's ally. Vladimir Putin and Serzh Sargsyan are said to have a close relationship—it's one that frequently plays out on television screens in Armenia during news broadcasts. Meanwhile, the only other political force with the capital in the region to sway the Armenia-Turkey, Armenia-Azerbaijan, and Armenia-Russia relationships is the United States. But the U.S., while maintaining very good diplomatic relations with Armenia, has more to lose by alienating Turkey, a top military ally at the gate of a Middle East currently in combustion. And so, for now, the scales continue to remain where they are, and the stalemate continues.

Moving Forward

It was mid-August when I left Yerevan, bound for New York. On most days during the summer, the sky is hazy, obscuring the view of Mt. Ararat, the mountain known as the landing place of Noah's Ark, which looms over the entire city. The Biblical mountain figures prominently in Armenian imagery, folk music and literature, and it occupies a leading place in the Armenian nationalist movements of the twentieth century. It is also a daily reminder of the impact of history: before the Armenian Genocide, the land around Mt. Ararat, and six Ottoman provinces to the west of the mountain, was inhabited by Armenians for well over a thousand years. The mountain is a daily reminder of the people, the land, and the historical prominence lost 100 years ago next April. On the morning of the flight, the mountain—and Lesser Ararat, directly adjacent to it—was in clear view. As the plane quickly passed over Armenian airspace, Ararat faded away. All I could think of was how Armenia would seek to come to terms with its history when history never afforded the Armenian people any distance.

2015 may present an opportunity to begin answering that question. The dynamism of Armenian communities around the world will be on display on April 24, 2015, the official day commemorating the Armenian Genocide worldwide. Pope Francis, in addition to the French president, has already pledged to attend, and many more leaders from around the globe have been invited. What will matter more in the long term, however, is whether Turkey, the United States, or other governments with important stakes in the region use the hundredth year since the Genocide as an opportunity to deliver a final answer on the lingering questions. Armenia's presentation will also be of critical importance: Will it present itself as a mature player, keen on having its human rights concerns heard and addressed in the international community, or will it deploy partisan rhetoric that plays directly into the Turkish government's strategy for deflecting claims of culpability? How the commemoration of the Genocide plays out next year may have reverberating consequences for Armenia's current geopolitical alignment.

Armenia must also more aggressively market itself. Despite its internal political sluggishness, it remains one of the safest countries in the region. Violent crime is almost non-existent, and the literacy rate is among the highest in the world. Yerevan is teeming with arts venues, restaurants, and universities, and each summer its streets are packed with tourists, mainly from Russia and other nearby countries. With immense potential for tourism growth if infrastructure around the country is improved, Armenia could be poised for a resource infusion that can put it back on track to becoming an economic hub—just as envisioned by World Bank economists in 2007. Its geographic location, a crossroads of civilizations for thousands of years, could become one of its strongest advantages: Paris, Rome and Vienna are about four hours away via air, while Tel Aviv, Moscow, Dubai and Abu Dhabi are all just three. With an ongoing liberalization of the country's air industry underway, more flight options will be emerging soon. Tourism and proximity to other places certainly aren't enough to completely alter the nation's course, but they may catalyze the beginning of a new era of participation in the global economy—something which Armenians, when given the opportunity in the past, have repeatedly shown they relish.

What Lawrence of Arabia Thought

One of the most interesting documents I unearthed during my summer research was an interview conducted by Lincoln Steffens, the American journalist who would later compile and publish *The Shame of the Cities,* a muckraking sensation detailing the doings of some of America's corrupt urban political machines. His subject for the interview was T.E. Lawrence, the enterprising colonel who fought the Ottoman Empire for the British Army and helped lead the Arab Revolt against Ottoman Rule from 1916 to 1918—the Armenian Genocide, which ended in 1923, was still in progress then. Lawrence would later be immortalized as "Lawrence of Arabia" in the 1962 film.

The interview was conducted in 1919, but was published in 1931 under the title, "Armenians Are Impossible." In it, Lawrence offered his extensive personal thoughts about the Armenian "race." Steffens called the interview the strangest he ever conducted: "[Lawrence] said, for example, that the Armenians were 'the last word in human impossibility.' They correspond, as a race, with 'the last man' in academic debate."

The "last man" Lawrence was referring to would almost certainly have been Friedrich Nietzsche's concept from *Thus Spoke Zarathustra,* the antithesis of the übermensch. He is the evolved man who is weak but is content to be weak, as long as he is comfortable at work and can enjoy his little pleasures: "The earth has become small, and on it hops the Last Man, who makes everything small. His species is ineradicable as the flea; the Last Man lives longest," says Zarathustra. Lawrence, Steffens said, seemed to have an "inexpressible sympathy" for the Armenians that also "gave him a human understanding for the Turks (and all the other near neighbors of the Armenians), who are forever trying to kill off this orphan race." Steffens was bemused, and he pressed Lawrence further, asking him if the solution to the question didn't necessarily require an Armenian state where Armenians would be made "fit to govern themselves...[with] industry, thrift and all the Christian virtues which go into making of good men and good citizens." Selected portions of Lawrence's fascinating reply are reproduced here:

> "There's no lack of thrift in the Armenians," he said dryly, "and, of course, you know that they are Christians, arch Christians?" ... "Armenians won't work," he said. "That is the trouble with your plan and that is the trouble with the Armenians. That is the trouble, really, with all these old races that have been civilized, learned the game and, having once dominated the world and worked it, have lost control, gone back, as you say; or, as I say, carried on. They have gone forward logically, psychologically, physiologically. They do not care for hard labor... But these forward peoples, the ex-civilized nations—they are not lazy. They are too intelligent to work for others. They are exploiters themselves, instinctive, inbred, incorrigible, hopeless... The living among the old races here are the survivors of a civilization, commercial in character, like yours... The modern representatives...are the inevitable, natural products of artificial selection of an order of society which imprisons the courageous, deports the original, depresses the mass, discourages any sort of

> variation from the average of the species and preserves the meek, mean, sly, shrewd and thrifty. For these are the commercially fit."

Lawrence continued, later on, to arrive at the conclusion supporting his "last man" theory: "The Armenians are the most intelligent, the most perfectly selected, the most highly developed race in the world—from the civilized point of view."

Steffens, the American journalist, must have been left speechless. It certainly wasn't a flattering account, and it didn't exactly portend good things for the future of the Armenian "race." In 2014, most modern sensibilities would probably find the liberties Lawrence takes in his description, rife with stereotype and caricature, rightly offensive.

And yet, Armenia seems to currently be living the implications of more than a few of Lawrence of Arabia's outlandish-sounding generalizations. As Armenia continues to swerve, employing skill and cunning to avoid being pinned down in the midst of a very unfavorable terrain, the largest question looms: Is survival Armenia's only grand strategy? Or does this "last man" of history have a fresh game of chess left in him yet?

THE ARMENIAN GENOCIDE CONTINUES

(*Yale Daily News, April 24, 2015*)

ON TUESDAY, 93-YEAR-OLD former SS member Oskar Gröning entered a German courtroom to face charges for his involvement in the greatest atrocity in history. He was complicit, prosecutors say, in the mass murder of Jews at Auschwitz-Birkenau in 1944.

For years, German prosecutors refused to try cases like Gröning's, saying the link to the atrocities was too tenuous. Not anymore.

One hundred years ago today—April 24, 1915—Ottoman Turkish authorities rounded up and executed 250 Armenian intellectuals and community leaders in Istanbul. They were the first victims among the 1.5 million Armenians who would subsequently be marched to their deaths in the murders and "deportations" that constituted the Armenian Genocide. In 1915, there were 2 million Armenians living across Ottoman Turkey. By the 1920s, less than 500,000 remained. Cities across Anatolia became ghost towns. Valleys were filled with corpses and bones. Today in these regions, local inhabitants can describe what happened. They will point you to "cursed ravines" they still avoid during their daily commutes.

These villagers, plus a handful of brave Turkish and Armenian journalists and activists, are perhaps the only people who will tell you what occurred. The Turkish government won't. In fact, saying the words "Armenian Genocide" can get you put in jail—or worse, killed at gunpoint. Not only does Turkey refuse to recognize what happened in 1915, but it also does its best to prevent other governments, including ours, from doing the same. When the Pope used the words "Armenian Genocide" last week, Turkey was furious. On Wednesday, Ankara prevented Bosnian politician Milorad Dodik from flying over Turkish airspace to personally offer his condolences at the Armenian Genocide Memorial in Yerevan, Armenia's capital.

Read any op-ed or historical account of the Armenian Genocide, and much of what's been mentioned here will almost certainly come up. But I'd like to argue something more: that the Armenian Genocide continues today. Historians, who are virtually unanimously in agreement about what happened, often call denial the "last stage" of genocide. In this case, it manifests itself in many ways. A few years ago, Turkey's president, Recep Tayyip Erdogan, threatened to "deport" the remaining Armenian citizens in Turkey. Last year, he called "allegations" that he had Armenian blood "ugly," insisting he was a "purebred Turk."

But there's something even more painful than outright racism from the leader of almost 80 million people. It's that today's Turkish citizens largely don't know what happened, because their government forbids the unfiltered teaching of history. I remember the first time I brought up the Genocide to a Turkish friend: she looked at me, staring blankly. She had no idea.

Armenia is a tiny country today because of the Genocide. At my Armenian church, I often still hear the names of cities from which survivors came: Erzurum, Van, Kharpert, Diyarbakir, Bitlis, Sebastia. The survivors and their children are old now, and many will take their memories with them when they die. They, and those who couldn't escape, were the "others" who had to disappear for modern Turkish political and cultural identity to be forged in the aftermath of World War I. It is an identity that leaves little room for minorities to this day, whether Armenian, Jewish or Kurdish—whose collective lineages are often repressed.

Turkey claims that, in the fog of war during World War I, Armenians and Turks suffered equally. It's a criminally ignorant false equivalence: Raphael Lemkin, the Polish-Jewish jurist who coined the term "genocide" in 1943, cited the Armenian case as the first example.

Four years earlier, as Adolf Hitler readied Germany for the ghastly extermination campaigns that were soon to begin, he assured Nazi party members of success: "Who, after all, speaks today of the annihilation of the Armenians?" he said. The Genocide has been a template for war criminals ever since.

Genocide denial is, as Stefan Ihrig recently wrote in the Huffington Post, "brutalizing the world," emboldening the enemies of humanity everywhere and making true reconciliation impossible: How do you mourn the dead and find forgiveness when the victims, deniers insist, never existed? And denial is also brutalizing the

Armenian psyche, which cannot get beyond distrust, paranoia and revulsion towards Turkey.

"Personally, I don't feel vengeance," Auschwitz survivor Hedy Bohm said of Gröning on Tuesday. "I don't want to see him go to jail. It's too late for it, he's too old. I'm just hoping that the law...will come to the judgment that he was guilty." Another survivor, Eva Fahidi, said the trial "is one of the most important events in my life."

Today, Armenian genocide remembrance day is about mourning and prayer. At 6:30 p.m., the Yale community will gather at Beinecke Plaza to remember those senselessly killed for the crime of being Armenian. But today, unfortunately, cannot be about reconciliation and healing. There can be no definitive healing until denial ends. When it does, the Armenian Genocide will finally be over.

COLUMBIA LAW SCHOOL, PERSONAL STATEMENT

(Spring of 2016)

"So ARE YOU happy or sad about finding a job?" asks a wide-eyed twelve-year-old, staring as we sit across from each other in my grandfather's old flat. I have just finished trying to explain what my work as a paralegal at the New York District Attorney's office, beginning in a month, will entail. Whether he was listening is unclear.

It is the summer of 2015 and we are in Yerevan, the capital of Armenia. The apartment would have been our home if my ambitious mother had not decided—at 36 and in the middle of a medical career—to drop everything and move to America.

"Why would I be sad?" I reply, wanting to understand why that registered as a possibility.

"Here," he begins to explain knowingly, "working as a lawyer's assistant means coming to work late and waiting for your boss to arrive. When he does, you light his cigarette, bring him coffee, and sit around all day until 5pm." He looks down before adding, "I never want a job."

This response from the lips of a twelve-year-old leaves me speechless. The Major Economic Crimes Bureau at the District Attorney's office offered a way to develop insight into how international and domestic financial crimes are prosecuted, by interacting with prosecutors directly. The position lay at the nexus of my academic passions: foreign affairs, jurisprudence, and the influence of law on society. At the bureau, my portfolio included international money laundering, securities fraud, and corporate theft cases. In law school, I anticipate researching the sociohistorical roots of Western states' disparate treatment of people from different economic and racial backgrounds—particularly in regard to federal aid, prosecution, and sentencing. After completing my studies, I hope to bring a deeper understanding of these inequalities into use in the practice of human rights law and diplomacy, whether this means pursuing criminal justice reform at home or helping to sway foreign policy in the interests of those displaced by war, labor exploitation, or environmental abuse. But all this is hardly a compelling answer for someone whose only conception of a "major economic crime" has come from his father's complaints that the country's president is shaking down the national treasury. Nor does Aram, my cousin, want to go to school. But he isn't to blame. He has already internalized what his father, relatives, and friends think and say every day: There's no point in trying here. Across the country, unemployment is high, and the corruption index rating is higher. But cynicism is astronomical. Nearly everyone has a theory to explain the present woes, but as soon as the conversation turns to solutions, talk ends abruptly. And as soon as you admit, in Armenian, that you are from America, a common refrain follows: Can you help get me a visa?

In the time I have spent in Yerevan, leading service projects with a foundation connecting students to their familial homeland through development missions for underserved communities, I have often found myself struggling to shake off an acute sense of loss, coupled with a nagging guilt. Each time I leave, I feel I ought to stay, and be part of both the joys and the hardships of Armenian life. This sense of partial exile—from my roots, from what could have been—follows me home every time, despite the opportunities this very privation has created.

And yet, those opportunities are what have enabled me to see a way beyond both stagnation and cynicism. Leaving behind high school student council meetings, I graduated to Yale Political Union debates and discussions, where each week was an exploration into privilege, into justice, into truth, into why. I sought to provide proactive answers whenever I found positive means of doing so: I helped reformulate Yale's approach to the ongoing issue of sexual assault on campus by working to streamline the anonymous reporting process; I became a weekly suicide hotline counselor through a nonprofit supporting LGBT young people in crisis. As in high school, I remained eager to lead and to inspire action in others: I was elected to run the Yale Political Union, one of the largest organizations on campus, as its Speaker my junior year, and I was chosen to mentor students as a Freshman Counselor my senior year. But Yale, as much through tortuous debates and real 3 a.m. crisis calls as through lectures and seminars in two rigorous majors, also refined the nature of my intellectual questioning. This is exactly why I hope to attend Columbia Law School next fall: to continue to ask and, when I can, to answer; to face the difficulty of truth inside and outside of the classroom; and to be able to confront, bearing all the hope that I can carry, whomever demands to know why they ought to try, with eyes wide open.

OXFORD UNIVERSITY, ARMENIAN CLASSICAL STUDIES MASTER'S PROGRAM, PERSONAL STATEMENT

(May of 2016)

EYES FIXED ON the characters just above the altar, I squint—as if the problem is merely one of poor vision, instead of comprehension. One letter appears to be an elongated English "r." This realization triggers photographic memories of a chalkboard from years ago, on which the Armenian equivalents of "a" and "b" are scrawled in the Sunday school teacher's elegant handwriting. I scan the chalkboard in my mind ferociously for more letters, but they are not there. Three letters. Not even enough to piece together a word.

This was a recurring predicament until only three years ago. I had heard and spoken fluent Eastern Armenian at home all my life, but remained illiterate in the language until my junior year at Yale University, when—in between classes, or for a few minutes each night before sleep—I began to teach myself written Armenian. Around this time, I also began serving as an acolyte in the Armenian Church parish of my youth, lighting a slow-burning yet increasingly indefatigable desire to unlock the meanings of the sung *sharagans* beyond the unconvincing English translations. And yet this sung language, classical Armenian, was doubly mysterious: not only was the script incomprehensible, but most of the words were, too. The chasm between modern Italian and ecclesiastical Latin serves as a useful, if rather imperfect, analogy. Yet at the time, the chasm between my Armenian and that of the church deacons' felt just as large, if not larger. But the determination to grasp this almost foreign-sounding tongue—and with it, the keys to the medieval world of the Bagratid Kingdom, of Vaspurakan, of

Queen Melisende of Jerusalem, of the Hethumids and Cilician Armenia on the shores of the Mediterranean—had already been firmly established.

Armenian youths are told since infancy that they belong to a civilization that has survived amidst invasions, wars, and genocide. They are told of the masters who produced the highest forms of Armenian intellectual expression in art, music, philosophy, literature, and theology. But, unfortunately, few young people in the diaspora have the tools with which to access much of these treasures. As I swung the thurible on the altar over two years ago, I resolved that I would not live this privation. I would find a way to properly claim my cultural inheritance.

Two years, two trips to Armenia, and one pilgrimage to the Armenian Quarter of Jerusalem later, my Armenian reading and writing skills in both the eastern and western dialects have improved dramatically. I read daily to continue progression in spelling and the pace of reading. I now seek to develop a stronger comprehension of classical Armenian grammar and syntax, beyond solely the Divine Liturgy of the Armenian Church, on which I continue to work. I am particularly interested in forming a deeper bond with the mystical "Book of Lamentations" and the broader works of St. Gregory of Narek, the 10th century Armenian saint who in 2015 was made a "Doctor of the Universal Church" by Pope Francis, joining thirty-five others throughout time and becoming the first non-Catholic to receive the title. There is a dearth of accessible literature on St. Gregory in the West, and I hope to become one of the rising scholars who might fill the void in a time of renewed interest in the value of St. Gregory's writings. I am also interested in advanced research into the political and religious activities of Cilician Kings Hethum II and Leo IV, especially in relation to efforts aimed at the reunification of the Armenian Apostolic and Roman Catholic churches during and after the Crusades, and the nature of the religious and political resistance they encountered.

Though I remain undecided as yet regarding whether to pursue doctoral research, the Master of Studies curriculum in Classical Armenian Studies at Oxford would form the backbone for all future academic or lay work in this field—and would certainly inform my decision about how to move forward. With its emphasis on formal training in classical Armenian grammar, followed by studies of homiletic, polemical, and historical literature and verse from the 5th to 14th centuries, the program offers a curriculum which is both focused on developing written language skills and expansive in its literary reach. I am particularly motivated by the opportunities for specialization in areas of unique interest to graduate students. I am also keen on delving into the first core course and simultaneously attending Oriental Institute colloquia on the Near East, to better historically situate Armenia amongst its Byzantine, Mongol, and Mamluk rivals. This upcoming academic year stands as likely the only occasion I will encounter to engage in this kind of work, as I currently plan to enroll in law school in the United States in the autumn of 2017. The opportunity to pursue the Master of Studies degree in Classical Armenian Studies at Oxford would be the fulfillment of a passion many years in the making. That the program is perfectly suited temporally and substantively to my research interests, and that it would allow for instruction from world-renowned experts in Armenian literature and religious texts, including the work of Grigor Magistros, serves only to further broader its tremendous appeal.

As an undergraduate at Yale double majoring in History and Ethics, Politics, and Economics (EP&E), my research interests in local religious ritual in the early modern English period and in the comparative study of the treaties of Machiavelli and Locke both demanded sustained efforts in close reading, as well as textual analysis. The process of uncovering and drawing new connections throughout the source material, together with an openness to the divergent paths in which analysis could lead, formed the very heart of my liberal undergraduate education. I synthesized and defended academic arguments in a variety of courses and subject areas. I anticipate these methods will once again be useful for the study of classical Armenian texts, particularly when a degree of familiarity with the texts to be examined in depth is reached. I am eager to once again rigorously engage texts in this way, as I am confident that the skills and knowledge acquired will be of great utility in any field of further graduate study; moreover, this time spent immersed in the Armenian language at Oxford would constitute an unprecedented step forward in my continuing academic (and self) discovery.

AN ARMENIAN PILGRIM IN JERUSALEM

(*Armenian Church Newsletter of the UK and Ireland, Issue 32, November 18, 2016*)

TALK GIVEN BY JOHN AROUTIOUNIAN, A STUDENT AT THE UNIVERSITY OF OXFORD, AT THE GALA FUNDRAISING DINNER FOR THE RESTORATION OF THE TOMB, CHURCH OF THE HOLY SEPULCHRE

FOR ALL OF us there are memories, once seared into our beings, which never depart. For me, one such memory begins on a hot summer day in Jerusalem's Old City, on a winding road opposite King David's Tower—a sweltering sea of hijabs, yarmulkes, burqas, and Franciscan habits. Of ultra-orthodox yeshiva students ducking into the Jewish Quarter, a pair of nuns rushing to make Mass, an imam taking a pause to wipe the sweat off his brow, an Israeli soldier gazing out from Jaffa Gate, machine gun in hand. And then, in this concentrated cesspool of devotion, of hate, of love, of distrust, of power, of sin and holiness, coming down the winding road is an Armenian Apostolic vardabed, in black robes, instantly noticeable by virtue of the distinctive head covering and the Armenian cross hanging around his neck. He is walking up through the crowd, and many heads turn to follow his gait. He is rushing from the Armenian Quarter, the ancient home of Armenian religious and pilgrims in the Holy Land, to the Church of the Holy Sepulchre, our Lord Jesus Christ's tomb, which Armenians co-administer along with, principally, the Catholic and Greek Orthodox Church. It is time for the weekly Armenian procession at the Holy Sepulchre, as it was the week before and every Sunday before that since time immemorial. I see all this and I think, as I frequently do now each time the memory returns: How did the Armenians survive here?

The answer, of course, is precisely how they survived everywhere else. But in this place—the most hotly contested stretch of land in the world, and the site of the ministry, suffering, death, and resurrection of the son of God—this question takes on a metaphysical significance.

Why has God, through their unspeakable tragedies and loss, continued to favor the Armenian people and Church, particularly at the sites of his only-begotten Son's life journey? A people so small, so scattered, so alone compared with the other mighty forces wrestling for control of this land.

It is a question as mysterious, it often seems, as others surrounding God's various choices—of the weak man Peter to be his disciple, or of the relatively unimportant Jewish tribe to be the bearers of His covenant in the Old Testament. Perhaps it has something to do with Armenia's unique history as a Christian people, an identity formed by the holy and sacred Armenian language, whose script was created by the fathers of the Church, by Armenian architecture and literature—indeed, all the highest forms of Armenian intellectual expression, which found their manifestations through service to God. And, of course, by the Armenian Genocide, the crucifixion and resurrection of an entire people and culture.

An excerpt from Isaiah 53 reads,

> Yet it was the will of the Lord to crush him with pain.
>
> When you make his life an offering for sin, he shall see his offspring, and shall prolong his days; through him the will of the Lord shall prosper.
>
> Out of his anguish he shall see light; he shall find satisfaction through his knowledge.
>
> The righteous one, my servant, shall make many righteous, and he shall bear their iniquities.
>
> Therefore I will allot him a portion with the great, and he shall divide the spoil with the strong; because he poured out himself to death, and was numbered with the transgressors; yet he bore the sin of many, and made intercession for the transgressors.

In the Jewish tradition, this image of the Suffering Servant is understood as the nation of Israel. In the Christian, as the figure of Jesus. Both are correct. But it is hard to read Isaiah 53 and to not also see a reflection of the Armenian nation, a Christian people spread around the world to be a "light to the nations," and to intercede for the world: "to be my salvation to the ends of the Earth." My pilgrimage to 2014, with a devoted group of student from the Armenian Church in America under Rev. Fr. Daniel Findikyan, opened my eyes to the reality that the trials of the world's oldest Christian people give us a special responsibility to stand up for the dignity of man and proclaim God's name to all we encounter. Perhaps this universal mission is why Armenians survive, and why they've survived in this of all places—Jerusalem.

My two weeks living in the Armenian Quarter, attending daily prayer and visiting places like Bethlehem, the garden of

Gethsemane, the Mount of Olives, and so many others convinced me that this is a trip every Armenian should feel obliged to take at least once in life. For Jerusalem is our Holy City in a way no other Christian people can claim—because through suffering and martyrdom of a brutality perhaps no other Christian peoples have ever seen, the Armenians are still there in the one and only Jerusalem, described so beautifully in one of the most haunting of hymns, from the Requiem Service of the Armenian Church:

> Ee vereenun Yerusaghem, ee pnagaranes hreshdagats, oor Yenovk yev Yegheeas gan dzeratsyal aghavnagerb eetrakhdeen.
>
> In the supernal Jerusalem, in the dwellings of the angels, where the prophets Enoch and Elijah live old in age like doves.

And one last thing—if you're blessed to have the privilege to make this pilgrimage, may I suggest that you choose to stay in the Armenian Quarter. The rooms are small and cramped, and there is no full-service hotel breakfast. But your path will more closely resemble the one taken by our ancestors over the centuries, who trekked from Cilicia, Van, and Ani just to see Jerusalem before they died. And you will be helping to ensure the Armenian footprint and bond with supernal Jerusalem—a bond virtually as old as the Christian story of Christ emerging from the tomb we are here to help restore tonight, endures forever.

DOLORES ZOHRAB LIEBMANN FELLOWSHIP APPLICATION, COLUMBIA LAW SCHOOL, STATEMENT OF PURPOSE

(November 2017)

I CLEARLY REMEMBER the afternoon in early 2016 when, sitting in the director's office of the Krikor and Clara Zohrab Information Center on 34th Street in New York, I laid out the plan. In a few months' time, I would begin a Master's program in Classical Armenian Studies at the University of Oxford, in order to improve my command of Armenian language and history. Upon completion, I would return home to undertake law school. Columbia, with its rigorous global bent, was my first choice. There, I would delve into international human rights law, arbitration, and diplomacy studies, with a focus on the nascent legal and civic institutions of Eastern Europe—as it continues emerging from the Soviet shadow and integrating with a globalized world. From here, I would return to Europe for practical experience in Armenia, to be followed by a combination of graduate work in international relations at Geneva's Graduate Institute and the completion of the doctoral research begun at Oxford. I would then plunge headfirst into a career working in consultancy and diplomacy, helping to bridge the gaping chasms between the United States and Eastern Europe, with particular regard to developing Armenia and other struggling nations requiring conduits to raise awareness in the West and put them on the agenda in capitals like Washington and Brussels.

Professor Daniel Findikyan—a personal mentor, priest, and Director of the Zohrab Information Center—listened intently to the ambitious plan. He then showed me some of the center's new acquisitions, established by Dolores Zohrab Liebmann in honor of her parents to serve as a hub for Armenian intellectual life in New York. As always, he promised to pray for me, and to support me as best he could.

Almost two years later, the plan remains on track. I am in the midst of my first semester at Columbia Law School, having returned in August from Oxford with the Master's degree. I will soon be pursuing opportunities at the United Nations and various courts of arbitration in Europe for the summer of 2018, with an eye toward further solidifying and developing language skills in Spanish, Russian, and French for effective cross-cultural legal work. This, together with coursework at Columbia increasingly shifting toward the study of the institutions of international law after the first year, will facilitate both future graduate studies and professional goals.

Whether the plan will remain on track, however, is increasingly in doubt. What I had failed to fully consider, long before the fateful conversation with Professor Findikyan, was how the funds for the preparation I was seeking would materialize. A mix of scholarships and my parents' savings saw me through five years at Yale and Oxford. Neither resource proved forthcoming for law school. The indefatigable, if sometimes foolhardy, Armenian spirit coursing through my veins determined this would be no obstacle, and I applied for federal loans to cover the entirety of Columbia Law's tuition. As I write this in November, however, after receiving the statement for the loans' first installment, and after multiple friends questioned my sanity for taking out over $200,000 in student debt, I am more uncertain than ever that there is a viable path for the career I had once sketched out.

None of this is to say, of course, that I intend to do anything other than forge ahead. But reality is set to interfere in the near future. My intent was to work at Armenia's Constitutional Court, or one of several civil society organizations, in 2019, and to transition into the final steps of my academic program in Geneva and

Oxford in 2020. Given, however, that the student debt will begin to be payable immediately upon graduation, and that deferment will only further hamper a career in international public interest work in the future, I will almost certainly have to enter the corporate legal services sector in 2019, and to stay for quite a few years after graduation. My hope would then be to pursue the remainder of my graduate study and enter the human rights field through international consultancy work, likely more than a decade later than I had planned.

It was electrifying to receive word of the Dolores Zohrab Liebmann Fellowship, because it presented a rare and incredibly exciting chance to rekindle my aspirations, and to reimagine a career in which I would not have to wait upward of a decade to begin having the kind of impact which I hope will define my life. The stipend included in the fellowship would allow me to engage in advanced research, during the academic year and especially during the summers. With knowledge of her family's history, steeped in the Armenian Genocide and the drive to overcome obstacles, and with Ms. Zohrab Liebmann's personal desire to see her generosity benefit those whose academic and professional trajectories hold promise, I am deeply moved by the prospect of applying to the fellowship she established.

I have endeavored to provide a frank and clear-eyed account of my work, my goals, and the very tangible and dramatic way in which the honor of being named a Dolores Zohrab Liebmann Fellow would reverberate across my path in law, academia, and public service. Through my time in high school in Kentucky, when I campaigned successfully to have the governor recognize the Armenian Genocide in one of the last remaining states yet to do so, to my years at Yale, when I undertook a rigorous course of study in two majors alongside a full roster of extracurricular leadership activities, to the present day, I have labored to realize seemingly untenable goals, and to channel my drive into action. If given this immensely meaningful opportunity, I would emerge with the tools for a lifetime of service.

[Editor's Note: *John received this fellowship for full tuition at Columbia Law School, the first-ever Law School student to receive such an award.*]

ISRAEL ORI INSTITUTE:
DEFINING STRATEGIC OBJECTIVES FOR ARMENIA'S FUTURE & REGIONAL SECURITY

May 19, 2018

The Very Reverend Fr. Daniel Findikyan
Primate Armenian Church of America, Eastern Diocese
630 Second Avenue, New York, NY 10016

DEAR FR. FINDIKYAN:

In 1704, Israel Ori—a pioneer of the Armenian national movement, born of noble stock in Armenia's rugged Syunik region—arrived in Rome to petition Pope Clement XI to adopt an ambitious plan for the liberation of Armenia from Ottoman and Persian rule. This was neither the first nor the last of his efforts: over several decades, Ori tirelessly lobbied royal courts throughout Europe and Russia, including that of Holy Roman Emperor Leopold I, French King Louis XIV, and Russian Emperor Peter the Great to assist in the cause of Armenian liberation. He obtained promises, and little else, for his "Armenia Plan," but his lifelong efforts inspired another visionary, Joseph Emin, and scores of future heroes. In 1991, for the first time since the fall of the Armenian Kingdom of Cilicia in 1375, Ori's dream was finally achieved.

A quarter century after independence, Armenia stands at a crossroads. In the last few weeks and months, the Armenian nation has stumbled upon a newfound, remarkable sense of hope, but the challenges remain enormous: endemic corruption in politics and business, grossly insufficient infrastructure, poor healthcare and life expectancy, dangerously low birthrates, few educational opportunities for Armenians outside the capital, and—most importantly—the Nagorno-Karabakh conflict and the ongoing security threat from totalitarian Azerbaijan and denialist Turkey. All this Armenia must grapple with on a daily basis, with dormant concerns involving Iran, Russia, the greater Middle East, the United States, and two competing unions, the Eurasian Economic Union and the European Union, constantly lurking at a stone's throw.

With the dawn of a new era in Armenian civic dialogue, the need is more acute than ever for a sober, comprehensive conversation involving the entire Armenian nation, in Armenia and across the diaspora, alongside those individuals and regional players with an interest in regional security and lasting peace. It is time for a new "Armenia Plan" that encompasses the entire region's dreams for stability, prosperity, and coexistence. This is the mission of the Israel Ori Institute: to provide a forum for a new conversation between various perspectives, individuals, and institutional actors. No view will be excluded from publication, whether from current or former members of government, partisans, clergy, academics, activists, journalists, nonprofit organizers, or individuals, Armenian or otherwise. The Institute espouses no ideology or affiliation with any party, government, or group. Its sole interest is the continued development of the Armenian nation along peaceful, democratic lines that serves as an example for both East and West. There will be three central eligibility criteria for publication in IOI media: rigorous research, civility in discourse, and an earnest desire to engage in dialogue and debate with fellow contributors. A call for the initial round of contributions to the website will be forthcoming in the weeks ahead.

IOI intends first and foremost to initiate a conversation accessible to all interested parties. But the project does not end there. IOI will seek to encourage conversation which:

- **Shines a light** on strategic issues often neglected in mainstream conversation, including infrastructure priorities like the North-South Highway and adjacent rail corridor, economic needs including access to credit and living wages, energy issues including the Metsamor Nuclear Plant and Armenia's hydroelectric potential, quality of life concerns including access to education, healthcare, and pensions, environmental stewardship, tourism development, and social issues;

- **Bridges the gap** between priorities in the Republic of Armenia and the diaspora, including language preservation and other challenges in countries including Lebanon, Iran, Syria, Turkey, Egypt, Georgia, Israel, Russia, Argentina, and Australia, as well as in Europe and North America;

- **Engages and educates youth** to develop an interest in and relationship with Armenia's future;

- **Raises awareness of the Nagorno-Karabakh conflict** and encourages critical thinking about how long-term peace can be established between Armenia, Artsakh, and Azerbaijan;

- **Probes novel ways** of addressing the injustice of the Armenian Genocide, and encouraging true democratic reform in Turkey and the rest of Armenia's neighbors;

- **Presses** international organizations, including the OSCE, and governments with a stake in the region to take a more active role in the region, and **creates a running dialogue** with policymakers in the Republic of Armenia.

The objective underlying each priority aforementioned is to more clearly define Armenia's strategic objectives as a nation eager to broker peace, enact twenty-first century reforms, and be a constructive member of the community of nations. IOI intends to be a think tank that helps to define theses strategic objectives, for use by members of governments, NGOs, and interested citizens and observers. Only by defining national priorities can progress be effectively measured and made in securing Armenia's future.

Fr. Findikyan, we write today to ask for your participation in this new mission as a founding member of the Israel Ori Institute's Board of Directors. The first engagement in which your presence will be requested will be IOI's weekend conference in New York in Fall 2018 entitled, "Reimaging Relevance: The Role of the Diaspora in 21st Century Armenia," during which the Board will meet for the first time. In the future, the Board will meet one to two times a year, and on an as-needed basis as it develops a global network of contributors and secures adequate resources to conduct its essential operations. We welcome any questions prior to your decision. We kindly ask that you inform IOI of your intent by June 2018.

We stand at the forefront of incredible developments in a globalized and interconnected world. We have already seen the potential of the revolutions in communication and organization actualized in movements across the planet. These changes, if harnessed correctly, have the impact to radically improve lives for billions. Armenia, with a population of 3 million and a diaspora of 8 million, must not let such an opportunity to strengthen and safeguard the future go to waste. We have an urgent mission to reengage Armenians and interested parties everywhere to define twenty-first objectives for a peaceful and prosperous future in the Caucasus and beyond.

We hope you will join us.

Yours sincerely,

John Aroutiounian, Executive Director

Israel Ori Institute—275 West 96th Street—New York, New York 10025

[Editor's Note: *Similar letters were also addressed to a number of other prominent Armenian-American intellectuals.*]

CHAPTER V

From the Depths of the Heart

Personal Letters & Communication

LETTER TO ABBY CAVE

(June of 2010)

Dear Abby,

It has been such an honor to spend the past 5 months getting to know someone so hardworking, so ethical, and so committed to her principles and beliefs. It has been so refreshing and uplifting, and I just need to take this opportunity to tell you how grateful I am for having received it.

Abby, you are a pillar of great strength. You held up our shift, and your insistence on responsibility is something I truly admire.

You are fun to be around, you are funny, you are witty. You make me smile when I need it most, and you are there to listen to a joke when I need it most.

Never exchange your morals for anything, Abby. I expect a great Republican Senator out of you! Always keep fighting and believing in your faith in God, your principles, and your ethics. You have, by your strength, strengthened my belief in these things.

And never feel like you can't talk when you'd like to. My ears and heart are always open, and I hope and pray we'll see each other soon.

Love,
John

LETTERS TO QUINTON CANNON (EXCERPTS)

New Year's Day, 2011

... I ALSO hope and pray that this is a good year for the world, and that 2011 will see a stop to the horrors of the past and a rebirth of love, empathy, and understanding. I hope 2011 ushers in a new era of God and Christian love around the world.

But I would be lying to you and to myself if I said I didn't have doubts, Quinton. Just this week—I'm sure you've heard—saw more violence and tragedy in America and around the world. A Congresswoman was shot by a lunatic. Churches were bombed. It all weighs so heavily—in addition to other wants—on my soul. I don't know what to think. This Christmas, I listened to Simon & Garfunkel's "Silent Night" a lot. It's one of my favorites. Thank you for giving me those songs, Quinny. Anyway, the song made me think of our current situation. The tumultuous '60s radio broadcast playing in the background is so much like what's going on today I suppose all we can do is hope and pray continually for a kinder, gentler world, and enjoy peace and serenity with friends and family. And always count our blessings.

September 16, 2012:

… Only a month, and I miss you so much already! As I write, I can only imagine the many new experiences you've already had and the innumerable others waiting for you in the two years upcoming. Living our lives in service to Christ is the utmost calling, and I simply can't wait to hear about them upon your return (and visit to Yale!).

I'm very anxious to hear about how your transition thus far has been and how the people you've met thus far are. On my end, the days are passing at a ferocious, unforgiving pace. Esther visited me over Labor Day weekend, which was a wonderful reprieve from my unrelentingly busy schedule and a great opportunity to reconnect.

In the maddening pace of things, I find my only solace in culture and faith—don't know where I would be otherwise. Sophomore year is truly the time to dig in—both academically and socially—in the stratified microcosm of society that is Yale. You're only afforded two to three years to figure your life out. What a frivolous, absurd society it is in which we live!

Now, more than ever, is a time to hold on to the source of meaning in life: faith, family, culture. I don't know how much news you hear, but American society (and the world at large) is in such disarray, Quinton. To have the strength to hold on now, and to keep the heart safe from the inhumanity the modern world wishes to impose upon the heart and soul, is each individual's greatest undertaking (in terms of difficulty).

I hope things are going really well, Quinny. I can't wait to hear from you. Keep wandering with your open heart and never lose faith—after all, as a dear friend once quoted for me, to wander is not necessarily to be lost (a paraphrase, but the point remains…). And, as always, lean on me any conceivable time I can be of help.

LETTER TO ANNA GHNOULY

(*April 15, 2011*)

THIS IS DIFFICULT from the onset, because I know that regardless of how much I say, so much will remain unsaid. But I suppose I should still try.

As I sit here on the beach, I realize that not a day has gone by since I last saw everyone that you, Quinny, or a select few other people haven't been the subject of my thoughts for at least several minutes each day. This is testament to the fact, I believe, that you have made an incredible mark on me that will never be erased.

It goes without saying, but you are one of the most remarkable people I have ever met in my life, Anna. And believe me when I say I haven't met that many. Your intellect, maturity, humor, kindness, good-naturedness, and humility amaze me. Regardless of how much your humble self refuses to acknowledge it, you're incredibly special and unique.

To find someone who is genuinely interested in pursuing more than the shallow satisfaction of life that so many are content with made me believe again in values that I always thought were right but that I had long lost faith in. Had you not come along, I doubt whether I could continue believing those things.

Anna, your ability to make those around you feel happy and appreciated is truly unprecedented. This is an ability and mark of your character that I cannot say how much I admire.

As I told Quinny, I spent my whole life waiting for friends who knew no boundaries of friendship—friends who I could trust like a brother or sister. At a time when I had already shelved my hope of finding such people, you and Quinton came along and changed my life. And I am more grateful for it than you will ever know.

I spent quite a few days, as the Page Program began to come to a close, crying out of a deep fear and sadness that I would never again get to experience the love and connection that I feel we shared. But now I am convinced that we will, while perhaps not under the same set of circumstances, continue holding on to our bond and taking every opportunity possible to meet. Starting with California and Utah this summer which I am determined to make happen. And a trip to Nantucket is also in order—when, I don't know. But I know that it will happen. I know you don't like the phrase "new change," and I don't either. But Anna, please never lose your determination to find the truth, no matter how hard it gets sometimes. You are incredibly strong-willed and hardworking, and I know you don't need me telling you that. I do it selfishly, because I know that if you lose that, I surely, won't be able to stand my ground much longer.

I want you to know how honored and touched I felt to have earned part of your trust, knowing how hard it must have been to let yourself do that. This alone was more genuinely gratifying and humbling than anything anyone could have done or said. What I felt between the three of us in Washington was unlike anything I've felt before in my life, and I am more thankful to you two than I could ever hope to say or write.

Know that you deserve only the best, in friendship, companionship, and life in general. Settling for anything less would be doing yourself injustice! And if I've played even a very small part in being the kind of friend that you deserve, I'm already extremely honored.

I hope this letter conveys at least a fraction of how much I value your friendship and how lucky I consider myself for having met someone like you. I hope I didn't sound too Patrick Montgomery-esque, a style I hate but so often find myself doing!

Can't wait to get home, open my mailbox, and read your letter! The time here in Florida has been wonderful, and has really given me a chance to—first of all—rest, but to also reflect and spend some time contemplating all that has happened and all that's to happen still.

I love you, miss you, and can't wait to see you the first chance we get.

At the risk of losing originality, seeing this was how I ended Quinny's letter, I will say simply thank you—Thank you for changing my life.

Love,
John

BIRTHDAY CARD TO BRITTANY GUNN (EXCERPTS)

(*May 16, 2011*)

... Brit-Brit, Happy Birthday!

We grew up so fast, didn't we?!

Just wants to put in words (though that's not really possible) how much I love you and wish that you have a wonderful birthday today and all year round.

You exemplify Mother Teresa's quote—and I am so happy and so lucky that I get to share your 18th with you, as we become adults (doesn't feel like it yet, though).

...You are, hands down, the absolutely best there is and deserve the greatest of birthdays. Good luck with all the performances this month, and Brit-Brit, always stay true to the amazing person that you are!

Sending all my love,
Johnny

TEXT COMMUNICATION TO STEPHANIE NEVEL-ALEJO (EXCERPTS)

Early 2011

... STEPHANIE, SCHOOL is so horrible it's beyond words. I got so fed up with AP bio that I dropped it; I'm now a teacher's aid that hour! (haha). I've reduced my school day to literally 3 classes... and it STILL feels like I'm there all day. I can't wait for May to graduate!! And, for that matter, MARCH for GAGA!!!!

Mid 2011

... THANK YOU so much for the sweet message. Everything is going well, just graduated last weekend (thank Almighty GOD) and am absolutely loving the 98 degree humid summer weather after a springtime of depressing rain and cold—I think the weekend you all were here was the only good weather I remember in KY this year up until this week—but then again, that could be because it was a highlight of the year in general! So I'm spending a lot of time at the pool this week and we leave for Florida on Saturday, so I'm looking forward to returning completely bronze!

Mid 2012

... STEPHANIE!! YALE round 2 is good, but hectic already—as evidenced by my 3am reply lol. Classes are keeping me up, but mostly because I'm prioritizing extracurriculars and keeping work until the end.

Where have all the study habits gone??

... I applaud you for getting out of the comp sci class. Who needs that s**t, anyway?? I'm taking 3 history courses this term lol. And Italian. Can't wait for all the job offers when I graduateeee!

Mid 2014

... THINGS ARE (finally) settling down a bit! The semester officially ended on the 8th with the submission of my last final paper lol...were quite the brutal few months. Took more classes than I'd ever taken before, including the notorious intermediate Microeconomics (rumored to be one of Yale's hardest...for humanities student like me, at least!). But I feel much better now having gotten through it...the low point of the semester was being awake at 4am studying and contemplating switching my (second) major from EPE (Ethics, Politics & Economics) to something easier and far lass marketable. I made it though.

Come at me, iBanking.

WEDDING GREETING CARD TO KELLY AND EDUARDO ANDINOS

(June 11, 2015)

MY DEAR KELLY AND EDUARDO,

My heart is rejoicing today! I wish you endless joy, happiness, and courage in your marriage—to last forever. As Roman Pope Francis once said, "In this day and age marriage and your will to serve God are truly heroic acts!"

My life has been greatly enriched by your friendship for which I am ever grateful, and hopeful that our bond will flourish forevermore. I pray for your union to be fruitful, for you and your family, and Our Lord Jesus Christ.

Love,
John Aroutiounian

Mark 10:9

LETTER TO ISABEL MARIN #1

(July 23, 2016)

Dearest Isabel,

This is my second attempt at beginning this letter to you, and in my continuing loss for words elected to appeal to St. Augustine:

> I have learnt to love you late, Beauty at once so ancient and so new! I have leart to love you late! You were within me, and I was in the world outside myself. I searched for you outside myself and, disfigured as I was, I fell upon the lovely things of your creation. You were with me, but I was not with you...you called me; you cried aloud to me; you broke my barrier of deafness. You shone upon me; your radiance enveloped me; you put my blindness to flight.—x.27, *Confessions*

Admittedly perhaps an odd way to begin an effort to let you know my joy and gratitude at the dawn of your beautiful marriage (indeed, I am not confident as I write these words that this version will survive the imminent proofread). But as you and Tom were likely traversing the Alps, my mind would drift to the rancor of my freshman, your senior, year at Yale—a time during which the flowing embers of a desire to better know and live in Truth were in jeopardy of extinguishment. How, I don't know, but it was at this juncture that I had the good sense to join the Federalist Party—yet I am unsure of what that itself would've meant in terms of the years that would follow had it not been for you. It was *your* dazzling intercession and attention then that was, and remains, the single most determinative influence on the trajectory of my college career, spiritual and intellectual life, and future goals. Though your regular role in reading over papers, advising on personal matters, or guiding the room's philosophical inquiry at Fed. Debates would wax and wane as the realities of your upcoming commitments began to intervene, you always made the time for me. And that which you set in motion through your lived philosophy of personal encounter, warmth, and sincerity went far beyond what a friendship, with its exchanges of conversation, ideas, or affection can typically achieve—you dramatically changed the orientation of my mind and its thoughts, and for all the forks in the road that have come since or will come, it would never be the same again. So perhaps, in this vein, Augustine seems more relevant, and explains why I felt this note of congratulations and admiration had to begin with an attempt at an expression of my gratitude.

I have and will continue to pray, Isabel, for your and Tom's happiness together and for your marriage to bear all kinds of fruit as an expression of God's love and charity for man. IT is not an easy time to be married both in terms of the habits that are "trending" in our age and in terms of the work that lies ahead of you two. But you've gotten a special blessing in the opportunity to study and live at Harvard together, and you two are without a doubt up to the occasion—and what powerful witness you'll be. I also hope so much that our friendships will continue and that this will give me the opportunity to truly get to know Tom as a friend. I pray that he always remains a worthy partner to such a incredible soul, and that the two of you always walk together on life's journey toward Jesus.

You should soon be receiving, if you haven't already, a small additional wedding present, of sorts. It is an Italian political philosopher Augusto Del Noce's collected essays, translated into English for the first time last year. He is one of the giants of continental political philosophy (and certainly of Catholic thought) of the past century, yet he is largely unknown in the Anglophone world. I've been tremendously impressed by the incisiveness of his thought and have learned a great deal—would love to discuss with you some day in the not-so-distant future, if you're up for it. My contribution to Tom's place ticket was insufficient and, in any case, I felt like I had to get you something specifically, as it provides an impetus for many upcoming conversations! Let me know also if you find it a bore!

Your friendship, even at points during which it felt distant (as assuredly it may have flet, given my below-average keeping up skills over the past two years), has meant more than you can know, Isabel. And it was an unforgettable honor to sit beside you at the elegant dinner on the night of your wedding, an event so beautifully and gracefully executed by you, Tom, and your families. That weekend, full of so many dear friends, in such a paradisiacal setting, and centered so tastefully on the truly awesome sacrament of marriage will long serve as an example of how moment in human time truly can reflect, in their radiance in our hearts, God's transcendent desires for all of us, and of how the ebullience of what are no more than specks in history contained in memory can, every time the need arises, put our "blindness to flight."

With love,
John

LETTER TO GRACE HIRSHORN

(Unfinished, 2017)

DEAR GRACE,

I think it was in the context of a viewing of Goya's *Saturn Devouring His* Son that my thesis advisor at Yale, Giuseppe Mazzotta (can't seem to remember—did you take his Dante class??), wistfully quoted the Metamorphoses: "tempus edax rerum"—time, devourer of all things. My man WB Yeats is also quite conscious of this in Easter 1916, the poem our dear Federalist Party knows I love so much! It seems only moments ago when we were at Yale for Burke weekend. Actually, this whole year has been such a raw, unprocessed blur—and yet, no time to take stock. "Minute by minute, everything changes—or, you realize, is liable to change. I think the realization of this is the first crack in the facade of childhood.

When we were on the Federalist floor, at the end of my meandering remarks—which I remember you noting were actually quite brief, given my speckled past on that floor—I think you asked a question. I could be misremembering, but I believe it went something like this: How do we take our axiomatic beliefs—the things that make up our core—with us? It was a good question—one for which I didn't have anything resembling a thoughtful, careful answer. So I mentioned the little wooden cross from Bethlehem I've worn around my neck on my travels over the past year, along with a medal of the Blessed Mother. I left it at that. What I didn't mention on the floor was this: that item is the little "Our Lady of Loretto" medallion with the plane on the back, which you sent me to protect my flight in a letter not two years ago. I felt a tad embarrassed, for whatever reason, blurting this out at the debate that evening. But I realized soon after that I very much wanted you to know that Our Lady of Loretto came with me to Hong Kong, Italy, Armenia, Georgia, Lebanon—so many of the places where I touched down this year. In fact, having a visible reminder of Our Lady with me during these travels immensely ameliorated my discomfort while flying—which had been getting pretty bad of late. So, in two words, thank you.

But my thanks extend well beyond that present, Grace. They extend to your consistent trust and friendship over the past years. At Yale, our adventures with the Federalists produced more than a handful of memorable evenings and conversations. You were always willing to engage, to chat, to plot! But then there were delightful chance encounters at STM [St. Thomas More], Stiles dining hall, followed by returning to the grind, or spontaneous trips to D.C. But I appreciate just as much the continuation of the friendship after graduation. I've been surprised, in ways good and bad, by the various degrees of effort and intention various friends have put into maintaining bonds after Yale. And I've found myself somewhat unexpectedly affected by this and quite disappointed by those who went missing, and deeply admiring of those who didn't. Your thoughtful letters—electric concoctions of the personal, the professional, and the intellectual—your though-provoking emails, and your prayer-filled check-ins often received altogether underwhelming replies from me, in the midst of various crises (sometimes of my own making!). But they never went unappreciated. They have never failed to lift my spirits, to get me to think, or get me to pray. And it has always been delightful to catch up in person, over Skype, or over the phone—still remember the Skype from Oxford, conducted at a bar while the drunkards were stumbling out! Each time, it has been so heartwarming to know that a fellow soldier continues laboring, continues fighting, though perhaps halfway around the world.

LETTER TO MARYAM

(February 8, 2018)

Dear Maryam,

Brace yourself: it's quite likely that you will feel as crazy once you finish this letter as I do right now, as I start it. It's also quite likely that you will read this before my letter in the mail, written in Armenian and covering much lighter topics, arrives. You might, as a result, develop a strong first impression regarding the level of drama that letters from me contain. I assure you this is an extraordinary case, and I ask for your patience in reading.

My most vivid memory from last month, January, is speaking with you from Lisbon. My friend and I had split up for the day to see different sights of personal interest. I went to the Gulbenkian Museum, and then to Jeronimos Monastery—I think I may have sent you a picture of the inside of the church, with a dark crucifix in the foreground, and another one of the abbey grounds. As I walked along the geometrically immaculate porticos of the cloister in the monastery that day, I distinctly remember familiar thoughts coming back to me: "What is God's purpose for me in this life? Am I meant to be married? Am I meant to be a priest? If only God could provide more clarity!" I texted my mother a picture of the scene, with a caption: "Walking here, contemplating life!" Since it was only the first week of the new year, I was full to the brim with thoughts and emotions from the past year—from the second half of my time at Oxford, from my stay at the Armenian monastery, St. Lazarus, in Venice, my summer travels, and my first semester of law school at Columbia. It was a grueling semester, as I've mentioned before. I was—and continue to be now—nervous about doing well academically, about student loans, about whether I would be able to work the heavy hours and bring in the large salary to keep my folks, and a future family, afloat. I was especially apprehensive because I felt that this kind of work wouldn't make me happy, yet few other options would provide for the kind of income necessary to pay off debts and proceed to have the life I'd imagined. I prayed for God's guidance and assistance, but I didn't fully trust in Him. I felt all the pressure directly on me, felt I needed to be in greater control over all the variables, in order to get to a place of security. Even as I shared these worries with my parents, and even as they promised that they would find a way to take care of my law school loans in case I wasn't able to pay them off immediately, I was unsatisfied, because I felt that in the long term, the only way to achieve security in New York as the only child of parents who weren't young would be to make a good deal of money in a fast-moving career. I did not operate as a man whose inner peace and comfort comes from knowing he has to do only what he can, and that he simply has to put his faith in the Lord for the rest. In any event, walking through the monastery in Lisbon that day, I was simply happy to have finished the semester, and was happy to have passed all of my exams. I knew the following semester wouldn't be as bad now, since I had proven to myself that I could do it (to these kinds of doubts, my grandmother always says, "Of course you can do it! You went to Yale! Just take good care of yourself!" But a part of you always worries you won't be able to, in fact, do it.) Yet I was weary still, as I was the week before when I was with my parents at our beach home in Florida—weary because so many questions still remained unanswered. And I was also physically tired: Shortly after the weekend I spent in Montreal (I think I also sent you pictures from that trip), I checked myself into the ER because I felt incredibly fatigued, and was told I had developed short-term anemia from an episode of upper stomach bleeding. The doctor said the cause was almost certainly a stress ulcer, but he scheduled an endoscopy for the week after my international trip to make sure.

But I am digressing: After the monastery, I walked over to the Torre de Belem, one of Portugal's most recognizable sights. The tower marked the point from which Portuguese sailing vessels would head out into the Atlantic Ocean in the 1400s, and from there to the New World. The sun's last rays were in the sky, the night was getting brisk, and the tourists were thinning out quickly. I had just arrived, and after surveying the scene, thought to myself, "Perfect." I think I've told you this, but few things please me more than being alone in places of historical and religious value. When I was a Senate intern in Washington eight years ago, I got to be by myself one night in the Rotunda of the Capitol Building—a place that's constantly bustling with tourists, and that requires several security checks just to enter. My job was one of the few that allowed unlimited access, as long as the Senate was in session, as it was that night. I was passing by the Rotunda to deliver paperwork to a side office around 11pm, and noticed the dimly lit, hallowed space—it was hard to miss. So I walked right over to the very middle of the room, laid down on my back, and stared up at the massive painting of George Washington on the ceiling of the dome that thousands of tourists would point to and photograph every day. That was the exact spot in which dead presidents had lain, the spot in which world leaders had given speeches. And I had it all to myself in that moment. A few years later, I stayed up very late in Rome one night, and walked over to St. Peter's Square in the Vatican, without another soul in sight. I remember wandering into the depths of Geghard Monastery by myself to discover a little stream inside, while rays of light broke through the cracks and dispelled the profound darkness of the space. I could go on, but you get the picture. And yet—partially remembering what you said to me once, and partially out of a feeling that was actually quite novel to me—I desperately wanted to share that moment at the tower in Lisbon. And that's when I sent you a message, and you indulged me with a response. I sat on the steps in front of the tower, without another person in sight, and took it in—but this time, I didn't feel alone. We spoke of Gulbenkian, and of medical school and law school. Amid my whining about the semester's unpleasant moments, you asked something like, "Well, what do you like?" And then, in response to my answer and half-baked plan for the future, you gave your approval, but also warned, "As long as you don't let the process destroy you." Obviously, these were snippets of a larger conversation, but the sheer incisiveness and wisdom in your comments were part of something I had come to notice time and time again over our conversations—whether through Skype, email, or messenger—over the past few months. You were always so genuinely interested, sharply observant, down to earth, and thoroughly unpretentious. I remember the conversation when I pompously mentioned Hegel and the Oracle at Delphi, when you very directly responded that you had never heard of either. Maybe you felt embarrassed or awkward, but I remember thinking, "I really like this girl!" Most other people would have immediately looked it up or pretended to know on the spot, and it would have been easy to get away with it while talking over text. But you were simply, succinctly, and refreshingly honest. And that night when it was just me, you, and the tower, I remember thinking, "She's so much smarter than most of the Yale douchebags I know!" One can always become more worldly: it's not difficult to travel, to read, to view art, and to build your "mental library" of references so as to sound cultured. It's extremely difficult, however, to develop curiosity, to develop passion for learning, to develop honesty and *parzutyun*. In the half year of our acquaintance, it became clear that you had all those in ample supply—and that you were unceasingly modest and humble in how you represented your own intelligence. Every conversation proved further that you weren't someone isolated exclusively in medicine. Maybe you hadn't majored in art in college, but you had a penetrating appreciation for what was beautiful, and you had a discerning eye when it came to analyzing the social and philosophical problems of the day.

Frankly, that evening also confirmed what I had come to realize over the several months in which we'd been speaking: you were frank, you were forward, you had gusto. It takes gusto to fly down to Buenos Aires and work the rooms upon rooms of established doctors, it takes gusto to reach out to people in Armenia and try to get your foot in the door with projects—particularly since Armenia isn't a place that's easy to break into from the outside. And it takes gusto to reach out to the son of a doctor you met, to set up Skype calls, and then to freely chat about topics from the abstract to the deeply personal over messages. It takes a level of confidence, and also a good amount of tenderness and openness. So many in modern Western society are so deeply neurotic, so deeply suspicious, so deeply vulnerable and afraid of genuine connection. You can be friends with someone for years, and then it hits you one day that you hardly know them—that your entire relationship was built on a performance, and that the real person underneath the act is completely unrecognizable to you. In Italy this summer, I started reading a German-Korean philosopher, Byung Chul-Han, who writes that even as Western society has gotten more efficient, more transparent, and more "open," we are more lost than ever when it comes to understanding ourselves and the people around us. And finding people who don't fit this mold has been, in my experience, exceedingly difficult to do—I can count on one hand, out of the many people from all over the world I consider friends, the number of people with whom I have ever established that kind relationship. In any event, it made me very happy that you, wittingly or unwittingly, agreed to be there with me at the Torre in Lisbon that evening. And I can confidently say that it was one of the few times traveling in which I was very happy not to be alone.

That night about a month ago left me with a wonderful feeling about where our friendship was going—I felt that I had, quite accidentally and unknowingly at first, stumbled upon someone with whom the connection wasn't going to be like most others. I had begun to detect that faintly months earlier, as I would read your kind, gentle, but also curious and probing emails. They were of a manner that demonstrated both a humane disposition and a finesse, whether intentional or not, in how you approached others. But what surprised me even more as the weeks went on was the extent to which you would feel comfortable engaging on rather sensitive topics, from questions of faith, to family size, to personal choices about sex and contraception. I've always told people, and have always told myself, that what I admire most in others isn't a superior intellect, or success. It's their faith. You see it emerge as a ttheme in novels like *Brideshead Revisited*, or the *Power and the Glory*. Few things have as high of a success rate in getting me emotional as when the usher asks me to walk around the church on Sunday with the collection basket (this is at the Catholic church across the street, my "backup church" when I don't get up in time for Badarak!). Every time I watch old people, disabled people, young people who clearly don't have much, putting their dollars and coins into the bin, I have to fight back tears. Every time, it shatters all the material impressions that build up in me during the week about what counts as success, about what counts as "winning" in this life. My mind's eye is refreshed anew, and Jesus' observation during the Sermon on the Mount that "Blessed are the poor in spirit, for theirs is the Kingdom of Heaven" is brought back into the center, for at least that moment. Anyway, nothing impresses me more than someone of strong and resilient faith. In conversations with you, I constantly found myself being taken aback by your faith, as well as your shrewd and obviously very insightful observations. You might be wondering why I was surprised, and the answer is simple: I had gotten to the cynical point in my life in which I just didn't expect it in people. This isn't to say I wasn't open to meeting people who would be impressive in these ways, but an insulating layer of cynicism develops over time. With each exchange we had, that layer broke a little more. And it was also surprising coming from an

Armenian girl. My parents have always reminded me of a promise I allegedly made when I was 6 years old to marry an Armenian. It's something I always hoped would happen, especially as I got older and realized how difficult it would be to live a life in which being and speaking Armenian played a major part with someone who wasn't. But, truth be told, I had grown increasingly doubtful that it would or could happen, because I knew that what I needed most, if I was to be married, was to find someone who put faith above all. Marrying someone who was culturally Armenian and Christian, but who didn't share my beliefs about the centrality of faith, and who wasn't prepared to live a personal and romantic life that was first and foremost an expression of God's love, wasn't going to fly. And, frankly, an overwhelming majority of the Armenian girls I have met don't have a deep understanding of the faith and what it requires of people in their daily lives. Both in Armenia and in the diaspora, the Christian faith is a historical element that is central to who we are as Armenians, but we're not so sure as individuals what that means for how we live our lives today. My theologically-inclined Catholic friends in college had guided me toward a much more examined faith, and toward a deeper understanding of the implications of Christianity for our lives. But I hadn't met many Armenians of the same stripe, so I had decided to keep an open heart and mind, but had also wound up telling myself that if I could find someone of deep faith and conviction from another background, perhaps I could convince them to live in Armenia with me for several years, and that would suffice. In any event, the point is that I wasn't expecting such depth from a chance encounter, and your being Armenian only seemed to lower the probability in my mind that you would be someone with whom I could develop a friendship based on depth of that kind. On this score, like so many others, I was blown away.

I relate to Tigran, the main character in *Kyanq u Kriv*, very much. Particularly the iteration of Tigran in the first half of the movie. When it comes to matters personal, I have spent years asking God for direction and guidance, but I have consistently felt too scared to act in any substantive way. My best friend in college was a girl with whom I had the kind of bond I was describing above. She was not Armenian. I took her to Armenia with me during the summer after our last year at Yale, and we had a fabulous time. I felt with her over the years of our friendship what I have felt with you over the past six months—that I could talk with her about anything for extended periods of time, and never feel the time go by. In ten days, we covered Paris, Munich, Vienna, and all of Armenia. I exaggerate—we left much unseen in each. But the whirlwind trip made me very happy. When she left to go back to work in New York, I stayed in Armenia for another month. The following month, I returned home and began work myself. Two months after that, she began seeing someone else. That was September of 2015. Last July, she married him. I couldn't make myself go to the wedding, even though I had promised her to fly back to the States from Armenia for it. I spent the week partying with friends in Beirut instead. To this day, I don't know if she ever figured out how I felt about her. And I'll never figure out why I so blatantly let the opportunity slip. The best answer I've been able to come up with is simply that I wasn't ready at the time, and it's not what God intended for my life. But, like Tigran, I couldn't escape the thought which his grandfather first articulated in an angry tirade: That I was spineless, and just as I had missed the opportunity with her, I would close my eyes to what God was calling me to do, whether that was to marry, or to join the priesthood. All the while, I was developing a deep restlessness with being alone and indecisive on the one hand, while I simply couldn't imagine a relationship or a marriage, much less having the courage to drop out of law school and enter seminary, on the other hand. Like Tigran, I would often even think about Armenian soldiers fighting in Artsakh, and I would say to myself, "There are millions of lawyers out there. Do something useful with your life: go fight with them. It's not fair that they are there, and you are comfortably here because your parents got visas to come to America." I would then have to remind myself that my career would be built around developing the ability to support Armenia and other causes I cared about, like the pro-life movement and education reform, more forcefully. But the guilt of not being more decisively involved always stuck with me. Other law school students don't seem to have a problem with doing their work, partying every weekend, and leaving the rest to fate. I wanted more meaning and impact for my life. That is something that continues to be true today.

The Lisbon trip came to a close only a few days after that night at the tower, and we flew back on Sunday, January 14th. The following day was Martin Luther King Day, and the day after that was the first day of spring semester classes. It was also the day of the endoscopy. That morning, I went to class, and then directly to the outpatient clinic. My last memory before being anesthetized was seeing the GI doctor, looking calm and pleased, giving the nurse a kiss—probably an episode of workplace sexual harassment! I woke up perhaps an hour later, and the doctor walked in with my mother. His face looked pained and concerned. "We found a mass between your esophagus and your stomach," he said. This was exactly three weeks ago, and I'm getting anxious just thinking about it again. In the post-anesthesia haze, I wasn't particularly impressed. I remember saying something like, "OK, well figure out what it is, and take it out." Over the past three weeks, it has begun to sink in, although it still hasn't fully. After two weeks of CT scans, PET scans, and MRIs, followed by a second endoscopy, the diagnosis finally became pretty clear last week. There is no spread to any other location, but there is a local tumor in that spot. And it wasn't until last Thursday, less than a week ago, that we met with an oncologist, and figured out what this meant. There would need to be chemotherapy, followed by surgery to remove it. The risk factors for this kind of tumor are a history of smoking, heavy drinking, acid reflux, EBV-positivity, family history, old age. I have absolutely none of them—the thing has popped up from nowhere. It's an uncommon tumor, but it happens in people under 35 in 2% of cases. So it's a rare occurrence for an already rare situation. It's like winning the lottery—except, well, the kind of lottery you'd pay just about anything to lose. It is patently absurd, from a rational, medical, or any other standpoint, for this to happen to a healthy 24 years old with no history of anything, and who was hiking on a remote, mountainous island in the Atlantic Ocean with nothing but a heavy backpack less than a month ago. But it has happened.

In the past three weeks, but especially in this last one, I have tried to regain my sense of self amid the fast pace at which everything is happening. I am praying more constantly and intently than perhaps ever before, I am seeing a priest who I have told about the situation. I have also told one of my college professors, who has become one of my best friends and mentors. But outside of my family, no one else knows. With so much up in the air, I don't see much of a point in telling people. I am not in a position to deal with avalanches of questions and concerns streaming in every day when I myself don't have anywhere close to all the answers. I had absolutely no symptoms, except for that one case of bleeding, which not even the chairman of the GI department at the hospital ever thought would be this: when we were trying to figure out when to schedule the first endoscopy, he said to me, "Enjoy your vacation, we'll do it after—I'm not worried." As I attempt to figure out why this happened, and what role this will play in my life, I am also trying to listen more intently than ever to what God wants in this, and out of this, situation. I have realized quite suddenly and horribly the extent to which everything—and I mean everything—totally hangs on God. This was true always, but I feel the truth of it now in a way I couldn't comprehend even a month ago. Gone are the concerns about law school, gone are the concerns about what the distant future will hold—I am simply praying and hoping for the strength to know what to do each day, and to make the correct decisions with my folks. Even that is very difficult, because each decision could have life-altering implications. And even as I grasp for meaning and understanding about why this bizarre situation is now suddenly upon me, I am made hopeful that God has a plan for this, as well. In the middle of all the scans and tests last month, I received an email from Columbia that I had entered the final round of consideration for a scholarship I thought I was a long shot for, at best. The scholarship would cover the entirety of my law school tuition—a pretty large sum. It's definitely not a certainty yet, but getting to this point was considered the hardest part of the process, and it gives me encouragement, regardless of how it unfolds in the end, that God provides when the need really arises. And I further hope that, in addition to seeing me through this, the Lord will use this, and use me, so that I am a vessel for His will being done. I am hopeful that He will give me the courage and strength I lacked before—the courage to make consequential decisions about what my life is to look like, so that it best serves Him. Already, more than ever before in my life, I feel utterly, completely, radically attached to Him, and though the coming months are bound to be scary and difficult, I know that He is what everything is about. When I was in Jerusalem with Father Daniel Findikyan in 2014, I remember standing outside the tomb of Jesus in the Church of the Holy Sepulchre and staring at the portrait of Him that hangs above the tomb. In that moment in the summer of 2014, I could only picture the scene when Peter, like Jesus, starts walking on water in the Sea of Galilee, but as soon as the first wind blows, he gets frightened, and as soon as he gets frightened and takes his eyes off Jesus, he falls into the water. When Jesus yanks him out of the water, He asks Peter with anguish on His face, "You of little faith, why do you doubt?" Though I have always had faith, there have been moments, whether in Jerusalem in 2014, or in many moments since, when I have doubted in thought or in deed. Though bad forces may try to use this period as a time in which to try to make me doubt more, God is also using this period as a time to draw me closer to Him, to His Word, and to His Will: "Thy will be done." Though I am uncertain about a lot of things, I am certain of this, and I have vowed to myself to obey and rely on Him completely through this process, and for whatever comes after it. School, for its part, feels like no burden at all anymore, and not just because I have new hope that the loans won't pose a problem. I am yet unsure whether I will take a medical leave or not, but I am not troubled at all by the possibility of extending law school by a semester, or a year. Much has been brought into perspective, and, for the good and bad that is to happen, I know that I will live in a different way as a result of this. I already do.

And yet, the process continues to be very difficult, owing in no small part to all the uncertainty involved. I don't know how I will respond to the treatments, I don't know how the surgery will go. So much is in other people's, and especially God's, hands. And there was one other piece of news delivered last Thursday that caught me completely off guard: The doctor, without even flinching, at one point mentioned, "We'll get a nurse to call you to discuss sperm banking." Although the chemotherapy that was going to be prescribed for me was not ordinarily supposed to cause long-term infertility, she explained that there was a chance that it might, and it certainly would reduce the quality of the genetic material for about the next year or so. "So you should be safe," she added. And then, she added a pretty dumb and insensitive joke: "Plus, in case your kids grow up and don't get in to Harvard, I don't want you to blame me." In my mind, I reacted with "Woah woah what?!" followed by, "I went to Yale, you asshole." But I was so browbeaten by that awful day that I barely responded to her. The following day, the "fertility nurse" called me four times, and I refused to pick up the phone each time. As I recovered from the emotional shock of all the news on Thursday, what I already knew became even clearer to me: I couldn't agree to sperm banking. For the past week since that appointment, my mother has been pleading with me to do it before chemo starts, but she and I come from different perspectives when it comes to these questions. I have long believed, as the Church teaches, that manipulating life is wrong: Abortion is wrong, contraception is wrong, artificial fertility treatments which separate life from the sexual act of reproduction are wrong. They are not in accordance with God's will from a Christian perspective, and I have known and believed that for as long as I could remember. So here was an extremely difficult question, on top of the many others already dumped onto my lap from nowhere, that I had to face and answer within a short period of time. I have reached out to my priest again, who I'll hopefully see before the end of the week, but I already know what he is going to say. My mentor, who I mentioned earlier, is a devout Catholic, and I asked for her counsel about this as well. Every reliable voice I trust in the Church says the same thing: you shouldn't violate the laws of God and nature, and you should trust in God that He will reveal and provide. And I will not go against God's law purely for the sake of my desires, or even the desires of my parents, for what the future ought to look like. And yet, it is very difficult: as the two of us have discussed in the past, I have only ever really seen two ways my life might unfold, based on my convictions and faith in God's plan. On the one hand, I envisioned a large family—something I did not have growing up, and something that fills me with tremendous excitement and joy every time I weigh it as a possibility. I envisioned a partner, a teammate, a wife who would feel the same way, and together, we would tackle every challenge, climb every mountain (figuratively and literally—I am a big fan of hiking, and had already checked out some gorgeous hikes in Sicily and Switzerland we could take on together someday). On the other hand, I envisioned the possibility of life as a priest with great promise, as well. I knew this path would disappoint my parents, because they want few things more than to see me married, with children. And I knew that, if I went down this path, I would want to dedicate myself totally to the Church, and to have an episcopal career, as opposed to the career of a lay priest. This would clearly mean forsaking marriage and children. Although the possibility of being alone in this scenario was somewhat frightening, I figured that the fellowship of priests and monks, combined with the heightened nearness to God, would make up for it—and I was excited by the possibility of devoting myself to prayer, to scholarship, and to ministry. But, over the past several years, I could not orient myself between these paths, despite many conversations with seminarians, married friends, and others. So I continued praying for signs and direction, and I continue praying for these things to this day. I suppose what this diagnosis, and this new reality, has done is it has brought these questions to the forefront. I now need to confront the real possibility that I may not be able to have children after treatment—and if I am not able to have children, then I will almost certainly decide to take holy vows. But even as I offer up the distress of this situation to God, and ask for guidance in this difficult hour, I know that the "freezing" option should be off the table—for if I am meant to have children, God will provide the circumstances for it to happen. And if I am not, then I will serve Him through the Church. I figure that all of this should become rather clear within the next year. But I confess that I am scared that I am finally being made—much sooner than most other people our age, especially for someone who has been so indecisive over the past several years—to go down a road that might close the door on something that I, and my parents, have so dearly wanted. And yet, there is no way out of this situation except through it, and instead of "taking out an insurance policy" on fate, like my parents want me to do with the banking option, I am telling myself as often as I can that I am determined to put my trust fully in God. Most people, particularly secular people or those who don't believe in the

Christian view of sexual ethics, would think I am absolutely idiotic for refusing to freeze totally healthy genetic material before treatment. I suspect my parents also think this. But I have faith that, no matter what happens, it is the right decision.

And so, I have been praying to God, to our Blessed Mother, and to my most beloved saints, and I have been thinking hard, asking God to give me strength and courage to follow through on my decision, and if He has any other ideas about what I should do in my effort to follow Him absolutely, to let me know. It was in this unbelievable process—a process that perhaps one day I'll be able to describe more fully, a process in which every day has felt like a lifetime—that it occurred to me, quite naturally, to write to you. You may think this entire letter is absurd, that it is a crazy case of over-sharing, that it represents the scattered thoughts of someone who is desperate or who has lost his mind in the admittedly strong heat of the moment. You may also think that this entire message is manipulative, and is meant to arouse pity, or guilt, or to twist your will into agreeing to something by referencing the faith we both hold dear. But please believe me: The entire point of this letter is to discern what the Lord's plan is.

And that purpose alone is why I ask: Will you marry me?

It is entirely true that, one month ago, writing a letter such as this, today, would not even have registered as a possibility in the most remote reaches of my mind. It is also true that, one month ago, I had absolutely no way of knowing what the next few weeks would hold. And I recognize that this entire letter may ruin our conversations, may ruin our friendship, may ruin any future possibility of meeting and deciding down the road that we may want to move things along in our relationship. I recognize that a more conservative and restrained person would prayerfully consider the possibilities, and might decide to go along with the sperm bank, "just in case." Or, someone might decide to take his odds and wait without saying anything, out of a fear of upsetting the other person or ruining his chances with her altogether. Indeed, my own self, one month ago, would have probably done one of those things. But as my heart has felt like it has been torn open again and again over the past month, it has also become much more open to the possibility that God, that the Spirit, is speaking in the most absurd and radical ways. If I were simply intent on having children, and were only searching for a vessel to bear them, there would have been simpler ways to do this. If I were only intent on finding a wife and starting a family, there are other people in my life who I know would be interested, and with whom I could imagine a stable, peaceful, happy existence. Even if this entire proposal seems ridiculous and unthinkable to you, please know that it is not a matter of someone who was searching for an easy way out of a difficult situation, for this isn't easy: I have spent several days not going to class and thinking about this. It is, perhaps, the riskiest option, since it risks alienating you permanently, which means the possibility of losing a friend, and losing maybe something much more than that further down the line. It represents my best effort to love God more than anything else, something I remember us both saying we valued and prayed to find in a partner—only days before the process which led up to the diagnosis last week began. I was moved, inexplicably, to write this, and to write it to you alone—and I am prepared to accept the reality, whether it turns out this is not God's will, or whether it turns out it is. Either way, it will be gratifying to tell God that, for once, I had the courage to take radical action, to risk embarrassment on a grand scale, in order to better discern what His Will is.

I don't need to tell you what the risks of saying "yes" are, of taking this leap with me, but I need to mention several of them, lest you think I haven't thought about them. First, it is unclear what is going to happen to me. If God wills it, even if I take a medical leave, I should be back in school for the coming academic year. I would be glad to discuss this—and many other aspects—more with you in person. Second, it is unclear whether I will be able to have children after the treatment. We would have some limited time, I believe, before the treatment began. But that raises a third issue—you may not be prepared for that now. And the possibility of having kids in the future, though the doctors say it's good, would be in the hands of God. Fourth, so much between us remains not discussed, and we don't know each other as well as people who have dated for months or more. You may find, upon meeting in person, that I am not to your liking. In this matter, I am reminded of my grandmother's response when I asked her if she loved my grandfather romantically when they were young. She said, "Inch ser? Gourgen uxaki lav mard er, amusnatsank, etpes el gnats." Anyway, I still think she was exaggerating, but the bottom line is you'd be taking a leap of faith, and maybe a foolish leap at that. I am sure there are other things on your mind, and there are also risks involved on my end, too. For both of us, we would be counting on the positive signs thus far to guide us toward a life of love, much more like people in the distant past would do than they do today. Not too long ago, in our native Armenia and all around the world, love only came into marriage after the sacrament and the ceremony. Curiously enough, divorce rates were much lower then, and couples were happier then. It's a different world now, and that different world has undoubtedly influenced many of our expectations. I certainly would have preferred to get to know you much better, to visit Vancouver or meet in Los Angeles, before even thinking about this step. But that isn't the reality that has been given to me, and perhaps it is better that way. All I know, Maryam, is that in this moment of fear, of confusion, of total dependence on God for guidance, something moved within me to give this a try. One of my best friends, who lives in Hong Kong, once said I was a "sapiosexual"—that I am attracted to minds and personalities. I think she had a point, and by that rationale, our conversations have provided me with everything I need to know to confidently be able to pop the question. Perhaps this was the only way to get me to summon the courage to act, and absent this opportunity, I would have spent many more years wasted. God only knows.

But I also want you to know—and I mean this with the utmost sincerity—that whatever your response is, I will be grateful for it. If you are willing, you don't need to bother with any kind of extended reply. Something as simple as a three-word reply, like "Let's do it," would do. I could be in Vancouver this weekend. Or you could be in New York this weekend. Or we could meet somewhere else. It would be whatever you wanted. Of course, there would be no time for the wedding that both of us doubtless always imagined. It would have to be a small, hastily arranged wedding, with our families. But don't think for a moment that this would be the whole story: After the treatments, hopefully in the summer or in the fall, we would put on the big show. Or multiple shows. Personally, I always envisioned a three-part wedding: one ceremony on San Lazzaro, the Armenian island in Venice, followed by a little Italy tour; then, another at Khor Virap in Armenia; and a third for friends in New York. We could add to, or change, the plan as you saw fit. Whatever and wherever you wanted, it would be done in a flash. Over the summer, after the end of your school year and before your trip to Armenia, we could spend time taking in some sun in Palm Beach, in Florida. Or we could head to Los Angeles, and hang out with my family out there. I have learned, because of good unexpected things that have happened as well bad, that excessive planning in life is useless. So I won't bother proposing what would come after the summer, because we would obviously have to take it slowly. I have several friends who have had kids during graduate school, and we could talk with them about how they have done it. We would absolutely figure out how to finish medical school and law school, and I know that my entire family, from coast to coast, as well as many friends (many of whom I would absolutely love to introduce you to!), will help in a variety of ways. If you wanted to take a year off from school, come to New York, and then return to finish the final year, we could do that. If you would like me to take another year off, come to Vancouver, and then return to Columbia Law, I would absolutely do that. In the future, if God were to will that we be able to have more children, we would figure it out incrementally, and I would go anywhere for you in order to make it work. I am getting far ahead of myself, and I also want to tell you that, in case the answer is "no," I will harbor no hard feelings whatsoever. Feel free to say "I can't," and leave it at that. You don't even have to do that: All I would ask is that you delete this letter, and let me know before Sunday that you've deleted it. If you feel angry or overwhelmed, and would prefer to stop talking altogether going forward, I completely understand. It would be completely reasonable and understandable, and I would still be grateful to you and to God for helping me discern, and I would accept whatever was to come after treatment—life as a priest, or possibly still married life. What I am trying my hardest to do in this situation is simple: to fully cooperate with God in discerning the purpose and plan. I hope that, in this ridiculous jumble of words, that at least that much is apparent.

I always knew that, were I to get married, I would sit down my fiancée long before the big day and make her a promise: We were going to have an extraordinary life. By this, I would explain to her, I meant a life that was decisively unconventional by today's standards. We would be going to the most interesting places, meeting and befriending the most fascinating people, doing the most spectacular things. I would tell her to brace for a life full of adventure, of travel, of intellectual engagement. I would ask her if she was comfortable with the possibility of public life—of my being involved in politics, in America or internationally. A life in which, while we did all this, we would strive to be witnesses for Christ first and foremost—in our family life, in our relationships with friends, and beyond. A life intimately connected to Armenia. I would say that we were forming a lifelong team, and that we would be bound to support each other in our personal goals and challenges, in our joys and hardships. And I would pledge to do everything in my power to be the kind of husband that always put her, the family, and—most importantly—God in the center. I would pledge that, if these three things ever came into conflict with what I wanted to do for my own ambitions, my personal goals would take a backseat immediately. I have always believed that all of civilization rests on the strength of women. They are the protectors of our hearts. I still believe this, and it is this same extraordinary life that I am offering before you now. The drama, the risk, and the adventure is just kicking in a little earlier than I had planned!

One of my favorite men in the twentieth century, and indeed, in history, is Saint Pope John Paul II. His personal motto as Pope was "Totus Tuus," which means "totally yours" in Latin, and references our Blessed Mother, Saint Mary. The Pope, along with innumerable people throughout time, have consecrated, entrusted, and devoted themselves to Mary, the Mother of God. Catholic, as well as Orthodox theology, has very often put forth the notion that Mary holds the key to a deeper relationship with Christ. As a human, she is a figure with whom all of humanity can relate, even though she was conceived without sin, unlike the rest of us. As the Mother of God, she holds a very special place in Jesus' heart, and Jesus does not turn her down. Totally giving oneself to Mary, then, is a beautiful way to totally giving oneself to Christ. I absolutely love that the Pope chose this as his motto, and I have prayed to the Blessed Virgin that she pray to Jesus in order to make me increase in love for Him, and to draw nearer to him. And tonight, as I finish this and head to bed, I will thank God for giving me the courage to write to you, I will pray for both of us, and I will say again to Mary and her Son, that I am totally theirs. If God wills it, and if you give me the chance, Maryam, then second only to God and your namesake, I will be totally yours, too.

John

LETTER TO ERIC SIRAKIAN (EXCERPTS)

(June 17, 2018)

Dearest Eric,

... I feel like me-you time got shortchanged, which is a shame a) because the point was to remind you that you're a *STAR* and b) because there remains so much to talk about. I suppose it's a reason for me, or hopefully, you, to come back soon.

I know I can be reserved in expressing my feelings, but *The Jungle* was the most moving thing I'd seen in a long time, and genuinely breathed new life into my legal and political ambitions which have taken a morale hit recently. I am so honored to have been a little part of the beginning of your illustrious career, from you Yale days to your West End premiere. It was a small part, yes, but a small part of a groundbreaking show and a part you fully mastered, without question! Excelsior! You were so deeply immersed in your role, and you can be sure that this came shining through. How exciting that it's going to run for a while, with the possibility of New York next!

There is so much more I want to say, but its my ambition to say it all in person before long. You were, at Yale and Oxford, such an integral part of my experience, and you continue to be, even when we don't speak for prolonged stretches. You are an absolute gem, and I am so thankful our connection endures.

We must, then, properly celebrate when I see you next—I will make sure of it. Until then, please know that the thought of you fills many of my unspoken moments with warmth for which I am ever grateful.

Yours, with love,
Ջոն ["John" in Armenian]

LETTER TO ISABEL MARIN #2

(*Easter Sunday, April 1, 2018*)

Dear Isabel,

It gives me such joy to know that I will now carry the memory of last night's glorious Vigil Mass, with you by my side and family and friends in tow as I was received into full Communion by Cardinal-Archbishop Dolan, with me always.

I am so utterly grateful for the gift of your presence as my sponsor, especially on rather short notice, so touched by your letter and presents, and so honored that Tom and dapper little Alexander could also attend!

And I am particularly humbled at this moment, Isabel, by your friendship. The question of the existence of God, particularly when it is cavalierly raised, is a maddeningly frustrating one. This I find to be so because, setting aside all the philosophical proofs, historical analyses, and theological pronouncements, a faithful heart is forged in hundred, if not thousands of moments of varying length and importance—moments which an atheist might call recurring episodes of confirmation bias, but which I know to be moments when the Divine Curtain lifts ever so slightly off the ground, to give a momentary glimpse of what awaits on the other side. This constellation of moments may include encounters with art, with fellow men, or with the voice of Christ Himself, emanating from the silence of the depths of the soul. To attempt to convey all this to a given interlocutor demanding answers in a minute, hour, year, or lifetime is an impossible task—more difficult than the most complex of formulas or theories—to say nothing of doing it convincingly! It is a task made attemptable only by a medley of Grace, personal charm, and superior fortitude of heart and mind.

These gifts, Isabel, you have been given in abundance, and with them you created many of the foundational moments during which my mind's eye noticed the Divine Curtain flutter. Know, then, that the process which came to its fruition when one, in the communion of saints, arrives at the Beatific Vision—was stoked in a tremendous way by you. For this process, which after some initial cornerstones lay dormant until the period between the first year of high school and freshman year at Yale, was reignited at that point in such a way that my love for the Church—the Armenian Orthodox Church, and soon afterward, the Universal Church, truly took flight. That, then, is the crux of the story, and I hope that knowledge of your role in it, by God's grace, is a source of joy. It certainly is for me, and I thank God for your continued presence, among many others, in my life, through battles and trials small and large. It is humbling to have such an exquisite foretaste of the communion of saints, with you leading the number—truly, when first asked who would be my sponsor, it hardly took seconds for the reply to generate in my mind!

Thank you, Isabel. To the slaying of dragons, to the unity of the Church, especially its Eastern and Western branches, to our law school endeavors, to family! Mary, Mother of God [John wrote Mary's name in Armenian here], pray for us!

As ever, yours,
John (*Հովհաննես*) [Armenian biblical spelling of *John*]

P.S. This card was made by one of the last printmakers of Venice, who has a longstanding relationship with the monastery of St. Lazzaro in the Venetian lagoon, home to the Mekhitarists, the only Armenian Catholic monastic order in existence. I found them whilst residing at the monastery last summer!

COVER LETTER: THE LEONINE FORUM

(*August 5, 2018*)

I WRITE TO express my enthusiastic interest in becoming part of The Leonine Forum's 2018 New York group. My interest stems from my personal, as well as professional, background. I am an Armenian Catholic, and was formed in faith chiefly through a close community of friends during my undergraduate years at Yale, where I was highly involved in both the university's debating society and in pro life activism. Since leaving Yale, I have worked for the Manhattan District Attorney's Office, obtained a Master's degree from the University of Oxford, and completed the first year of studies at Columbia Law School. In New York, my hometown, I have had the opportunity to become well acquainted with Schuyler Hall, which now serves as my go-to location for spiritual direction. I hope to enter legal practice in the areas of international law and diplomacy, with a geographic focus on Eurasia and the Middle East.

As I begin the second year of law school—having faced numerous personal challenges over the past few years—I find myself yearning to reengage with, and to be surrounded by, peers who share both faith and a common sense of mission. At Yale, it was this sort of community that saw me through four years in a setting largely unfriendly and challenging for people of faith. New York City is but a magnified version of the college campus. To once more have the privilege to gather for discussion, learning, and fellowship with Catholic Christians in stations of life similar to mine would be a tremendous blessing. Four friends who participated in the Forum's 2017 New York group—Andrew Laird, Grace McInerney, Courtney Horton, and Zach Horton—all lavished praise on the program and spoke of how their lives were enriched by participation this year. I am certain that, in much the same way, I would stand to benefit both professionally and personally through participation in the many sessions with peers and community leaders, covering a wide range of topics and disciplines, to be held this year. I am most curious to obtain insights into how Catholics successful in a variety of fields have led integrated lives of faith. Regardless of my vocation, I am certain that the information and personal experiences shared in these sessions will be widely applicable in the situations I encounter.

I am a great believer in the importance of creating and maintaining strong community. In this era of constant dislocation and instant communication, it is critical that individuals maintain communities of those who share their values, whether they are physically close or distant. It is through this belief, and the steps I take every day to live out this belief in my life, that I also hope to give back to The Leonine Forum and its members—by being a fellow soldier on whom others in this unique network can lean. It is a paradox of history that our interconnected age features so much social decomposition and personal fragmentation. It is a prime moment for the Church to act as "salt, light, and leaven" in emphasizing the transcendent meaning of human dignity across the world, in shining a light on those forgotten in a society that worships power and ability above all, and in breaking through polarized discourse to reorient our politics toward the pursuit of true human flourishing. But this can only be achieved by prayerful individuals, guided by the Holy Spirit, laboring each day in solidarity with one another.

It is in the hope that The Leonine Forum can be a great source of strength and fellowship in the furtherance of these goals that I submit my application for consideration. I deeply appreciate your time and attention.

Sincerely,
John Aroutiounian

THE LEONINE FORUM INTERVIEW

(*August of 2018*)

Q1: *Please tell us a little bit about yourself.*

JA: I'd love to. As you have pointed out already, I'm at Columbia Law right now. I just began my 2L Year, so just completed the foundational curriculum, and getting to branch out a little bit and explore some of the course offerings I'd like to focus my career on—European Union Law, International Law, Human Rights Law—so actually those are the classes I'm taking right now. Prior to this, I was at Oxford, completed a Master's for a year in Classical Armenian Studies. And that sort of came about as a result of, I would say, a prolonged search to rediscover and to further deepen my Armenian roots. My parents are immigrants to the US. I grew up speaking Armenian at home, but my reading and writing skills were poor, and I sort of taught myself the alphabet over the course of a number of years. And then got to the point where I said, "Okay, I really want to pursue formal study in Armenian," and so eager to study classical, early Armenian, also the medieval language and, more broadly, sort of political and ecclesiastical history in the ancient Near East, from around 300 to the early middle ages. So it really broadened down to not just Armenian history and language and culture, but also early Christian studies, which was really great. And I'm considering, after Law School, depending on how things go [smiles]—we can talk about that some other time—doing maybe a PhD in that. So if law doesn't work out, that's my fault back [*laughs*]. Prior to that, I worked in New York for a year as a paralegal in the District Attorney's office in major collar crimes—sorts of securities fraud, international money laundering cases. And prior to that, I was at Yale.

I've had, kind of, a very bouncy life. I grew up here in the [New York] City. My parents moved to the US from Armenia—well, the former Soviet Union—in 1992. I was born in the City, and then they went through the process of retraining as doctors, and that process led us to Kentucky. I went to Kentucky for five years for high school, during which time I was a page in Washington for a semester, so I lived in D.C. for a semester. And then eventually when I got in to school in the northeast, we moved back up here and we've been here ever since.

Q2: *So New York City is kind of home now?*

JA: Absolutely. New York (City) is my hometown, and although Kentucky retains a sort of a very critical place in my heart, this is home for now. We'll see about the future. I, you know, might consider going back to Kentucky. We have a family member and home in Florida, so we might move there in the future. I might stay in New York. But quite truthfully, I am thinking about maybe working and practicing in Europe after graduating, so have a lot of options...a lot of things up in the air right now. Still sort of discerning vocations, too—that's a whole other aspect of this—sort of trying to decide that. So there are a lot of...it's almost not even sensical to talk about plans right now, because, you know, so much is in flux.

Q3: *All sounds exciting! How did you first hear about Leonine Forum and what made you interested in applying?*

JA: Andrew Laird is the first person who mentioned it to me and then, as I got to know it, and asked some of my other friends who had been involved this past year, they all had tremendously wonderful things to say about. The Leonine Forum seems like exactly what I am looking for this year as I sort of have settled down into the field of law school. I'm not as anxious about handling the workload. It feels like the optimal time to. Because, honestly, a good chunk of my friends here in New York are people from my childhood friends from growing up in the City, or people from Yale who moved down the City—about half the graduating class moved down to New York after graduating—and certainly a few people at law school. But by in large I feel as though for this new stage in my life, I don't really have a core group in New York, other than the people from all these other aspects of my life.

And I kind of want to turn the corner in terms of getting to know a new community in New York and really calling it my own. And also, to have that infused with a sense of Catholic mission and purpose is incredibly important to me in this stage in my life. My religious community and the people who shared beliefs with me in college ended up being my closest community, and I want to re-create that in New York, to the extent possible.

Q4: *What challenges do you see in your everyday life that you hope Leonine to help answer?*

JA: Maybe somewhat related to my previous answer. New York, I think, is—and certainly New Haven (and Yale) was as well, in its own way—but I think New York presents its own challenges for a person of faith. I think it can be an incredibly difficult place, I've found that somewhat. I'm lucky enough to have a very supportive and faithful family, and church community. But all that being the case, I still find I need more structure, and I need a community of people who can both hold each other accountable and help each other out. I think that's a big challenge for any Catholic young person today, but I think it's particularly magnified in New York, because of the, kind of, hyper concentration of opportunity and pitfalls the City provides. So I think that's the biggest challenge I have. I'd like to create more structure in my spiritual life and in my faith life, but I also recognize that a key part of that isn't just doing it on your own—it has to be in community. So really developing that community is sort of one of my major goals for this coming year.

Q5: *What you think you might bring to the group, or how you see your contribution?*

JA: Absolutely. So my long term passions have been US and international politics, foreign relations. These are the things I kind of love, and I know that the group usually has people, as well. And doesn't Fr. Roger Landry involved in this group? He is obviously very involved with this kind of issues. Those are the kind of intellectual worlds I frequently find myself interested in and called to, and sort of steeped in. And so, I hope I can certainly bring a little bit of experience in some of the fields I find interesting that might be interesting to others in group discussions or in different kinds of settings in which the Leonine Forum meets. Also, the friends I make and keep by stay very loyal to over a long period of time. And, I really hope that this group provides a medium through which those kinds of friendships can be built. It sort of feels weird to say, but I think I'm a good friend, and I'd like to be able to make new friends in the City with whom to develop those sorts of long lasting and meaningful relationships.

Q6: *Finally, how you see Catholic social teaching intersecting with your professional life, civic life?*

JA: So, I think anybody who's interested in civic life, and in sort of "public square," and who has strong Christian, Catholic faith, goes through different stages in how they interact and how they deal with living in such a pluralistic country and society that frequently the culture is quite hostile. So, you know, I went through a period where I was sort of pushing people's buttons on Facebook and launched these, sort of, [*laughs*] Facebook tirades and discussions with people. I had a phase in my life where I did a lot of that. But as I look forward to how I want to structure my career and my life—if I do end up in public service or some kind of a political or civic role—Catholic social teaching, even before I was a Catholic, was a key part of how I viewed myself and my role personally in the world, and in interacting with friends on a sort of local basis, and how I viewed what I wanted to contribute to the world in a career, in a profession, or in public life. I always, from a young age, would organize pro-life rallies, discussion groups in Kentucky; I organized this big, like a 50-person group from my high school to the state capital. So that's been an issue that's been very front and center in my thinking as a young person, and still is. But really the totality and the whole of Catholic social teaching, as I've studied it more and learned it more comprehensively, really animates the kind of change I want in effect in the world. When I think about policy issues and how to resolve and how to approach them in the United States and in other parts of the world, my first reference point is Catholic social teaching. And so I really hope that my career becomes a vessel through which to serve the Church's teachings, and by default to serve God, as well.

A lot of people in our generation, I think, suffer from a crisis of meaning, and a crisis of, well, what can I do that will leave a legacy or that will, you know, at the end of the day, leave a record I could be proud of. And I think if you structure your life around Catholic social teaching, and if you implement it at least somewhat dutifully in your career, then at the end of the day you will have something that you can be meaningfully proud of. So, that is kind of my hope and my aspiration for my career.

LETTER FOP INTERNSHIP AT FRESHFIELDS BRUCKHAUS DERINGER, LLP

(*August 11, 2018*)

Dear Ms. Champion:

The transcript from Columbia Law School attached reflects the proudest year of my academic career to date. Looking over the transcript, this sentiment may ring strange, as the page is mostly populated by "B" grades earned in the courses of the foundational first year curriculum. And it is certainly true that I achieved far better marks during my undergraduate and graduate education prior to law school. But this year posed a new challenge of an unprecedented kind.

In the middle of my first semester at Columbia, I developed a life-threatening stomach condition that caused blood loss, leading to acute anemia. I began to take my fall semester exams only one week after being admitted to the emergency room, blocks from campus, with dramatically low blood levels. During the entirety. of the second semester, I received intensive treatment to stabilize the condition—treatment that is well-known to severely impair both physical and mental function. All of the developments over this stretch of time are documented and accessible upon request. At various points during this period, withdrawal from school seemed the most viable option, yet I chose to remain and complete my studies. As a result, each hard-fought credit that appears on the transcript is a point of pride—indeed, far more than all the "A" grades I earned at Yale as an undergraduate, or the scores earned at the University of Oxford as a Master's student.

I ranked the Summer Associate position at Freshfields in London as my first choice during Columbia's Early Interview Program earlier this month. I did so because my time living in the United Kingdom convinced me that working in transactional practice in Europe is precisely how I would like to begin my career. And I am confident that there is no better place to begin than at Freshfields. Speaking with Omar Pringle during my interview only confirmed me in this conviction. With its global reach and reputation, and with its currently expanding presence in the United States, I can think of no better time to be in London as an American lawyer to help to serve as a facilitator of this growth. I also hope my Italian, Spanish, and Russian language skills will prove valuable in the European work I may be assigned.

Should additional supporting documentation be desired, I am happy to provide contacts for my physician, and for my instructor in Columbia's "Legal Practice Workshop" course as a reference.

I very much appreciate your time and consideration.

Sincerely,
John Aroutiounian

LETTER TO KIRSTEN SCHNACKENBERG

(*September 2, 2018*)

Dear Kirsten,

This is a Christmas card, I know, but I love this depiction of our Blessed Mother at the Met so much that I couldn't resist sharing, even in September!

I wanted to send you this little "care package" with some of my favorite goodies of the "eve" of this new chapter of your life in Chicago to let you know you're very much on my mind as you begin this exciting journey. I hope the snacks—ha!—are a tiny reminder of how much I'm rooting for you in your personal, career, and spiritual life.

I am ever grateful—even if I'm not the best in expressing it—for your friendship and support for now seven (wow!) years. And I hope you won't forget that you've always got a friend and a fan and a friend only a call or short plane ride away.

The crazy events of life have taught me that you can never know how long "always" will be, or what unexpected things can be thrown your way. You know that better than almost anyone: "minute by minute [things] change," to quote Yates.

All I can recommend is this: pray to her, listen to her, and always keep Mary close to your heart.

Your friend,
John

LETTER TO ISABEL MARIN #3

(*February 27, 2019*)

Isabel,

I hope you won't find what I've done too large and unacceptable a departure from the accepted norms. It is often my practice to write out a letter on lined paper first, to edit, and then to transfer to paper like this. In this instance, I've ended up with a bit more than projected and I've not, unfortunately, the energy given the current state of affairs to complete the transfer.

So I've taken the unprecedented (at least for me) step of sending someone the lined draft. Perhaps it will be more interesting that way to read, but frankly it's probably just going to be more strain and annoyance to get through, for which I apologize! It is undated, but it was written on the same day as the above.

Sending my love to your entire family, very much including your parents, who I ridiculously neglected to mention specifically in the papers enclosed!

God Bless,

Ave Maria,

John

Dear, Dear Isabel,

I write from what I can only describe as a very small, dimly lit clearing in an otherwise perpetually dark and unforgiving forest—the canopy is so thick that it leaves one with the impression that the sun has finally expired, and the short period of calamity preceding the ultimate demise of a world deprived of its animating energy source has begun. One gropes around in the sheer wilderness, enduring the haunting sounds of strange creatures and, quite literally, not knowing what he is going to fall into with the next step. Sleep brings little relief, as it is always brief and of low quality, without the presence of light to regulate the body's neurochemical secretions. And so, only faith and hope light the way, along with dwindling patience. From the clearing at which I've arrived, I am just able to tell by looking up that the sun hasn't yet burned itself to oblivion, or if it has, we are in the period in which its last rays are still traveling toward an oblivious Earth. Moreover, I haven't the slightest inkling as to whether this clearing is a sign the forest is reaching its terminus, whether perhaps more realistically, this "bald patch" will continue for a while longer before the darkness falls away, or whether the abyss is once more right around the corner, and whether I should be preparing for the moment when

God, whose explicit consent makes each breath possible, decides to withdraw His consent.

Your presence in my life, Isabel, has from its inception been a wellspring of beauty, charm, and inspiration. From your conceptual assistance through our discussions in the Trumbull library, whether I would hopelessly crank out D.S. papers at 2 am on Friday mornings—Trumbull's plush chairs, uniquely fruit-filled breakfasts (consumed moments after the papers were finished), and, most importantly, its resident senior Federalist who was always willing to provide the pep talk needed to get projects over the finish line made the library the obvious favorite—to your unrelenting support and encouragement over the past several months, no other person has made more of a difference. No other friend has shown to the same extent that they have not forgotten. And, when you're going through something like this, I have found that to be the most important thing. Though I have not been in much of a position to respond, I have so deeply cherished every text, missed call, letter, and the countless gorgeous packages you have sent my way. I have an inbox full of missed calls and messages spanning months from various friends and relatives—to most of which I will issue perfunctory replies when and if my patience for that sort of thing returns. I hope you'll understand why I couldn't allow myself that kind of reply to you, Isabel. Even a call would be half-baked under the circumstances. If this has caused you undue worry, I am sincerely sorry—but I hope you know that no one else has, or likely will, receive as honest and comprehensive an account of the situation at hand.

I am on medical leave from law school this semester. This certainly wasn't "the plan," but a bizarre series of events—as strange as those precipitating the original diagnosis in January of last year—took place between December 2018 and January 2019. On December 12th—an auspicious date, not chosen by me, as it is Our Lady of Guadalupe's Feast Day—I was scheduled for surgery to remove the remains of the tumor that had been bombarded with drugs, for almost a year, with decent results. As soon as the effects of the anesthesia had lifted, I awoke and began feeling around. "Where are all the tubes and pipes?" I inquired of the only person in the room. "The surgery wasn't done."

My first reaction was elation at having retained my stomach, a good chunk of which was supposed to be excised. The bad news quickly followed: the procedure was scrapped because the surgeons, upon initial inspection, found evidence of spread to the liver, which "is a whole different ballgame" and for which surgery is rarely, if ever, indicated. Had the surgery gone ahead, then, there is a solid chance I would not be alive to write this now. That certainly warrants an "Ave."

The following week we were back in the office of the oncologist who had treated me all year.

Despite the egregious bedside manners (and other problems with her "care," which shouldn't be discussed as they may be relevant in legal proceedings in the future), we had stayed with her because of the tremendous resources her institution offered. But on this day, she entered even more nonchalantly than usual, told me "this disease will take your life" after having asserted mere weeks earlier that "you'll forget this ever happened" shortly after recovering from surgery, and proceeded to ask when it was I'd like to come back to start chemotherapy again to keep things at bay. It all felt beyond surreal. We said we needed a few weeks to consider options. "Come back in a month," she said.

A week later, shell-shocked Aroutiounian family tried to celebrate Christmas at St. Patrick's, where we'd last been with you in April. The seating was assigned, we were assigned choice seats overlooking Cardinal Dolan's pulpit and the Our Lady of Guadalupe Chapel.

Over the next two weeks, we scoured the world for treatment options, leaving no stone unturned. I won't exhaust you with the details. And then, in the middle of this search, another body blow:

around the second week of January, my liver erupted with tumor growth. So much for "come back in a month." Scans revealed a dire situation—the disease was progressing rapidly, to every doctor's utter shock. Just a few days later, I could barely eat, sleep, walk, or even breathe. On the 24th, I was admitted to the hospital and started on a concoction of medications almost immediately. Each time I managed to fall asleep, I wondered to myself whether I'd be opening my eyes again.

The pure strangeness of all this, from the moment it all started the day after a serene trip to the Canary Islands in January of 2018, is not lost on me. This tumor almost always strikes the old; I have no family or behavioral history of any kind; since high school I have gotten myself tested for all kinds of cancers with a hypochondriac's tenacity; my parents are cancer specialists. In its way, the strangeness of this malady as it has affected me, together with the overarching strangeness of being itself, only further solidifies my faith in God. Some will say this is the thought of a weak and desperate mind, unable to hold in his hands the reality of a cruel and unresponsive universe. I reject this dismissal. Not only would its validity require, in my view, suicide on the part of any thinking and compassionate man, but its acceptance would necessitate a blind faith in the patently illogical on the part of these logic-driven atheists most likely to think this way. Over the last two months, I have come face-to-face with varieties of suffering I never dared to think existed, and the only people who've seen this toll have been my poor parents, who are similarly facing the prospect of their world crashing all around them. In some ways, I am sure their suffering is even greater than mine. But even they cannot comprehend the extent of it, just like I likely can't comprehend all of theirs. To be utterly tripped of, quite literally, everything almost overnight builds [? John's handwriting unclear] your character. But in its strangeness, this suffering has not only solidified my belief in God the Father—but has brought me so much closer to Jesus, His Son, the Holy Spirit, and Jesus' Blessed Mother. They are ever-present in my consciousness in a way I have never before experienced—even compared to last year, when I first perceived a deepening relationship.

It is an exaggeration, though just barely, to say "everything" was taken away. I am so blessed to have the family and friends I have, and I thank God every day for faith, as well, without which I surely would have collapsed in the forest a long time ago. And I am now in the hands of a creative oncologist who is trying some very interesting things. Though each day still brings a cornucopia of side effects—the worst are the debilitating fatigue and nausea, which have me feeling at least 83 years old, as opposed to the vigorous 65 I'll admit to feeling most of life—the liber's calmed down considerably, though that could change any day.

As to the future, no doctor would look at this situation and offer a sunny prognosis, but without knowing what's to come I am simply grateful for being not where I was a few weeks ago. Interestingly enough, I am far less fearful of death now than I was when perfectly healthy—perhaps because I haven't absorbed the magnitude of what may come. Still more likely, perhaps, the situation is like being in the thick of war, when all fear usually dissipates and man becomes totally fixed on what is placed in front of him in each moment and how he must act. But above all, it is my faith in Jesus and in the fundamental intentionality and rationality of the universe which attenuates fear at this point.

Life at present is rather grey: going out, even for a walk, is uncommon; there is a weekly doctor's visit, sometimes two; my emotionally battered mother is at home, taking care of the situation the best she knows how; I hang out on a comfy chair in the living room, uneager to move much. I am taking a lot of naps, which isn't a bad thing from a healing perspective. But it's rather annoying to feel so weak all the time, particularly when it's so bad that it robs me of the presence of mind needed in order to read, write, or stay attentive to something. I am grateful for that presence of mind given today so I could finally write to you.

I know I have tried to convey on many occasions how inimitable and inexplicable a force you have been for me over the past seven years, Isabel. Far from diminishing over time, distance, and the weight of large events, as is so often the case among friends, your heart, decency, and spirit continue to be sources of inspiration and strength unmatched by any other friend. Though most of this missive was spent recounting the tedium of my recent ordeals, it is *this*, which I chiefly wanted to convey. I can only hope I did not fail too harshly.

Please, a hug and my best to Tom, and a kiss for (still-little?) Alex! If you could pray for the side effects mentioned and for the current regiment to work to its full extent, I'd be enormously grateful.

John

"*The most important virtues in life:*
FAITH, LOVE & SERVICE"

–John

Made in the USA
Middletown, DE
16 August 2023

36842260R00183